FIRST POSITION

FIRST POSITION

A Century of Ballet Artists

Toba Singer

Foreword by Bruce Marks

Westport, Connecticut
London

Library of Congress Cataloging-in-Publication Data

Singer, Toba.
    First position: a century of ballet artists / Toba Singer; foreword by Bruce Marks.
      p. cm.
    Includes bibliographical references and index.
    ISBN 978–0–275–98391–8 (alk. paper)
1. Ballet dancers—Biography. 2. Ballerinas—Biography. I. Title.
GV1785.A1S56 2007
792.802'80922—dc22
[B]   2007022977

British Library Cataloguing in Publication Data is available.

Library of Congress Catalog Card Number: 2007022977
ISBN-13: 978–0–275–98391–8

First published in 2007

Praeger Publishers, 88 Post Road West, Westport, CT 06881
An imprint of Greenwood Publishing Group, Inc.
www.praeger.com

Printed in the United States of America

The paper used in this book complies with the
Permanent Paper Standard issued by the National
Information Standards Organization (Z39.48-1984).

10 9 8 7 6 5 4 3 2 1

For the Four J's (*in order of appearance*): Jean, Jack, Jim and James

Dancing is like writing in the sand.
—Virginia Johnson

Contents

Foreword *by Bruce Marks*   ix

Preface   xiii

Acknowledgments   xvii

1. Erik Bruhn   1

2. Alicia Alonso   15

3. Rudolf Nureyev   29

4. Margot Fonteyn   43

5. Mikhail Baryshnikov   57

6. Anna Pavlova   71

7. Li Cunxin   85

8. Gelsey Kirkland   99

9. Lázaro Carreño   113

10. Natalia Makarova   125

11. Maya Plisetskaya   139

12. Carlos Acosta   153

13. Muriel Maffre   169

14. Arthur Mitchell   185

15. Carla Fracci   199

Contents

Notes	213
Bibliography	223
Index	227

Foreword

Dance is an ever changing art. And although some elements of the art form and what defines excellence never change, other aspects have changed enormously.

The "look" of a ballerina today is not the "look" of decades ago. Dancers' bodies have evolved into leaner, finer instruments. And male dancers have acquired line that once was reserved only for their partners. Everyone is turning more and jumping higher than ever before. Is the dancing any better? Not a question I would care to answer, but I do know that I loved the dancers of the middle of the last century and also those that followed: Ulanova and Fracci, Fonteyn and Farrell, and yes, Youskevitch and Baryshnikov.

I do believe, however, in the importance of dance scholarship. Writing on dance can illuminate the past in a way that archival or dance film alone cannot. One would think that film or still photographs would be preferable to the written word in describing what a dancer does or did, who they were and why they are now revered. It is, in fact, complementary but cannot tell the whole story. I have seen Pavlova on film and understand that it is only a shadow of what she was, only one aspect of her art. I can, however, understand that she lived in a time that was *hers*. The *style* of her time along with the ballet technique and, indeed, every other sensibility was different. There are no films of Nijinsky, but if there were they would convey only certain aspects of what and who he was. The still photos are beautiful and intriguing and hint at some aspects of his genius.

What a film can't give us is the context of the artists' work. It cannot provide the background of achievement up to the moment that the lens opens and then shuts. Dance is a living art form that must be seen as part of its moment in history. It is the writer who can give a life in dance a fuller context.

In the dance world, a world of non-verbal communicators, we must recognize the importance of the written word. So much has been written about music, visual arts, film, and theatre. The lack of a large body of criticism and biography keeps dance in its place, a place near the bottom of the totem that is the arts.

The 15 portraits that you're about to read represent artists from eight countries (five Russian, three Cuban, two American, and one each from Great Britain, France, Italy, China, and Denmark). Only one was born in the nineteenth century: Pavlova. There are eight women and seven men, and at this writing only three are dancing: Acosta, Baryshnikov, and Maffre, but all have danced. Eleven are living and four deceased. I have worked with seven (Baryshnikov, Bruhn, Fonteyn, Fracci, Kirkland, Makarova, and Nureyev) and known 10 (add Alonso, Mitchell, Plisetskaya). They are, as a group, as varied as the art form itself.

It is clear that there is great value in what Giorgio Vasari did in his portraits of the painters of the Italian renaissance, and heartening to know that we have begun to do the same in dance. Many of those included are world famous, but some are known only in the dance world, a small world indeed, and even I, having been involved in this art form for 57 years, found one individual I had not previously heard of.

I can only assume that those included are the dancers, directors, teachers that interested the author. They are all worthy of our interest.

In compiling a series of portraits like these one offers not only biographical material but, more importantly, insights into the artists themselves. What is clear from these 15 lives is that each, emerging from his or her own ethos, represents a personal "dance culture."

Some of those portrayed think of themselves in service to the art and others see the art form as a vehicle for their talent. There are the searching artists like Kirkland, always trying to find the heart of the movement and filled with doubt about themselves and their approach. There is the confident Carreño whose background is in the Russian system of Vaganova and yet teaches the quick allegro that is synonymous with the technique developed by Bournonville and Cecchetti. Fracci, for example, claims Cecchetti ancestry as well since she was trained by Pavlova ballerina Esme Bulnes, while Bruhn started with Bournonville and then credits the Russian, Vera Volkova, with his later achievement.

We learn more about each individual artist: Fracci and her approach to acting, Muriel Maffre's take on continuing education. We find out about Lázaro Carreño's fusion of Russian training and Cuban temperament. There are tales of Fonteyn and Nureyev, Bruhn, Nureyev and Tallchief, Kirkland and Baryshnikov. Perhaps these stories are available elsewhere, but here juxtaposed they give the relationships new context.

At any rate, it is a pleasure to introduce these artists to you. Many of them have changed my life, the way I danced, and the way I have directed. Perhaps they will change your life too.

Bruce Marks
Orlando, Forida
31 January 2007

Preface

~ ——————————————————————————————— ~

When my son James Gotesky began to study dance, it became clear to me that every one of his teachers taught based on a different tradition—an asset or a liability depending upon the school's overall pedagogical philosophy. There is nothing approaching a unified pedagogy to guide dance education in the United States. Where schools are associated with companies, teachers may prepare students to dance according to that company's style, but with the exception of the School of American Ballet, such preparation doesn't amount to a philosophy unless the philosophy is pragmatism. In the mid-1990s, I saw a film made in 1986 by my friend Frank Boehm about the life of the Ballerina Assoluta, Alicia Alonso. The film focuses in part on the pedagogy of the Cuban system of dance training. It confirmed my suspicion that Cuban dancers are outstanding because someone in Havana was in a position to elaborate a national curriculum, put it in place, and test it in life, thanks to the propitious confluence of proper training, an artistic vision, a zest for hard work, and the commitment of a revolutionary government based on the idea that workers and farmers who produce for society deserve only the best in return, especially in art and culture. After attending the Prix de Lausanne competition in 2000, and having a chance to observe ballet students from all over the world while I engaged in an ongoing discussion there on the subject of dance pedagogy with Antonio Castilla and Larisa Skylanskaya, I wanted to investigate the question more fully and write about my findings.

I made a couple of pitches for a ballet book to Praeger. The one that was accepted was not the first proposal on ballet teachers, but the one I proposed on a collection of biographical sketches of dancers. I knew that underlying and intertwined with the stories of dancers' lives are the histories of their training, rich with lessons.

My only question was: How does one choose 15 dancers from thousands? If you start with the *best* dancers (assuming that agreement can be reached on what is ultimately a matter of taste), names such as Sylvie Guillem, Yuri Soloviev, and Olga Spessivsteva would head the list. Paris, Milan, Havana, London, San Francisco, New York, Toronto, Tokyo, Shanghai, Rio de Janeiro, Johannesburg, St. Petersburg, Amsterdam, Frankfurt, Houston, Monte Carlo, and Stuttgart could each contribute a dozen names! To make the process as democratic, objective, and authoritative as possible, I polled a cross section of choreographers, teachers, administrators, and ballet students, active and retired dancers, balletomanes, dance historians, and writers. They served as my nominating committee. Collectively, they submitted approximately 300 names. The list was broad and centrifugal, so much so that the only name that appeared on every nominator's list was "Mikhail Baryshnikov."

I telephoned Frank Boehm. He is not only a filmmaker: in his capacity as a choreographer and producer, Frank has auditioned as many as 500 dancers at a time for as few as eight jobs. I asked for his help. Over a cup of coffee at the XO Café in San Francisco, Frank asked what I wanted my ensemble of dancers to "say" to the reader. I answered that I wanted each of them to give voice to or transmit to the reader something key about the process of becoming a ballet artist, supported by an honest recounting of their training and what they gained from it. I wanted readers to meet virtuoso dancers who for the most part came from ordinary backgrounds, but whose outlooks were forward looking, and whose overall contributions were social and historical as well as aesthetic. I wanted to know how each one strived for authenticity, not only as an individual, but as an ambassador of the changing culture of dance.

The three year period during which I wrote *First Position* coincided with my son James' developing dance career at Houston Ballet. When appropriate, I shared with James and his fellow company members what I was learning from the dancers in my book. Houston Ballet was my laboratory: I was invited to observe class there, and saw dancers rise, rededicate themselves, and mature as artists and human beings, or retreat from the many challenges that are relentlessly posed, fall away, and go on to pursue other interests. The ballet masters and mistresses and the administrative and artistic staff of the company followed my progress with great enthusiasm and never failed me when I asked for assistance.

The poet Rainer Maria Rilke defines fame as "the sum of all misunderstandings that collects itself about a name." *First Position* is not a book about fame. Each chapter represents a sketch of a dancer's life and begins with a quote intended to capture the special qualities of that dancer, but in order to minimize the misunderstandings Rilke refers to, I have omitted labored descriptions of the dancers' body of work or praise of it. I wanted to use the space allotted me to relate the story of each dancer's experience as much as possible in his or her own voice. I worked to push past the false consciousness that derives from celebrity to mine the particular nuggets of creativity, curiosity, fervor, and quixotic hope that tend to dissolve into the general when one invokes the overused term "passion." The cultivation of a ballet dancer requires a hothouse environment of rigorous training, mental focus, singularity of purpose, and coaching. The ballet artist, as distinct from the dancer, would seem to naturally hunger for the nourishment of that environment, while at the same time mesh with an auxiliary set of gears that motors him or her out of the hothouse and into the world of human frailty and triumph. It is this special auxiliary motor that I wished to explore in each artist. I was fortunate to have been able to conduct face to face and email interviews with seven of the eleven living dancers, as well as more than ten interviews with individuals of special significance in their lives, giving me access to intimate thoughts, feelings, and observations that are current, but unavailable from other sources.

In *First Position*, the reader meets 15 ordinary people who love or loved to dance. Having come from better or worse circumstances, they decided to place their lives at the service of their art. By virtue of their own gravitas and a majesty that cannot be measured in material units, they seized hold of what was in an earlier era a rather antiseptic art form reserved for kings and queens, to breath life into it and begin the history-altering process of rendering it the collective property and experience of all of humankind.

Acknowledgments

Sandi Kurtz of the Dance Critics Association pointed me towards Praeger. Bruce Marks offered counsel and wrote a thoughtful and thought-provoking foreword. Mary Ellen Hunt sent predawn support and resource information via email and over coffee. The criticaldance.com editorial staff offered encouragement, patience, and a generous attitude regarding copyright. Richard Gibson offered counsel. Frank Boehm, Cher Delamere, Janet Falk, Rita Felciano, Sonja Franeta, Jim Gotesky, Mark Hall, Bitsy Myers, Lorraine Padden, and Justin Woo read to me when I couldn't turn pages and hold a book at the same time after wrist surgery. Benjamin Pierce introduced me to his life companion, Muriel Maffre. Muriel Maffre shared tea, touring, stimulating conversation, and humor in two languages on two continents. Bernard, Monique, and Isabelle Maffre and family, and Marc Gamar and Nat London, offered hospitality, translation, and transportation assistance in Paris. Carla Fracci, Barbara Gronchi, Beppe Menegatti, Cosimo Manicone, Gillian Whittingham, Rosella Simonari, and Patrizia Vallone offered hospitality and assistance in Rome. Carlos Acosta, Suzanne Banki, Janine Limberg, Antonio Castilla, and Ivana Garcia and family provided hospitality and assistance in London. Lanie Fleischer, Janette Hawkins, Arthur Hughes, Margaret Marchisio Luca, and Carlo Romairone provided hospitality and assistance in New York. Karen Hildebrand of *Dance Magazine* gave valuable direction in conducting the Lázaro Carreño interviews. Tiekka prieve was generous with her time, and Dina Makarova offered editorial and photographic assistance. Laura Alonso, Lupe Calzadilla, Lorena Feijoo, Javier Gálito-Cava, Freddi Kirchner, Claire Sheridan, and Oscar Trujillo in San Francisco and Justin Coe and Covadonga Garcia Mar in Madrid gave their time and translation assistance con muchas ganas. Lauren Anderson,

Lázaro Carreño, Andrew Edmonson, Joanna Tschebull, Shauna Tysor, Melissa Carroll, Cassandra Patterson McClurg, Kathryn Crowder, and Susan Zárate gave their time, hospitality, and assistance in Houston. Joy Melvin, Muriel Maffre, Chris Hardy, Jason Bell, Guy Harrison, Asya Verzhbinsky, Kate Crady, Jim Caldwell, Li Cunxin, James Gotesky, Thomas Tavis, and Lázaro Carreño, Barbara Milberg Fisher, and the staff of the San Francisco Performing Arts Library, Samantha Cairo-Toby, Kirsten Tanaka, and Eric Brizee, the staff of the New York Public Library Dance Collection, Tom Perrier, Phil Karg, and Thomas Lisanti, who helped and helped generously with photographs. Judy Chen assisted me with endnotes technology. The "nominating committee" of Melisande Amos, Frank Boehm, Deborah Brooks, Karen Brown, Lisa Claybaugh, Edward Ellison, James Gotesky, Kimberly Graves, Marc Greenside, Mary Lou Della Puietra, Edward Ellison, Mark Franko, Mary Ellen Hunt, Lauren Jonas, Alegría Garcia Mar, Shannon D. Mitchell Hyatt, Augusta Moore, Juliet Neidish, Lorraine Padden, John Philbrook, Matthew Rehrl, Dean Spear, Mayo Sugano, Stuart Sweeney, Hanna Takashige, Francis Timlin, and Katita Waldo. My husband Jim Gotesky and son James Gotesky read or listened to many drafts and offered boundless support. Dr. Ellen Dolson, Dr. William Green, and Dr. Richard McDonald, Dr. Stuart Werboff, the California Pacific Medical Center nursing staff, and occupational therapists Kathleen Parker and Troy Shelton for helping put various moving parts and systems back together. My editors at Praeger Press, Eric Levy and Elizabeth Potenza, were patient about deadlines during what must have been for them a record number of author medical crises. Their enthusiasm for the project was unflagging, and in Eric's case, continued even after he moved on to other pursuits.

1

Erik Bruhn

His technical credentials include a fine dramatic sense and an ability to leap with a high-arching grace, to turn with cat quickness and fluidity on the ground or in mid-air, to project emotion with vivid movements of arms, legs and body...he somehow rivets an audience with the promise of action before he has danced a step...he spends restless nights reviewing roles in his mind. He has surprisingly little of the vanity that goads most performers; he does not want audiences to pay, he says, "only to see me jump"...He would rather "be bad in a good ballet than be great in a bad ballet."

—*Time* Magazine[1]

How could six-year-old Erik Bruhn have guessed that the curio ballet world that he entered in Gentofte, Denmark, was the sanctuary of a four-century tradition that began in the Royal Court of Frederick II? In 1816, the French dancer Antoine Bournonville became director of Copenhagen's Royal Theatre. His son August succeeded him in 1829. Born in Copenhagen in 1805, August was his father's first student. He studied in France, returned to Copenhagen, and then danced with the Paris Opera, where he developed the revered technique characterized by simplicity of preparation and line, and airily light combinations borne on quicksilver feet, known today as "Bournonville."

Erik Bruhn, a diffident boy, had four high spirited sisters, and sought refuge in the garden from his domineering and jealous elder half-sister and the torpor of his parents' disintegrating marriage. His mother, Ellen Evers Bruhn, a hair stylist, worked in nearby Copenhagen. Ernst Bruhn, Erik's kind but ineffectual father, worked sporadically and drank heavily. The Bruhns' separation before Erik's sixth birthday was their noblest gesture of mutual goodwill.

Erik Bruhn as James in *La Sylphide*. Photo credit: Rigmor Mydtskov. Courtesy Dance Collection, New York Public Library.

Erik's teacher worried that he was mentally slow, and recommended a special school. Instead, Ellen Bruhn enrolled him in dance class. After a few months, it was obvious that Erik was not mentally retarded, but had been suffering in a family that failed to nurture his deepest needs for self-expression. Erik quickly learned the dance combinations. His balance and articulated line were unusual for a child his age. After two years, responsive to his beloved Aunt Minna's bribe of one *krone*, he auditioned for the Royal Copenhagen Ballet School. Born on October 3, 1928, Erik was 10 when he enrolled. He distrusted the school's mire of courtly traditions and puffery, but in less than a decade, he would be its most celebrated alumnus.

In his first two years, Erik's social self lagged behind his dancer self. He wished to vanish when all eyes were on him, but eventually learned to utilize performances to open up. Inclined to rebel against studio discipline, he says of his teacher Karl Merrild:

> I hated and loathed that teacher...I made him so angry that he nearly had a nervous breakdown! When I turned 14, I remember not obeying him in any way...he used to beat us with a stick to make us jump...I was given a warning...when this happened, I stopped being a problem—not out of fear, but because I felt satisfied to have made my feelings known...I didn't have to continue.[2]

Bruhn later manipulated others to his advantage, but as a student he toggled between gregariousness and steeliness, intimacy remaining a temptation. Though Bruhn did not excel academically, his ballet accomplishments were stellar. By 1943, his teachers pronounced him a master of the Bournonville technique. His greatest challenge then surfaced: revealing his feelings through his character. Of the three "schools" of ballet—the Russian Vaganova, the Italian/French Cecchetti, and the Danish Bournonville, the latter wants ballet to inspire its audience with the desire to rise to its feet and dance. It rejects the notion of the virtuoso dancer whose "tricks," leaps, multiples of turns, and complex lifts, are contrived to "wow" audiences. Steps are seen as inseparable from the work as a whole. No elaborate preparations alert the audience to show-stopping feats. Bruhn could turn more and jump higher than what was considered Bournonville-appropriate, and enjoyed pulling an extra turn or two out of a musical phrase. He believed that holding back deprived the audience of the dancer's unique artistry.

"Ballon" is what makes the leaping dancer appear to hover in the air. In Bournonville, lightness characterizes all movement. In other techniques, *ballon* rests on the strength of the *plié*, a simple-seeming knee bend. Done correctly, the *plié* allows the dancer to pump "air" into the jump from the body's center. Without a confident relationship with the floor, the jump won't float, and the dancer courts injury. As Bruhn danced roles out of the Russian tradition, lifts caused him knee and back problems which he attributed to a weak plié. He began to learn the Vaganova technique from Russians with whom he danced, who in turn emulated the silkiness of the Bournonville style. Bruhn thus synthesized discreet schools into a workable body of technique to serve the art, instead of elevating each school into a sectarian icon of its own. Music was his confessor: "Hear the music for the first time every time you dance to it...then you find more of yourself *in* the music."[3] Bruhn disdained choosing a lifelong companion, but was able to "marry" and remain faithful to the dancer's most fickle but indispensable partner—music. He began and ended on the right beats but took liberties with the phrasing to innovate, dramatize, and color his characters, tailoring the choreography to his and his partners' sensibility and mood, and the temper of the audience.

The royal court authored a set of a semi-feudal power relationships and practices that have dictated the training and career protocols to which dancers are still subject. A company receives state or private funding. Artistic directors may be more or less despotic, but certain practices are ironclad. The dancer is always grateful to the artistic director, regardless of his or her opinion of him or her. Convinced that they can replace one dancer with another with no impact on the box office receipts, artistic directors' decisions are rarely informed by their debt to their dancers. It is easy to forget that ballet is a collective endeavor, requiring collaborative coaching and preparation that can make or break a company. The company's needs and the artistic director's creative impulses are coefficients of a mysterious algebra that dancers hope will work for them, but that relationship of forces favors dancers only to the extent that there are strong unions.

Royal Danish Ballet audiences first saw Bruhn in 1946 as Adonis in Harald Lander's ballet, *Thorvaldsen*. Afterwards, Lander, the company's artistic director, offered him a contract. Recognizing that his advancement depended upon ending his social isolation, at 18, Erik went to London's Metropolitan Ballet for the summer. The Metropolitan was a startup company of young, enthusiastic, international dancers and choreographers. Among them was the captivating Bulgarian 20-year-old, Sonia Arova. Arova's career plans were dramatically altered by World War II. Her ballet teachers had arranged for her to study in Paris, grooming her for the Opera Ballet. Dressed as a boy, Sonia was smuggled out of Paris to London during the German invasion, where in 1942 she was hired by the International Ballet. Just prior to Bruhn's arrival, she had joined the Metropolitan as a principal.

Arova and Bruhn felt an instant mutual attraction. London offered the romance of Sadler's Wells, access to dancers such as Margot Fonteyn, Moira Shearer, and Jean Babilée (whom Bruhn referred to as "the very first dancer I felt I could really look up to"),[4] and guest dancers from the United States, including Kathryn Dunham. The Metropolitan offered Erik a principal contract, and he longed to take it. It was not only Bruhn's loyalty to the Royal Danish that made him hesitate. There were consequences: not returning would cost him his lifetime pension and the security of an established company where he would be treasured. Once home, he wrote to Harald Lander to explain his decision to resign from Royal Danish and accept the Metropolitan contract. The astonished Lander invited him in for a conference, after which he granted the equally astonished Bruhn a six months' leave of absence. Bruhn walked away with the best of both worlds: job security and the rare opportunity to dance the best roles with a new company in an international dance capital. At 18, such good fortune may have teased out Bruhn's lifelong tendency to play a "running bases" game with devoted friends, major dance companies, the finest partners, and a roster of passionate lovers and admirers.

Within the first six months, Bruhn danced the Blue Bird pas de deux and excerpts from "Aurora's Wedding" from *Sleeping Beauty*, as well as *Les Sylphides*, *Spectre de la Rose*, and the second act of *Swan Lake*. John Taras set his ballet *Design with Strings* on Erik and Svetlana Beriosova, and Frank Staff choreographed *A Lovers' Gallery* on him. Sonia and Erik's partnering in *Spectre de la Rose* was a study in onstage serendipity. Offstage, their intimacy was intense, but Arova noticed a moodiness driven by something unreachable in Bruhn. At that stage of their relationship, she didn't know about Erik's "Black Swan," the doppelganger within that was at least as forceful as his warm and welcoming self. Women were objects of Erik's manipulation. He was brutally frank about why: "There was a period of time when I couldn't stand being with women."[5]

Critics gave Bruhn's performances the highest marks. Leaving Arova was no easier than returning to Copenhagen. She was off to Paris to pursue dancing with Paris Opera. Erik gave her an engagement ring, and invited her to Gentofte to meet his family.

The impact of Bruhn's six months in London was not lost on Harald Lander. Coincident with the return of a much more outgoing Erik was the start of Léonide Massine's tenure as guest choreographer. He cast Erik as The Hussar in *Le Beau Danube* and in *Symphonie Fantastique*. Bruhn utilized these roles to unlock qualities of enchantment, beguilement, and wit hidden beneath his solemn personality, and was praised for his sweeping line and light-footed technique. Lander mounted "Bournonvilliana" in June of 1949, seen by the American impresario and president of the Ballet Theatre Foundation, Blevins Davis. Founded in 1940 by members of the Mordkin Ballet, Ballet Theatre was the predecessor of today's American Ballet Theatre. Lucia Chase and Richard Pleasant became its artistic directors. After watching Erik rehearse, Davis invited him to dance with ABT. Backstage, August Bournonville's last student, Hans Beck, told Erik that Bournonville would have predicted, as he had of Beck, that Bruhn would "go far." Buoyed by the accolades, Bruhn considered his options. He was obliged to finish the Denmark season, and had promised to join Sonia in Paris the following summer. He asked Harald Lander for a year's leave of absence. Though Lander threatened to withhold Erik's soloist promotion, in the end, Bruhn was promoted to principal *and* received approval for a year's leave!

Sonia and Erik met in Paris to follow a false lead from Serge Lifar that he could hire Bruhn (and they hoped Sonia, too) at Paris Opera. In the end, both dancers found that neither would be hired because they were not French nationals. Blevins Davis, also in Paris, left a message for Bruhn that he had booked passage for himself and Erik to the United States. This was presented to Arova as a fantastic coincidence, but she suspected that there was more to the story. While devastated that she and Erik wouldn't marry that summer, she accepted the sudden departure graciously, aware that it would have been futile to hold Erik to their earlier plans. They took leave of each other as fiancés, intending to marry. While their careers brought them together on a few very happy occasions, their shared dream of marriage never materialized.

Back in Denmark after the ABT season, Erik learned that a palace coup was afoot at Royal Danish, resulting in Harald Lander leaving for Paris with his wife, the exquisite dancer Toni Lander. Bruhn joined the chorus of those complaining about Lander's artistic mismanagement, even issuing his own press statement. Niels Bjørn Larsen succeeded Lander. A pro-Lander faction remained vocal, and Bruhn was ultimately ridiculed for his indiscretions with the press, making him all the more eager to return to ABT. Bruhn requested his third (and per company policy, final) leave of absence, this time granted with the proviso that upon return, he would stay for at least two years.

With displays of fine technique, Bruhn had begun to win a following in New York, but when he returned to Denmark, the press was still hostile, and friends and family a bit chilly. He used his time there to improve, dancing major roles in *Swan Lake*, *Sleeping Beauty*, *The Nutcracker*, *Les Sylphides*, and *La Sylphide*. It was as James in *La Sylphide* that Bruhn advanced light-years. A fastidious technician, Bruhn had great difficulty with theatricality. Not knowing the back story of the character made it nearly impossible for him to mime or act the role:

> When I made my debut at twenty-two in the full-length *La Sylphide*, I was terrified. And because I was terrified...it seemed I could dance but I couldn't act. I decided to think carefully about James—about who this man was...It was more a question of getting to the psychological root of the character, of making this person become a living human being, rather than some dusty relic of the past...I portrayed a James that was acclaimed on all levels.[6]

Years of training are written into the bones of dancers, and summoned via "muscle memory." One can easily take for granted an array of skills that teachers impart. Bruhn benefited from an excellent Russian teacher, Vera Volkova. Born in St. Petersburg in 1904, Volkova studied with Agrippina Vaganova, and was considered one of her best exponents. She danced and then taught in Shanghai, at Sadler's Wells and La Scala, before coming to the Royal Danish in 1951. Bruhn recalls that some of his happiest moments were with Vera. Bruhn and Volkova discussed at length how best to train the muscle groups. Because Bruhn had a sunken chest, Volkova suggested that he visualize a button at its center, and then raise that button. Within a year, Bruhn had corrected his placement. Bournonville training results in a lengthened line that shows all flaws. With Vaganova training, a musculature develops that masks most flaws. Volkova wisely combined both techniques. Nonetheless, over time, Bruhn felt that Volkova was suffocating him. Thinking too much about his dancing was causing him stage fright, and he would refuse to dance, angering Volkova. After a name-calling spat where a purse was thrown, the friendship shattered just as Bruhn was to return to Ballet Theatre. With some geographic distance between them, Erik realized that he owed Volkova a great debt. Later, they resumed what became a very close friendship.

While Erik divided his time between Copenhagen and New York, Arova was dancing with smaller companies in London, Tokyo, and Paris, where she met Blevins Davis. Cognizant of her engagement to Erik and her talent, Davis spoke with Lucia Chase, and within two weeks, Arova was invited to join Ballet Theatre. Erik was delighted, but his circumstances had changed. He was now flanked by an entourage of new acquaintances. Sonia felt sidelined. It was obvious that it was impossible to pick up where they had left off. Though Erik still adored and would have married Sonia, he no longer truly craved a permanent arrangement, which he communicated to her by letter. There would be no wedding, but Sonia and Erik continued to work together.

The *pas de deux*, a duet that showcases the female partner, relies on the male presenting her at her best. It may appear that the artistry is hers, but that is only partly true. The male partner must cover the flaws of the female partner, and be strong enough to lift her if she does not jump high enough. He must adjust his tempo if she veers off the music, and "learn" her body. Her weight may be oddly distributed, or her tutu so large or rough-edged that it blinds or cuts him. He remains composed in rehearsal, always a gentleman when her errors are addressed. He sends her flowers on opening night. One hopes that the sentiments on the accompanying card are genuine. If not, the entire *pas de deux* can suffer, and he, not she, is labeled "not a very good partner."

Alicia Alonso, Nora Kaye, Lupe Serrano, Mary Ellen Moylan, Alicia Markova, Maria Tallchief, Rosella Hightower, Natalia Makarova, Carla Fracci, and Gelsey Kirkland all praised Bruhn as a fine partner. However, his public candor regarding *their* weaknesses gave off more than a whiff of misogyny, apparent in Bruhn's words about the electrifying Alonso:

> In 1951, we did a Don Quixote *pas de deux*. In rehearsal, I noticed that the tempos were unbelievably slow. That's what Alicia liked. When we came to the performance, I couldn't bear the thought of dancing to such slow tempos. So, because I was very young and a little brash, I went to the conductor and told him to speed up the tempos. Naturally, I didn't tell Alonso. The conductor asked me if I had told Alicia, and lying, I said yes. Well, from the first bar of the music, Alicia knew that something was wrong, and being Alicia, she paid no attention to the music and did her variations in her own tempo, disregarding the music completely...Of course, she was quick to realize who had requested the changes, and during the performance she whispered in her lovely Latin way, "I am going to *k e e l* you!"...Alicia didn't kill me, but the tempos were restored to the way she liked them.[7]

Erik Bruhn and Natalia Makarova in *Epilogue*. Photo credit: Dina Makarova.

In 1955, Bruhn partnered Alicia Markova in *Les Sylphides*. She openly shared what she had learned from Fokine about the piece. Bruhn's success qualified him to dance Albrecht to her Giselle. As he learned the role, a drama was unfolding between Bruhn and Lucia Chase, who asked Bruhn to return to ABT the following season as a second soloist with a higher salary, citing lack of seniority for not promoting him to first soloist. Bruhn argued that if he could be cast as Albrecht to Markova's Giselle, he was entitled to the rank of first soloist. Chase threatened to pull him from Albrecht if he did not sign the second soloist contract. Markova informed Chase that *Giselle* with Markova could not happen without Bruhn as her partner. *Giselle* went up with Bruhn as Albrecht. Igor Youskevitch and Alicia Alonso had just announced their decision to leave Ballet Theatre for Ballet Russe de Monte Carlo. Chase apologized to Bruhn, and offered him a principal contract!

Bruhn's new "exclusive" contract with American Ballet Theatre meant putting all his chips on one number, a practice he had artfully dodged up to that point. A principal dancer reprises roles that have brought acclaim. Dancing them night after night took a toll in injuries, stress, and behaving badly toward Lucia Chase, who pushed him hard.

In 1958, Bruhn asked Chase to add Birgit Cullberg's *Miss Julie* to the repertoire. To test his acting skills, and investigate his anger at women, Bruhn wanted to dance Jean, the valet who seduces his aristocratic mistress. The acclaimed French dancer Violette Verdy danced Julie, and called her collaboration with Bruhn one of the greatest in her life. John Martin wrote in the *New York Times*, "Mr. Bruhn, as the valet, proves himself once again to be a superb actor-dancer and an artist of the first rank."[8]

Deep in debt, ABT suspended operations for two years. Bruhn returned as a principal to Royal Danish in the midst of another gigantic succession battle. Within a week, his contract was cancelled, but with a lawyer's help he signed a three-year contract to dance three months of his choosing each year.

In 1959, when a formal invitation to join New York City Ballet arrived, Bruhn accepted it. He had danced Balanchine's choreography, but hadn't worked with him directly, and was eager to increase his range. The dancer most identified with New York City Ballet, Maria Tallchief, was returning from maternity leave. Of Osage descent, she had studied with Bronislava Nijinksa and Balanchine, danced with the Ballet Russe de Monte Carlo, and joined NYCB's predecessor, Ballet Society. Bruhn admired Tallchief's talent, and found her individuality tantalizing. For Tallchief, Erik was irresistible.

Bruhn regularly dined with Lincoln Kirstein, the company's co-director. They often disagreed, with the tone of their discussions turning hostile—until Kirstein no longer invited Bruhn to dinner. Then, Balanchine's assistant, Betty Cage, called a meeting of Bruhn, Balanchine, and Kirstein. Balanchine accused Bruhn of acting the star and expecting big money and billing, and demanded to know what he wanted from NYCB. Astounded, it occurred to Bruhn that perhaps it hadn't been Balanchine's idea that he join the company, but Kirstein's, and because Kirstein had soured on him, he might find himself out of a job. Bruhn said that it was his understanding that Balanchine had invited him to join the company, for which he was deeply grateful, as he hoped to profit from Balanchine's genius. However, if Balanchine didn't know what to do with him, then it seemed to Bruhn that he should leave immediately. Balanchine, amused, admitted that he had misunderstood everything. Bruhn was instructed to learn many new roles, and told that he and Tallchief would open in *Swan Lake*.

Companies claiming no stars suffer from the paradox that such a populist feint reveals more about the tyranny of ballet than it obscures. No amount of "Americanization" deters audiences from confusing danseurs nobles and prima ballerinas with princes and princesses. A virtual galaxy of *female* stars emerged at New York City Ballet over the years; among them Tanaquil LeClercq, Maria Tallchief, Patricia Neary, Patricia Wilde, Patricia McBride, Allegra Kent, Suki Shorer, Suzanne Farrell, and Gelsey Kirkland. Balanchine specially coached or set ballets on them. A question mark was placed over his "no stars" policy with respect to men when Balanchine invited Mikhail Baryshnikov to join the company in 1978.

Balanchine made calculated changes that pointed up Maria's work by reducing Erik's role. Bruhn described these engineered catastrophes as "the most destructive and negative" in his life. Performances ran back to back, with changes thrown at him from one to the next. He habitually took himself out of shows. Dancing with Tallchief was exhilarating—and more—as their relationship extended beyond the footlights, but by February 1960, Bruhn had had enough. Tallchief was also at the end of her tether, and said to Walter Terry, "I can stand being listed alphabetically if I must, but I will not be treated alphabetically."[9]

ABT was back on its feet by 1960. Bruhn joined the company's Soviet tour with Tallchief as his partner, and was a guest of the Bolshoi the following season. The tour brought Tallchief and Bruhn closer, but once again, intense intimacy turned Bruhn from fire to ice. Bruhn said,

> We had gotten too involved...Toward the end of the Russian tour, things got out of hand...At the end of the tour...I told her that I no longer wanted to dance with her, talk to her, or ever see her again.[10]

Tallchief tells it this way:

> The trouble is, Erik lets you fall in love with him and then...goodbye!...He is a desperately lonely man. He always was and he always will be.[11]

By 1961, Bruhn was considered by many to be the best male ballet dancer in the world, a *danseur noble*. Bruhn put it this way, "When you've become a box-office name, your fellow dancers are afraid to say anything. And even more, directors or managers never say anything—so long as the house is full. So, everything falls on you."[12]

In spite of Bruhn's disaffection, he continued to partner with Tallchief during the 1960–61 Jacob's Pillow season, where their quarreling resumed, and Bruhn ended their working relationship for good. Tallchief's parting words were, "Alright, I'll find a new partner. There is a Russian who has just defected."[13]

The new prospect was the 23-year-old, Rudolf Nureyev, whose defection rendered the words "defector" and "ballet star" nearly synonymous. Nureyev confided in Tallchief that a major motive for leaving the Soviet Union was the wish to meet and work with Erik Bruhn and study with Vera Volkova. Tallchief received an invitation from Bruhn to be his partner at Royal Danish. He stipulated that their collaboration would be strictly professional and *not* personal. Nureyev accompanied Maria, and Erik found his insouciance delightful. In the hothouse climate of giving one another class, studying with Volkova, and performing, a jealousy developed between the three, forcing them to sort out their personal and professional issues. In the end, Tallchief's notices in

Miss Julie outshined Bruhn's. She returned to the United States, and
Nureyev remained in Copenhagen until invited by Margot Fonteyn to
dance at a gala for the Royal Academy of Dancing. When Nureyev
returned from London, he moved into Bruhn's Gentofte home. Bruhn
sustained a relationship with Nureyev through all the ups and downs,
including Nureyev's greater stardom, even as he lacked Bruhn's polish
and subtlety.

The Bolshoi postponed Erik's guest appearance, which he took
as a slam against his friendship with Rudolf. So they left for Paris, where
Erik would rehearse with Sonia for a London performance of *Flower
Festiival in Genzano* and *Don Quixote*. Though Arova invited Bruhn to
stay with her, when she learned that Nureyev was in tow, she booked a
hotel room for them. Rudy seemed ill at ease with Arova, while Erik
was genuinely pleased to see her again. All three traveled to London
together.

An injured foot prompted Erik to propose that Rudy replace him as
Tallchief's partner on "The Bell Telephone Hour" in New York, which
was a huge success. Rudy and Erik returned to London, and took an
apartment together. Walter Terry wrote: "A beatnik and a prince have
taken London by storm."[14]

Ninette de Valois called Bruhn the "greatest and noblest example of
the Danish school."[15] Yet, when forced to choose a guest dancer (Royal
contract dancers must be British), she was beguiled by the onstage
romance of the Fonteyn-Nureyev partnership, and wholly insensitive to
the offstage Nureyev-Bruhn rivalry: she chose Nureyev. The rejection
was fatal for Bruhn, as he had left Ballet Theatre for the Royal, and was
loathe to return to Copenhagen in defeat.

Bruhn offers this insight:

> What happens with me is that I collide with things....that's what happened
> between Rudik and me—a collision and an explosion which could not last...
> Still, we remain friends and we have continued to go through a great deal
> together, and on many different levels.[16]

Bruhn joined Stuttgart Ballet, where Nureyev would also be dancing
during the 1962 Ballet Festival. Partly in response to Rudy's presence,
but also because the challenging work he was doing under artistic director
John Cranko's direction terrified him, Erik began to experience debilitat-
ing stomach pain. When Cranko expressed doubts that he was truly ill,
Erik walked to his car, and drove from Germany to Copenhagen. Adding
to his discomfort were back spasms. He partnered Sonia at a gala before
the King and Queen. Nureyev joined them, and they returned to Gentofte,
where, during their visit, Erik's mother died of a blood clot in her lung.
In keeping with his mother's deathbed wish, he danced in *Carmen* the very
next evening.

Bruhn traveled to Milan to partner La Scala's celebrated *étoile*, Carla Fracci, whom he had met through Christopher Allan, an ABT press attaché and devoted friend. Bruhn says,

> To dance with Carla was...a love affair consummated on the stage...but when we danced that *Giselle* in Milan in 1963, we were both ready for what happened between us. The moment was there and we were both prepared for it.[17]

Erik accepted Balanchine's invitation to return to City Ballet for the 1963–64 season. Tallchief also returned. Erik began to experience knife-like stomach pain before and after performing, but rarely onstage. Balanchine taught Bruhn the role of Apollo in a single afternoon, along with the roles of the three female Muses. Bruhn called the experience "transformative." The following Tuesday, Bruhn discovered his name on the schedule for the evening performance, but refused to dance without having had a rehearsal with the Muses, and Balanchine wouldn't allow one. Balanchine had told Erik earlier, "You are *the* Apollo!"[18] Erik never got to prove him right. Blaming Balanchine, he left NYCB, and endured agonizing pain for 12 years, until treated for what was later diagnosed as an ulcer.

Invited by Claude Bessy to partner her in Paris Opera's *Giselle*, Bruhn maneuvered to partner Yvette Chauviré instead. The next season, Bruhn divided his time between the Royal Danish, Harkness, and National Ballet of Canada. At Canadian National, he staged a new *Swan Lake,* which, according to Rudy, was suspiciously similar to one they had attempted and failed to mount in Vienna. While critics debated the merits of Bruhn's interpretation, the box office receipts swelled to a record high.

In 1967, Erik finally agreed to return to ABT under the condition that he partner Carla Fracci in *La Sylphide* and *Giselle*. He also accepted the directorship of the faltering Royal Swedish Ballet Company. He reshaped the school, hiring Betty Oliphant to teach and Nureyev to stage *Nutcracker*. Though it nearly cost Bruhn his health to tame the unruly company, it won the Gold Medal in Paris for best foreign company. He partnered Carla Fracci in the film version of *Giselle*, where Bruce Marks danced Hilarion, Toni Lander, Myrtha, and Eleanor d'Antuono and Ted Kivitt danced the peasant pas de deux. Toni Lander presented Bruhn and Fracci with the 1969 Dance Magazine Award, saying,

> Erik was...born to dance. He had everything...physique, technique, talent. From the day he took his first step in the ballet school, it was obvious to everybody that here was the great hope of Danish ballet. Whatever he did became beauty and perfection...always the perfect cavalier to his ballerina and he has that certain way of presenting her...so that she looks absolutely gorgeous, and because of this perfection as a partner...Erik has been testing

all kinds of styles, adding new forms to his own vocabulary, while bringing so much of himself to other people.[19]

In 1970, Bruhn returned to ABT. He ended up in the hospital on opening night of *Giselle*, and Ivan Nagy partnered Makarova for Bruhn. The rivalry Bruhn provoked by maneuvering around Fracci hit a new low at the Kennedy Center, where he had Lucia Chase tell Fracci that he would partner Makarova in *La Fille Mal Gardée* instead of her.

Of their partnership, Makarova said,

> We had many wonderful conversations about *La Sylphide*, and I would say that dancing this ballet, as well as *Giselle* with Erik was a high point in my career...he was an ideal partner—elegant, refined, emotionally generous. We had a beautiful rapport. There is nothing empty about Erik. Every time we see each other, I learn something from him. He has intelligence and sensitivity...Sometimes he would correct me, and everything he said was just right—precise and full of good taste; but then Erik is an artist of the first order.[20]

In 1971, Christopher Allan issued a letter announcing Erik's retirement. Erik attended the ABT opening on January 8 at City Center, where Niels Kehlet was put in for him as Carla Fracci's partner. The audience rose in a standing ovation to honor Bruhn, and Carla Fracci made her entrance in *Coppèlia* with tears in her eyes. Bruhn became Artistic Director of National Ballet of Canada in 1983, and remained there until his sudden death on April 1, 1986.

2

Alicia Alonso

❦ ———————————————————————————— ❧

Unless all signs fail, here is truly a classic dancer, in the sense that Alicia Markova is a classic dancer. Her exquisite performance of Carlotta Grisi in Anton Dolin's Pas de Quatre is no less than a forewarning that before long she is going to step with full grace into Grisi's most famous role of Giselle.

—John Martin, *New York Times*[1]

Alicia Ernestina de la Caridad del Cobre Martínez y del Hoyo owned no practice clothes. When she began studying ballet, class was given on a theater's stage, not in a studio. In an odd way, the playing field was equal: in 1931, when she was nine years old, Alicia was new to ballet and ballet was new to Cuba. It had been introduced to the island by the Russian, Nikolai Yavorsky. The Cuban Pro Arte Musical society doyennes who engaged him expected Yavorsky to turn their daughters into graceful debutantes: that a well-bred young lady such as Alicia might pursue ballet *as a career* was unthinkable!

Most of Alicia's family dated back to the sixteenth century Spanish conquest of Florida. When Spain was forced to cede Florida to the United States, the Arredondo family resettled in Cuba. Alicia's father, Antonio Martínez de Arredondo, a veterinarian, was a paterfamilias in the colonial tradition: Boys mastered the ways of the world, which included a higher education. Girls mastered the household arts, staying out of harm's way. Alicia was born in Havana on December 21, 1921. Ernestina del Hoyo y Lugo, Alicia's mother, encouraged her daughter's interest in dancing.

Because of her dark eyes and love of movement, Alicia was nick-named "Unga"—Spanish for "Hungarian." She danced the rumba and Yoruba-rooted Conga, learning to play maracas and, during a trip to

Alicia Alonso as Juliet in *Romeo and Juliet*. **Photo credit: Walter E. Owen. Courtesy Dance Collection, New York Public Library.**

Spain, the castanets. Alicia and her sister Cuca learned the folkloric Sevillana and Malagueña there, attuning them to placement of the upper body and head. The Spanish costumes left a deep impression on seven-year-old Alicia.

At eight, Alicia began ballet class at Pro Arte Musical, where Yavorsky was an exacting taskmaster. When Alicia became a target for his taunts, Cuca threatened to pull her sister out unless he apologized before the class, which he did. After that, Alicia stayed after class to work a bit more. By regaling her with tales about Nijinksy, Karsavina, or the "floating" Pavlova, and the revolutionary choreographic innovations of Michel Fokine, an opponent of the privileged and elitist Imperial Court, Yavorksy managed to repent for his earlier malfeasance. Fokine and Pavlova had protested the shooting of demonstrators during the 1905 revolution, and defied the Czar's orders to dance, helping to organize a dancers' strike for better working conditions. The lessons of Yavorksy's stories were not lost on the young Alicia.

Pro Arte Musical was itself an elite institution, yet by no means immune to the deprivations resulting from the 1929 worldwide economic depression. There were no pointe shoes, but a member brought a single pair back from Italy to be given to whomever they fit best. Alicia ended up being Pro Arte's lucky Cinderella. Going on pointe convinced her to become a professional dancer. Who knows whether there would have been ballet in Cuba today had the Italian slippers not fit Alicia's feet! Still, Yavorksy seemed to ignore her as he rehearsed others for the end-of-year recital. Then, in a hallway, while she was practicing steps she had watched Yavorksy teach, he suddenly appeared. She halted in terror, but he bid her to continue, and later decided to add her to the grand waltz in *Sleeping Beauty*—the first classical performance by Cuban dancers. It was December 1931; Alicia had just turned 10. Within a year, she was dancing the Bluebird variation in a full ballet performance. "Among my pupils," said Yavorsky, "are many who are doing three years' work in one...Among my top pupils are Delfina Pérez Gurri and Alicia Martínez."[2]

Alicia's father couldn't understand her dance obsession, and her mother worried that she was missing out on the normal social life of girls her age, but as soon as she left for a party, Alicia ran to the studio instead. When a roller skating accident caused her to stop dancing, she gave away her skates. She stopped riding horses so as not to compromise her turnout.

Under the stewardship of Laura Rayneri, Pro Arte Musical changed from an exclusive membership society to a theater that attracted the very best talent and sold tickets at prices that the general public could afford. Rayneri's youngest son Alberto Alonso joined the ballet school in 1933. Ballet's athleticism attracted him, and his self-confidence became a pole of attraction for other boys. Having male students meant more ambitious programs could be mounted. In 1935, Yavokrsky staged *Coppélia* with Alicia dancing Swanilda and Alberto dancing Franz. It was her first full-length ballet: a perfect showcase for her acting and pantomime. After the show, in a display of great gallantry, Alberto's brother Fernando congratulated Alicia. Born into the same social class, Fernando and Alicia were childhood acquaintances. He was aware of her fondness for ballet, but until that evening hadn't seen her perform. Enchanted by Alicia *and* ballet, Fernando decided at the advanced age of 19 to study at Pro Arte Musical. With Alicia coaching, he quickly internalized the discipline required to become a professional. In 1935, the Spanish dancer Antonia Mercé, known as "La Argentina," appeared at Pro Arte. Mercé auditioned Alicia for her company. When they later met amidst a crowd of autograph hounds, La Argentina recognized "the one with the big eyes" whom she had advised to "work very hard." Her encounter with La Argentina, and Alberto Alonso and Delfina Pérez Gurri's successful auditions in Europe, prompted Alicia to confront the limitations of remaining in Havana. Yavorksy's classes had become stale. To grow, she needed to take class and perform with more advanced dancers. At 15, she found herself in long discussions with Fernando about love, marriage, careers, and the social unrest that was consuming their island. The tyrant Gerardo Machado had imposed martial law, hoping to stem an advancing tide of labor uprisings, student strikes, and protests by poor peasants in the country-side, demonstrations that occasionally disturbed the sleep of Alicia's family and their Vedado neighbors. The rebellion was contagious. Alicia's protest took the form of breaking with those social conventions that regarded a theatrical career as the first step down the primrose path to harlotry. She and Fernando decided to move to New York.

Fernando went there first to find work. Alicia followed by boat, chaperoned by the wife of Cuba's Consul General. The couple married shortly after Alicia's arrival. The New York of 1937 had been hit hard by the Depression. An atmosphere of rebellion prevailed there too. There was a willingness among New York performing artists to experiment with dance forms that broke the old rules. The modern dance influences of Isadora Duncan, Martha Graham, Doris Humphrey, and Charles Weidmann were changing the face of dance. The ornamental aspect of ballet was rejected in favor of the unadorned and avant garde modern dance trends. A new dance company, "Ballet Caravan," came to the attention of the public at a benefit for Spanish Civil War anti-fascist fighters. New talent headed for New York, including great dance teachers. Alicia regarded the city as fertile ground for growing a new dance culture. She also discovered her own fertility: she was pregnant, and at 15, was looking forward to a gestating baby *and* a professional dance career.

Fernando was hired into the corps de ballet of Mordkin Ballet Company for its 1937-38 tour. In 1924, Mikhail Mordkin, a former premier danseur with the Imperial Moscow Ballet, opened a school in New York and started the company in 1937. Alicia networked with the New York ballet world via Fernando, and by rehearsing what he was learning, acquired its ballet repertoire, including Giselle, the role for which she would be best known. The couple's daughter Laura was born in 1938. After Laura's birth, thanks to the Federal Dance Project, Alicia was able to take class for 25 cents with Enrico Zanfretta's at Rutgers Church. She met Leon Danilian and Maria Karnilova there. They admired the gifted young girl who worked tirelessly on what would become her hallmark *batterie*: quick, clean, strong beats that gave her feet the rapid lightness of moth wings.

Fernando's job with Mordkin ended, and he joined *Three Waltzes*, a musical at Long Island's Jones Beach Theater. Alicia and Laurita went with him to rehearsals, and not because Alicia was a clinging vine. She used the time to practice on a bridge leading to the stage. Marjorie Fielding, the dance captain, noticed Alicia, and asked her to teach class for the performers' children, including her own daughter, Lorrie. Fielding and her co-director husband, Charles Barnes, added a number to the show for Alicia, and so it was that Alicia Alonso made her U.S. debut at Jones Beach.

Fernando and Alicia could now afford ballet lessons, and had positioned themselves to hear about more and better jobs. They were hired for the Broadway musical, *Great Lady*. Alicia toured Philadelphia, New Haven, and Boston, and learned how to mount a production. It was only her flawed English that kept the curious young woman from feeling completely at home in the United States.

Great Lady received good reviews for its dancing—and no wonder! The cast that *New York Times* critic Brooks Atkinson praised included Nora Kaye, Jerome Robbins and Paul Godkin, as well as Alicia and Fernando. Alicia and Fernando then danced in *Stars in Your Eyes* with Ballet de Monte Carlo's Tamara Toumanova. Alicia utilized her Broadway jobs to strengthen her classical ballet technique, and it paid off: she was offered a scholarship to the prestigious School of American Ballet.

Lincoln Kirstein and Edward M.M. Warburg, the school's founders, asked Vladimir Dimitriew to come to New York to become its director. The Russian-trained George Balanchine, Pierre Vladimiroff (a former Pavlova partner), and British dancer Muriel Stuart were the first teachers. Students quickly acquired lightness, speed, precision, balance, and a talent for choreography, but needed a company to showcase them. In 1934, the American Ballet Company was formed. Resident at the Metropolitan Opera House, it performed until 1939 as Ballet Society, and then was reborn in 1948 under its current name, New York City Ballet. In 1936, a second touring company, "Ballet Caravan," was launched. Touted as reviving the "American spirit," Ballet Caravan would experiment with the new post-Depression genres. The "American spirit" degenerated into jingoism when Kirstein declared that every dancer had to be or become an American citizen. Finally, his reactionary fiat was overturned, and the company reprised its original goal of honing an American dance tradition. Joining its 1939 cross-country tour forced Alicia and Fernando to reorganize their lives. Laura was 18 months old. Relying on other dancers to look after her at rehearsals was no longer practical. They decided to entrust Laura's care to her Havana grandparents, an arrangement that made it possible for Alicia to have a career.

The company's first tour by train and bus—and taxi, in an instance when Alicia, Fernando and the company pianist missed their train— consisted of 35 one-night stands, and offered the rare opportunity to dance a great variety of roles. Alicia returned to New York a soloist, and danced the Mexican Sweetheart and The Mother to Michael Kidd's Billy in *Billy the Kid*. She was learning choreography at a breakneck speed. In Cuba, she had become accustomed to short classical variations. In the United States, she was learning long, fast-paced, asymmetrical works to contemporary, sometimes atonal music, where she relied on her own counting system. It was a challenge to filter into a company where dancers had been close friends for years and spoke rapid-fire English, leaving shy Alicia out of the repartee. She disliked the North American custom of married women taking their husbands' names, and said, "So now I am Alicia Alonso and no longer Alicia Martínez."[3] So, when she read a review describing Ballet Caravan as a company of "fresh young American dancers," she was surprised to find herself agreeing that she had become a genuine contributor to the new "American" idiom.

After the tour, Alicia and Fernando danced in a Havana Pro Arte concert, visited Laura, and returned to New York to audition for a new company, Ballet Theatre. Founded by Lucia Chase and Richard Pleasant in 1940, Ballet Theatre would later become American Ballet Theatre, and offer a broad repertoire, including classical, contemporary, modern, and character works focusing on Black and Spanish dance. Eugene Loring, Michael Fokine, Anton Dolin, and Antony Tudor headed its roster of choreographers. Among those who joined immediately were Adolph Bolm, Agnes de Mille, Mikhail Mordkin, and Bronislava Nijinska, John Kriza, Muriel Bentley, Jerome Robbins, and Alicia. Fernando joined several months later. The backstage atmosphere was more inclusive than Mordkin had been, and Alicia renewed her friendships with Nora Kaye, Maria Karnilova, and Jerome Robbins, all very young and looking out for one another. Alicia's new ballet teacher was Alexandra Federova. Using the Cecchetti method, Federova demanded proper alignment and fluid movement. From Federova's son, Leon Fokine, Alica learned *caractère* according to Eastern European folkloric traditions. She crammed as many classes as she could into a day. When not dancing, she was poring over dance books. Critic Olga Maynard rated her dancing of The Bird in *Peter and the Wolf* "equal–and sometimes the superior—to some Diaghilev soloists."[4]

Soon Alicia was chosen over the company's soloists, reprising the roles she danced in Loring's *Billy the Kid*, with him dancing Billy. Of Alicia, Loring said, "She radiated a sense of sun...a kind of full-blooded honesty."[5] She was cast as the renowned dancer Carlotta Grisi, best-known for her interpretation of Giselle, for which Alicia would become equally, if not more well-known. Alicia and co-stars Nan Gollner, Nina Stroganova, and Katherine Sergava took 17 curtain calls on opening night. She didn't trust the heady feeling, and committed herself more fully to the hard work of perfecting her technique and artistry. There was just one problem: she had begun bumping into things for no apparent reason. Something was wrong with her vision, and she consulted an eye doctor. He happened to be in the audience on an evening when dizzying black blotches appeared before her eyes, and was summoned backstage. Alicia had suffered a detached retina of the right eye, and was scheduled for surgery the day after she performed in Ballet Theatre's last full spring program.

If the eye were a conventional camera, the retina would be the film upon which images are imprinted and sent to the brain to develop. The eye cannot work without its retina intact. After her retina surgery, Alicia was ordered to lie still, as any stirring could cause another detachment. Her life in motion came to an abrupt halt, her head immobilized by sand-bags. She incurred permanent loss of the peripheral vision in the eye. When she returned to class, her retina detached again. On her doctor's advice, she returned to Cuba to rest after the second surgery. A respected Havana ophthalmologist offered a frightful diagnosis: she had sustained another detachment in her right eye *and* a detached left retina as well. She was hospitalized for surgery on both eyes. With both eyes swathed in bandages, she recuperated at the home of her mother-in-law. The doctor's strict orders were: "You must not cry, you must not laugh, you must not move. And you must never dance again."[6] In the dance world, that pronouncement is not as uncommon as it is fatal. Many a dance teacher relates ruefully how a torn radial crucial ligament ended his or her career in a flash of pain. But there had been no damage to Alicia's body or spirit, so she heard none of the intended fatalism in her doctor's words. They were heard as more of a challenge than a sanction. At 19, she was as determined as the girl of 13 who ran to the studio instead of a party. She used her long, dark confinement to mentally summon her muscle memory, so as not to have to rely on her eyes.

At rehearsal, ballet dancers walk around randomly, wrists lifted as if by strings, the "strings" wagging the hands in a mysterious sign language, fingers, heads, and eyes turned skyward, as if trying to recall a name. This "marking with the hands" is among the most important of activities for dancers. Alicia lay perfectly still, except for her fingers. As she listened to music by the composer, Adolphe Adam, she concentrated on marking the steps to *Giselle*, bending her fingers into pliés, floating them into jumps, "throwing" them into grand jetés, and spindling them left or right to signify *en dédans* (inside) or *en déhors* (outside) turns. Fernando was both audience and repetiteur, miraculously offering corrections. Three-year-old Laura, whom she pretended to see through her bandages, was her companion. When the bandages finally came off, Alicia was rewarded with having most of her sight in her left eye, but none in her right.

Alicia's body felt like it was not her own. She had to return to the studio as quickly as possible to get it back. After not having taken barre for an entire year, and in defiance of her doctor's orders, she slowly began to "find" her alignment. Difficulty seeing had made her crane her neck forward. She had to relearn its placement, and re-chart the "box" of space that a dancer visualizes around her. Alicia exchanged ideas in salon discussions with other artists, and choreographed her first work, *La Condesita*, to music by Joaquin Nín. She staged a production of *Aida* for a New York troupe on tour. She began teaching class at the School of

Language and Art. That was before the 1959 Cuban Revolution and subsequent U.S.-imposed embargo, when there was a rich exchange of culture between Havana and New York. Without consulting her doctor, Alicia accepted a position as guest artist at Pro Arte in 1942. She danced the pas de deux from *Aurora's Wedding*, and in *Les Sylphides*, and in works that Alberto set.

During a hurricane, Alicia ran outside to rescue her Great Dane and the dog's puppies. A glass door shattered, hitting Alicia in the head, shards cutting her everywhere, with blood streaming down, but her eyes were unaffected. She made her case to the doctor: since the blow to her head did no damage to her eyes, could she dance again? His reply was "It's up to you."[7]

Alicia returned to New York's Ballet Theatre in the fall of 1943. During her absence, the company had gained size and stature. Impresario Sol Hurok was changing its image from "All-American" to International. Two new prima ballerinas, Alicia Markova and Irina Baronova, along with Anton Dolin, assumed ranking positions as stars. The company had lost Eugene Loring, Donald Saddler, and Michael Fokine. New additions were Rosella Hightower, Barbara Fallis, Janet Reed, Sono Osato, and Léonide Massine.

When Markova fell ill before a *Giselle* performance, Alicia was put in for her. In spite of having painstakingly learned the role during her blindness, she began to "see" how little she really knew about it. She set about getting the training she needed from Fedorova, but also took a page from Pavlova's training with Cecchetti, setting up a regimen that enabled her to concentrate on a different element each day. With the company's big shift from an ensemble repertoire to a star-driven eclecticism also went its singularity, a loss felt at the box office. In the fall of 1945, Alicia and Andre Eglevksy headed the cast of *Giselle*. This time, audiences did not see a Markova understudy. They saw Alicia as she saw Giselle, devoid of guile, purely a creature of the joy and passion bred of country life. Belief in herself allowed Alicia to overcome blindness; Giselle's mission was just a tad more challenging: to overcome death.

What earned Alicia a prominent position in American Ballet Theatre's galaxy of great dancers? She had technique, versatility, and theatricality, but mostly, it was her willingness to work hard, alone and with her partners, for the interpretation the choreographer's work merited. As she learned more of the company's repertoire, she began to appreciate the importance of a good partner, and saw partnering as a conversation through movement, the interpenetration of contrasting personalities to tell a story of romance, intrigue, anger, or frustration. Her partnership with Igor Youskevitch, a dancer of the Russian aristocracy whose imperial breeding was ever present in his work, was highly praised. What audiences and critics didn't know was what a huge effort it took for both dancers to accommodate to each others' style, mood, and work habits.

Alicia Alonso with Igor Youskevitch in *Giselle*. Photo credit: Ballet Theatre Foundation. Courtesy Dance Collection, New York Public Library.

Youskevitch was a trained engineer and liked to have every moment planned to the last detail. Alonso was more spontaneous: once the plan was in place, she liked to freely use variables in the music and stage elements to reinvent her interpretation. Still, their partnering was so exquisite that George Balanchine set his renowned *Theme and Variations* on them. Alicia had an opportunity to open in the world premiere of Agnes De Mille's *Fall River Legend*, the dramatic story of Lizzie Borden. Alicia threw herself fully into becoming Lizzie, who had been driven to such despair that she hacked her evil stepmother and ambivalent father to death. Alicia viewed each role as a means to grow, a step out of blindness into light. What a letdown it was when Lucia Chase announced that due to a fiscal crisis, there would be no 1949 season!

Ironically, ABT's temporary closure offered Alicia and Fernando an opportunity they had hoped for. Because of the speed with which they had left Cuba, one might have thought that they had never given the island so much as a backward glance. That was not the case, however. While away, and on return visits, their awareness of the artistic treasures they'd left behind grew. They had left their child there, and were for some time conceiving of a second "child," a world class ballet company on Cuban soil. Alicia saw no reason why Cuban-born dancers should have to leave the island to learn ballet technique. She and Fernando invited several laid-off ABT dancers to join them in Cuba. They viewed the Latin, and particularly Cuban, personality as distinctive—warm, expressive, and rippling with Yoruba-inflected musicality. Here was the chance to provide an artistic platform for it. Alberto's directorship of Pro Arte had set the stage for experimental works in the folkloric tradition. Alicia and Fernando named the new 40-member company "Ballet Alicia Alonso." Fernando and Alberto were its artistic directors, and Alicia its prima ballerina. There were 16 Cubans, and a shank of ex-ABTers: Igor Youskevitch, Helen Komarova, Paula Lloyd, Michael Maule, and Royes Fernandez. They were joined by Dulce Wohner Anaya and Enrique Martínez, who performed principal roles. The musical directors were ABT ex-pats, Max Goberman, and Ben Steinberg.

Pro Arte generously supplied pointe shoes, costumes, sets, and a discount on the rent. Soon its repertoire included *Giselle*, *Petrouchka*, *Coppelia*, and the Black Swan pas de deux. The company held its debut on October 28, 1948, at Pro Arte, with Alicia and Igor Youskevitch heading a bill featuring the Pas de Quatre, from *Swan Lake*, *Giselle*, *Peter and the Wolf*, and *Les Sylphides*. Without really knowing the political terrain, the company launched a tour of Latin America. They arrived in Caracas in the midst of a military state of siege. The University of Puerto Rico bailed them out, chartering a plane to bring them to its Rio Piedras campus where the company was given keys to the city. A few of the American dancers decided to leave at that point, and when the remaining dancers returned to Cuba, the company decided to tour the island's outlying provinces. This offered the many Cubans who had never stepped inside a theater a first chance to see ballet. Hundreds turned out. Back in Havana, the company gave a free outdoor performance attended by 30,000, where audience members filled every available inch of space. In January, 1949, the company went on an 11-country tour of Central and Latin America, mostly to small towns, as bookings in large cities were impossible without money to pay for agents and publicity. Alicia decided to fill a hole in one of the programs with a performance of *Dying Swan*, but she had no money for a costume. Her mother, an ingenious designer and seamstress, was traveling with the company and noticed that the white, sheer hotel curtains had an oversized double hem. When Alicia returned from rehearsal, the new costume and curtains looked splendid! The company received rave reviews. Among the new dancers were Lupe Serrano, Felipe Segura, and Nicholas Magallanes.

Stranded in Chile for a month without money to pay their hotel bills, the Argentine government flew them to Buenos Aires, and underwrote hotel expenses, while the Cuban government did nothing to help them. Word reached Havana of their triumphs and their debts, and grass-roots support took the form of an organization composed of artists, distinguished women, and university students who urged the Cuban government to supply funds. After all, tattered, inflammable sets could not travel to New York City, where Sol Hurok was eager to book the company into a tour. In 1950, when the government finally coughed up a monthly stipend, most of the dancers collected their back wages and looked for work elsewhere, leaving the company nearly devoid of dancers. Alicia and Fernando opened an academy linked to the company to train its future dancers, with Fernando as school director and Alicia's sister, Cuca Martínez, as its administrative director. Fernando began developing a curriculum that leaned on classical training, enhanced by a sensibility redolent of Cuban warmth, flexibility, and theatricality.

To earn wages to invest in the new enterprise, Alicia returned to Ballet Theatre in 1950, which became a conduit for stellar talent that ended up in the Cuban company. The birth of the company coincided with the political ferment that would eventually lead to Cuban workers striking at their workplaces—mostly sugar refineries owned by U.S. interests. Marches in Havana and clandestine guerilla warfare in the Sierra Maestra hastened the overthrow of the hated Batista dictatorship. At a huge rally to commemorate the 100th anniversary of the death of Jose Martí, the company performed a work choreographed by Cuca Martínez.

In 1955, Batista withdrew the company subsidy, instead offering a small sum for Alicia, and another for the school. These "gifts" were contingent upon Ballet de Cuba, as it was now called, being willing to join Batista's National Institute of Culture. Alicia publicly rejected the offer, which she characterized alternately as bribery and charity. The company would never become an arm of the government! Her declaration initiated a whirlwind of protest, and out of it, the Committee for the Defense of Ballet was formed. Following each performance on the company's tour of the island, Alicia made a presentation to the audience about the ballet's financial needs. Members of the F.E.U (Federacion Estudantil Universitaria-University Student Federation) organized a mass rally at the University of Havana on September 16, 1956, where Alicia danced in *Les Sylphides*, and closed with *Dying Swan*. The audience of 30,000 rose to its feet, shouting "¡Brava!" and Alonso announced that this was her last *Dying Swan* as long as Batista remained in power.

Alicia left Ballet Theatre to join Ballet Russe de Monte Carlo, where she would not be required to dance more than six months out of the year. In the fall of 1957, the Cuban company danced *Coppélia* in Los Angeles, and Alicia danced in the Soviet Union—the first ballerina from a country with a pro-capitalist government to dance there. A three-week tour turned into a ten-week, 17,000 mile tour. After the Riga show, the corps dancers carried Alicia to her dressing room on their shoulders. In class, she stood at the barre between Ulanova and Tikhomirnova. The newspapers praised her "sculptured poses," and the "stability, preciseness of the smallest movements and the brio of her pirouettes."[8] While in Chicago in 1959, Alicia learned that the Batista dictatorship had been overthrown by a revolution led by Fidel Castro. She expressed her hope that "the grave injustices in Cuba would come to an end."[9] In February, 1959, Alonso received Dance Magazine's highest award, the Silver Trophy. Its inscription read: "To Alicia Alonso for illuminating the purity of classic dance with her radiant warmth—a dazzling combination which recently brought surprise and delight to still other audiences in Russia." In her acceptance remarks, Alicia predicted "the changes [in Cuba] will result in a new ballet company for the world."[10]

Laura Alonso was raiding the refrigerator on a Sunday morning, when there was a knock at the front door. She found herself face-to-face with the Commander in Chief, Fidel Castro. "Is your mother home?" he asked. "No," she stammered. "Well, is your father home, then?" "Yes, he's upstairs in his room."[11] Fidel rushed past Laura and climbed the stairs to find Fernando sprawled in bed, reading the paper. Sitting on the bed, Castro asked, "How much will you need for the next ballet season?" Fernando quickly calculated and named a figure. Fidel considered the estimate, and then said, "We'll double it. But it has to be the best company in the world, with dancers from all of the Americas." Alicia got busy traveling to identify candidates to audition for the generously funded Pan-American company.

Alicia's work with Ballet Russe and as a guest artist with other companies picked up steam in the early 1960s. She appeared in New York's Central Park's open-air theater before thousands. She and Youskevitch toured Latin America, and Ballet Nacional de Cuba hosted the International Ballet Festival. Alicia and Royes Fernandez replaced Alicia Markova and Erik Bruhn in ABT's 20th Anniversary *Giselle* at the Metropolitan Opera House, and received stellar reviews. In the midst of a free exchange between dance artists from around the world, politics intervened. The 1959 Cuban Revolution expelled the corporations—majority-U.S.—which had bled the economy dry and exploited Cuban workers. In 1960, U.S. President Dwight D. Eisenhower declared an embargo on export to Cuba of all but food and medical supplies. In 1961, President John F. Kennedy broke diplomatic relations with Cuba. Ties between the two countries were severed after the U.S. CIA-engineered Playa Giron invasion failed to overthrow the revolution. The U.S. then launched a secondary boycott of any country that traded with Cuba. The resulting pauperization only served to increase Cuba's determination to become independent. The Cuban Communist Party debated the pitfalls of its forced reliance on Soviet aid. The embargo severed the continuity between the Ballet Nacional and the U.S. dance world at the very moment when the best ballet training in the Americas was to be found in revolutionary Cuba.

Laura Rayneri de Alonso donated the Spanish colonial townhouse next to Pro Arte to the revolutionary government. It became the home of the Cuban National Ballet. Alicia charted an ambitious course of outreach to working class communities and agricultural workers in the country-side. Laura worked with her mother to initiate "Psycho Ballet," a revolutionary program enabling blind and disabled children to explore dance movement. The company consciously sought members from Cuba's large black population, whose culture was rooted in the Yoruba tradition, and performed on jury-rigged stages at factories, orphanages, and on loading docks under the aegis of the successful literacy campaign which drew international acclaim. "Ballet" was one of the first words newly literate adults would read and write. Dancers joined work brigades and Committees in Defense of the Revolution. Laura Alonso and Lupe Calzadilla offered evening ballet classes to workers, who learned reper-toire in two weeks that had taken the company years to master.[12] Even with the shortfalls in harvesting 10 million kilos of sugar cane in 1970, and the rectification campaign and "special period" that followed the col-lapse of the Soviet Union owing to Cuba's overdependence on subsidies from that country, free, world-class ballet performances were accessible to everyone.

In 1962, Cubanacán, formerly a country club, became the new, larger site of the National School of Ballet, where any child who passed three levels of dance training could receive an academic education, including dance, music, theater, painting, and sculpture.

The company toured Eastern Europe during the first years of the embargo, winning top honors at the Varna competition. It wasn't until 1966 that it performed in such U.S.-allied nations as France, and then at Montreal's Expo '67. Alicia reunited there with Maria Karnilova, Lucia Chase, and Eleanor D'Antuono, a deeply emotional experience, as actually seeing them was nearly impossible: Alicia was almost completely blind.

When cataracts prevented her from being able to "spot" (keeping the eye trained on one place while turning), she practiced turning with her eyes shut. Still, in spite of her efforts, she danced one entire performance with her back to the audience. One time, the power failed in the theater,[13] but unaware, she continued dancing. For Alicia, blindness did not signal the end of her career; it was just one more hurdle to overcome. She used the imagery she culled during her first eye surgery. She trusted her part-ners to cue her, especially Azari Plisetski, Igor Youskevitch, and Jorge Esquivel, who was recruited to the ballet school when it toured his orphanage. Agnes de Mille, a juror in a Moscow competition, said, "Who can explain...how she manages space, without guide as to direction or distance? What incomparable bravery. She has the most beautiful feet in the business. These days they bear not only wings but laurels for valor."[14] Wherever Alicia or the company danced, the reviews were unstinting in their praise. In *Dancing Times*, Janet Sinclair and Leo Kersley wrote, "For dancers, Cuba is the promised land."

At 51, Alicia could see only a pinpoint of light. When the company flew to Bulgaria, where nine dancers won awards at the Dance Festival, Alicia flew to Barcelona for eye surgery. She regained partial vision in one eye, the other remaining sightless, and did not dance for two years. In 1975, she danced Jocasta in *Oedipo Rey* and the title role in *Carmen*, and the U.S. State Department reversed an earlier decision by granting Alonso and Esquivel visas for the ABT gala, where they received a 20-minute standing ovation. It was her first time back in 15 years! Reviewers called Alicia "timeless," and the event a "watershed moment." In 1978, the company, including Laura's son, Ivan, danced Antonio Gades' *Blood Wedding* at the Met. To dance, Alicia had overcome social sanctions, Batista's avarice and blackmail, blindness, age, and even a political embargo.

In 1974, she and Fernando divorced. Alicia later married the dancer Pedro Simón. At 85, Alicia is nearly completely blind, and Simon squires the company. Cuba has made an effort to export its dancers, as it has its doctors and teachers. Nonetheless, some dancers have cited the wish to dance with other companies as a reason for defecting to the U.S., which, in the language of the U.S. press, becomes a quest for "artistic freedom," even as most of the dancers discover that U.S. companies and training don't measure up to their Cuban-cultivated expectations. At the same time, the BNC is less racially balanced than in the early revolutionary period, and faces shortages of necessary items. Even so, the Cuban National Ballet Company remains one of the most respected companies in the world, and the life and career of Alicia Alonso, its Ballerina Assoluta, is reflected in her own words in Frank Boehm's documentary film "Alicia":[15]

> Every performance is an opportunity, even if there is just one person in the theater. If that person leaves the theater happy, having seen the beauty, you have achieved your life's purpose. Nothing you can earn, nothing you can own in your life can compare with that feeling. *This* is the life of an artist![16]

3

Rudolf Nureyev

He had the charisma and the simplicity of a man of the earth and the untouchable arrogance of the gods.

—Mikhail Baryshnikov[1]

Farida Nureyeva gave birth to her third child and first son, Rudolf, on March 17, 1938. He was born in a rail car on the Trans-Siberian Express while his mother was en route from her home town of Kushnarenkovo in the Urals to a small village outside of Vladivistok, where Rudolf's father, a Communist Party Red Army functionary, was assigned. Nobody can pinpoint where on the 3,900 mile route or in what jurisdiction Rudik was born. Perhaps this serves as a metaphor for the young Tatar's life, most of it spent stateless, as an international icon of the ballet world, with defining moments occurring in transit, between nations, in theaters and studios and even on back streets, the borders and boundaries of which must have seemed inconsequential to Nureyev, who wanted nothing more than to dance for the entire world.

His ancestry on his father's side could be traced to Genghis Khan and the thirteenth century Mongol conquest of the Russian steppes. The word "Tatar" is derived from "Tartarus," the territory of "fierce people" just below Hades, where the Titans were to be found. When it suited him, Nureyev would proudly cite his Tatar roots to justify an entire repertoire of uncivil behaviors.

His parents, raised as devout Muslims, married in 1928, the year that Stalin initiated a string of schematic five-year plans vaunted as the means to realize the goals of the 1917 Russian revolution. Hamet and Farida shared an earnest belief in the potential of communism to transform their impoverished lives. They hoped that Hamet could obtain military

Rudolf Nureyev in *Corsaire*. Photo credit: Henrietta McDowell. Courtesy San Francisco Performing Arts Library & Museum.

schooling first, and then Farida would pursue her dream of becoming a teacher. He completed his education, but two more children came along after Rudolf, and she reassigned her hopes for her own education to her children. When Rudolf was 16 months old, Hamet transferred to Moscow, whereupon the family's fortunes improved considerably. During the German invasion in 1941, the family was evacuated to Chelyabinsk, about 850 miles east of Moscow, and ended up living in Shuchye, in a mud brick house with a lime bark roof, dirt floors, and no electricity or running water. Nureyev remembers his days there as an "icy, dark and above all, hungry"[2] time, and would later refer to his childhood as his "Potato Period." Christians who shared their small home with the family rewarded the children's prayers with bits of potato or goat cheese, inciting Farida's atheist and communist anger. To Rudolf, the reward justified uttering the arcane words.

Rudolf took refuge from the terror of the war, rural poverty, and grim surroundings by listening to the radio. Music enchanted him: "I looked upon music, from my earliest days, as a friend, a religion, a way to good fortune."[3]

Soon Rudolf's family would move again, to Ufa, the capital of the Eastern republic of Bashkir, where Rudolf's uncle Nurislam and his family lived. In 1942, the town, an industrial center, was key to the war effort. Many heavy industries had been relocated in the mineral-rich Urals, home to the oil refineries and power plants. Food for the large family was scarce, and Farida sold her absent husband's clothes or walked the two-day journeys to town, 24 miles away from where they lived, to feed the family. Leaving the woods at night, she would sometimes see glints of light, which she mistook for fireflies but later realized were wolves, and yet her resolve never failed. She worked first at a bakery and then a refinery. The children took charge of their own upbringing, reading library books or playing checkers by the light of a Primus lamp in the evening, and attending school by day.

Rudolf began kindergarten owning no shoes. His sister Lilya carried him to school on her back. According to Rudolf, children made fun of him, calling him a beggar. Former classmates now say that it was not so much for his apparent poverty that they ridiculed him (everyone was poor), but for wearing girls' clothes. Later in life, Rudolf attributed his need to acquire things and accumulate vast amounts of money to the humiliation he experienced in childhood. Never assured of an evening meal, he made certain to eat breakfast, and another free breakfast served to him at school. It was in school that Rudolf learned Bashkirian and Tatar folk dances. He was a quick study, learning the steps on his first try. He would practice at home, singing the music he had heard earlier in the day. He made friends with Albert Arslanov, who also loved to dance, and the boys participated in a children's ensemble that performed for hospitalized soldiers. The two boys were even filmed dancing for a newsreel. Neighbors recommended that Farida send her gifted child to Leningrad for a *real* dance education.

Rudolf's school days were shared with Albert, but he also spent time alone on a perch above the Ufa railway station, watching the trains and imagining them taking him to destinations he had learned about from Jules Verne books. Even as he dreamed of leaving, life in post-war Ufa was changing, as so-called undesirables, exiled from St. Petersburg and Moscow, arrived and began sharing their intellectual and cultural bounty with the town. A visit to the Opera House on New Year's Eve of 1945 (his mother having managed to get the entire family in on one ticket) convinced Rudolf that the enchantments found there were his dream for the future. The ballet he saw that night, *The Song of the Cranes*, starring Zaitouna Nazretdinova, transported him.

> Something was happening to me which was taking me far from my sordid world and bearing me right up to the skies. From the moment I entered that magic place, I felt I had really left the world, borne far away from everything I knew by a dream staged for me alone…I was speechless.[4]

By the time Rudolf was nine, his father had returned, and while they shared daily routines together, Hamet was not very interested in his son's dance activities. His sister Rosa on the other hand, was also dancing, winning some contests, and teaching Eurythmics. Rosa brought home dance costumes, and Rudolf would spend hours examining them. His dreaminess puzzled his classmates, and they would gang up on him to provoke a response. He avoided them, but when forced to retaliate, he would throw himself on the ground and cry like a wounded animal, exaggerating the insult, then quickly calm down after his point had been made. In 1948, he won his first dance prize—in a Young Communist League contest among amateur groups of the Zhdanov district. A dancer from Ufa Ballet who set a piece for the children encouraged him to study at Teachers House with Anna Udeltsova, a former Leningrad ballerina. Udeltsova insisted that Rudolf audition by performing a gopak and a lezginka. Stunned by what she saw, she told Rudolf that he had "a duty to learn classical dancing" at the Maryinsky school in St. Petersburg (then Leningrad). After 18 months, Udelstova referred Rudolf to Elena Konstantinovna, a former coryphée member of the Kirov. Twelve-year-old Rudolf was the best student in her very disciplined class. The teachers and the accompanist invited him to tea and took care of his creature comforts, but Farida, while favoring him, made no special effort to encourage him as a dancer. He very consciously took charge of his own advancement. When his father caught him in a lie to cover sneaking in an extra dance class, he beat Rudolf. It is not clear whether the beating was punishment for lying or his passion for dance, an interest his politically-minded father regarded as frivolous. When Rudolf asked Hamet to inquire about the Kirov school, he relented when he saw how much it meant to his son. Instead of admitting that he could not afford the 200-ruble train fare to Leningrad, Hamet himself lied to Rudolf, reporting back that it was too late—the Ufa children had already left for the audition.

Thanks to his interest in geography and maps, it wasn't long before Rudolf realized how attainable Leningrad was and redoubled his resolve to get there. His determination was aggressively discouraged by Hamet. By the age of 14, he had become "nervous and explosive," according to his friend Albert.[5] He didn't care what his classmates thought of his behavior and bragged about his physical prowess in rude, tearful outbursts. While he excelled in literature, geography, and physics, like so many dance students who regard time in the classroom as wasted, Rudolf would dreamily sketch the outturned legs of ballerinas instead of taking notes, and use his pocket change to buy photos of famous dancers. In his classes at the Pioneer Palace, he demanded that the teachers give him corrections, even when he acquitted himself perfectly.

The children had many performing opportunities. Rudolf disliked performing at the opulent officers' club. He took great joy in dancing with the traveling theater that balanced a board between two trucks transporting dancers, their costumes and props to small towns, so that workers and peasants could watch them perform folkloric dances. Rudolf celebrated his 15th birthday one month after Stalin's death, which coincided with the opening of the 1953 inauguration of a ballet studio at the Ufa Opera House. He was admitted to the ballet school there on the recommendation of his teacher, Elena Voitovich, and shared a dressing room with the Ufa Ballet dancers. Soon he was given walk-on roles, for which he was paid. He began studying with a new teacher, Zaitouna Nureevna Bakhtinyarova, who ran a tight ship and didn't care for Rudolf's outbursts and undisciplined behavior. To discourage it, she made him take class in the hallway, explaining to him that she was hardest on those who showed promise. Rudolf was taking three classes a day—not easy, as he had to sneak out of the house moments after his father left for work, often arriving late. He focused on what he couldn't do—aping his friend Albert's elevation, while Albert admired Rudolf's pirouettes. By 16, Rudolf's dancing and teaching at various workers' collectives was earning him almost as much money as his father was bringing home. Hamet grew more accepting of his son's unusual vocation.

A temporary job with the corps de ballet offered Rudolf an opportunity to dance in the opera *Ivan Susanin*, but it coincided with Rudolf's high school final exams. He failed his exams, *and* failed to report his failure to his parents. Luckily, the failing grades were camouflaged by a company summer tour that took Rudolf and Albert 750 miles northwest of Ufa to the Oka River. On a night off, they took a bus to Moscow, visiting Moscow's museums and bookstores.

Rudolf accepted an invitation to become a company apprentice, and studied with the ballet master Viktor Pyari who criticized him for working "from the outside in,"[6] mimicking work he'd seen rather than building a sturdy platform of technique.

At 17, he learned that, pending an audition, the Ministry of Culture had approved his scholarship to Leningrad. Initially, the school had turned down his application based on his age. The upper age limit was 14, but after some politicking from Bakshir to Moscow, and a fortuitous tour there, where Rudolf replaced an injured dancer, and maneuvering to dance for the Leningrad school administration in a hotel room, he was accepted without having to audition. At the same time, one of his teachers was lobbying the Bolshoi to take Rudolf, and they agreed, but offered no scholarship. Then the Ufa Ballet offered Rudolf a contract, which he would have immediately accepted had it come along earlier. Instead, he went to Leningrad. By the late nineteenth century, St. Petersburg's Leningrad Choreographic Institute had attained first rank in academy training for aspiring dancers. It was renamed the Vaganova Choreographic Institute in 1957 to honor the eponymous teacher, Agrippina Vaganova, whose meticulous method is now taught the world over. "Vaganova" trains dancers to work the body around the spine, encouraging ample response to the music, delivered with faultless technique. Male dancers are very much center stage, taking grand leaps, multiple turns, and costumed as daring, dashing princes, rogues, or loathsome evildoers.

Rudolf took leave of his father and tearful mother at the train station, and having boarded a local instead of an express, ended up standing for what was a 16- instead of 8-hour run to Leningrad. When he arrived on August 25, 1955, he learned that in spite of assurances that he would not have to audition; crossed signals from parallel tracks of the bureaucracy required that he dance before a panel of the school's administrators and teachers. Vera Costravitskaya auditioned him along with a group of Latvian boys, and prophesied, "Young man, you'll either become a brilliant dancer—or a total failure." She then reconsidered and added, "Most likely, a total failure."[7] She assigned him to the sixth level, where most of the boys were 15 years old and taught by the school's director, Valentin Shelkov. It wasn't long before Nureyev and Shelkov established a relationship of mutual dislike and distrust. Rudolf would say of Shelkov that he was "a boss, not a ballet master."

Soviet ex-patriot dancer, Valery Panov wrote:

> The "regimen"—that is *conformity*—was held up as the highest good of all our work, while artistic brilliance that challenged the "norms" of deportment was positively persecuted. The more gifted a pupil, the quicker the authorities were to expel him if he was rude, childish, or incompetent in general subjects—most of all, if he violated the regulations.[8]

Panov's words could describe most schools in *any* system, but the Stalin-engendered bureaucracy was especially ill-suited to Rudolf's temperament. As in Ufa, he placed himself at odds with classmates and teachers, breaking as many rules as he could, especially those governing eating, bathing, or conventions requiring that he change clothes in front of others.

The academy's 11-hour day began with ballet history, music, or art, followed by two hours of ballet class. After lunch, there were academic subjects and character, fencing, makeup, piano, or French lessons. Rudolf was least interested in Soviet history and most interested in literature, art, and dance history.

After Rudolf broke one of the school's cardinal rules by staying out all night, he found his meal ticket and mattress missing. He mocked the rules in front of his classmates, resulting in a visit to Shelkov's office, where the director snatched Rudolf's address book out of his hand.

Rudolf then demanded to be promoted two levels into the class taught by Alexander Pushkin. Shelkov assented, happy to be rid of the trouble-maker, and took advantage of the occasion to predict only the worst for Rudolf's ballet future.

Another Pushkin protégé, Mikhail Baryshnikov, said of Pushkin, "He had patience, his rapport with the students was very low-key...He was teaching you how to dance, not making you dance."[9] A men's teacher of the highest rank, Pushkin was the scion of the exemplary technique handed down by generations of Kirov teachers. Unlike Shelkov, Pushkin revered the capacities of his students, mining their strengths, never raising his voice. He said almost nothing, convinced that explanations were redundant: it is the work itself that teaches musicality and the broad artistic demands of the art form.

Pushkin's quiet, confident temperament made it possible for Rudolf to work with complete focus. For example, he found cabrioles difficult, and would repeat them *en face*, heading directly into the mirror, to see every detail of his mistakes. To compensate for having left Shelkov's class, he would ask level six students what they had learned.

The students were given supernumerary roles in Kirov productions. Rudolf committed every step to memory. He wasn't satisfied with his grasp of the music, and sneaked into the theater whenever he could. He frequented the Hermitage, Philharmonic, Pushkin, and Gorky theaters. He cultivated a friendship with Menia Martínez, a Cuban student, whose lively appearance and personality were magnetic. She could sing and dance the Conga and other Yoruba dances, a standout in the very ways that meshed with Nureyev's narcissistic requirements. She would be the first of a certain type of woman to whom he would gravitate: attractive, distinctive, somewhat aloof, yet completely enthralled by, and in most cases in love with, him. Others would include Margot Fonteyn, Jacqueline Kennedy, Lee Radziwill, Clara Saint, and Maude Gosling. Menia's father was a University of Havana professor and editor of the Cuban Communist Party newspaper. She introduced Rudik to her Leningrad family friends, Mikhail Volkenstein, a physicist, and Estella Alenikova, an editor, who spoke several languages and enjoyed discussing Pushkin, Shakespeare, Dostoyevksy, and Göethe with Rudolf when he visited their dacha in the mushroom picking season. Rudolf began taking piano lessons with Marina Petrovna Savva, who played at the Maly Opera Theater.

The November 1956 20th Party Congress "Khrushchev Revelations" partially exposed the Stalin bureaucracy's lies and political thuggery: assassinations and outright murders of hundreds of thousands of workers and peasants, revolutionary oppositionists inside and outside the Soviet Union, and the wholesale repression of Soviet national minorities. While the revelations had little impact on the world of ballet, the public pretense of redressing Stalin's crimes opened up space for companies to tour beyond the borders of the Soviet Union, and conversely, for artists from the capitalist countries to appear before Soviet audiences. A U.S. touring company of *Porgy and Bess* stopped in Leningrad and saw the Institute's *Nutcracker* while they were there. *New York Post* columnist Leonard Lyons wrote that he saw "a Tatar boy, whose headpiece hampered his vision," lift an "Oriental girl...He could not see that the grip was uncomfortable" for her.[10]

Under Pushkin's stewardship each spring, students prepared a final exam variation. Pushkin assessed Nureyev as unready to perform at the year-end showcase. Undeterred, Rudolf learned the "Diana and Actaeon" solo variation from *Esmeralda*. He worked and showed it to Pushkin, who immediately reversed himself and encouraged Rudolf to dance it at the showcase.

Rudolf remained in level eight for two more years, during which time he demanded Pushkin's full attention as he devoted tremendous energy to working past the limitations imposed by his medium height of 5'8" and somewhat short legs. Yuri Soloviev was the school's star dancer; Nureyev's stormy presentation was the very opposite of Soloviev's clean style. Rudolf would dance and even stand on demi-pointe to extend his line, and bested the girls in high extensions. In his third year, he was presented at a yearly competition with the Moscow Bolshoi school. The Bolshoi was favored with more funding, and because of its location in the capital, held in higher regard by the regime. Among those chosen to represent the Kirov school were Alla Sizova, a frequent partner of Rudolf's, Marguerite Alfimova, Yuri Soloviev, and Natalia Makarova. Moscow presented Vladimir Vasiliev and Ekaterina Maximova. Sisova became ill, and wasn't able to dance the "Diana and Actaeon" pas de deux, and so Rudolf performed the men's variation only. He is said to have "astounded the hall." When Sizova felt better on the second night, she and Rudolf danced the *Corsaire* pas de deux, and the primed audience demanded an encore. Rudolf's certainty of style, emotion, and spell-binding command of space demonstrated by his grand jetés, burst beyond the confines of the rehearsal studio and onto the stage like a comet.

Rudolf and Alla were the only Leningrad students invited to be part of a documentary film on Soviet ballet. Rudolf was offered soloist contracts by both the Bolshoi and Stanislavsky theaters. He was hoping that the Kirov would also offer him a contract, though his eye was on the Bolshoi because its roster of ballerinas included Gallina Ulanova and Maya Plisetskaya, and also because it had been first among the dance companies to tour the Western nations. After he reprised the *Corsaire* excerpts at a graduation showcase, the celebrated 46-year-old Natalia Dudinskaya made an almost unprecedented offer to Nureyev. She said, "Stay here...and we'll dance *Laurencia* together."[11] The only known precedent was the invitation tendered by Matilda Kschessinskaya—prima ballerina of the Imperial Ballet and the Czar's former mistress—to Nijinksy, upon his graduation.

Rudolf Nureyev with Margot Fonteyn in *Gayneh*. Photo credit: Henrietta McDowell. Courtesy San Francisco Performing Arts Library & Museum.

Rudolf returned home for the summer, certain that he had a place at the Kirov, only to receive a telegram from the Ministry of Culture informing him that he was being reassigned to Ufa Ballet to compensate the government for having paid his tuition. He rushed off to Moscow to lobby officials, and while there, angled to convince the Bolshoi to renew its contract offer, which they did. He then went to Leningrad to ask for Pushkin's help, where he learned from the company's new director, Boris Fenster, that "there was never any question" regarding the Kirov. Rudolf turned down the Bolshoi—again. He believed that turning down the Bolshoi twice and an earlier decision not to join the Komosol (the Communist Party youth organization) hurt him politically.

Rudolf feared leaving Leningrad—even for a vacation—and was determined to use the time before the dancers returned to prepare for the upcoming season. He would make his debut on October 25, 1958, dancing the *pas de trois* from *Swan Lake*. Less than a month later, he did indeed partner Dudinskaya in *Laurencia*, as she had promised. She had danced *Laurencia* earlier in her career with the noted Vakhtang Chaboukiani. Rudolf would be Dudkinskaya's last Frondoso—and according to Sasha Minz, Nureyev danced it "like an eruption of Vesuvius." His technique still needed polishing: he fell slightly out of his turns, jumped with unsteady landings, but his theatricality and fearlessness sent shock waves through the audience.

It wasn't long before Rudolf and Alla were assigned a two-room apartment, into which his sister Rosa also moved. Rosa's provincial ways embarrassed Rudolf, and to escape unwelcome reminders of his past, he began to stay at the Pushkins' apartment. Pushkin's wife Zenia (called Xsana for short) indulged him in every way, cooking and cleaning for him, nursing him through his first injury, and dispensing a mixture of discipline, scant advice, and affection. In later years, he would confide to Menia that the two had also shared a sexual relationship. Xsana saw it as her role to prepare and steady him for a career where one must be variously humble, aggressive, patient, unyielding, or reverential— according to the circumstances.

It is safe to say that Rudolf's relationship with male dancers was strictly competitive. His female partners found him temperamental and difficult to work with, but patient and even pedagogic in his approach to the artistic process, resulting in a rewarding experience and feelings of great fondness and even passion for him.

Rudolf had assumed that some day he would marry Menia, who joked about it but never seemed seriously interested. Indeed, she decided to return to Cuba following the victory of the 1959 revolution. Rudolf said that he would see her off in Moscow, even if it meant missing a performance. When the moment came, he was nowhere to be found, and a disappointed Menia went to the train station alone. Everyone was assembled at her departing train, including the ever-vigilant Shelkov and Dolgushin, but Rudik was nowhere in sight. When at last Menia took her seat, Rudolf burst out of nowhere, wearing a triumphant smile. He had hidden in the bathroom of the *Red Star*. They spent the eight hours en route to Moscow in each other's arms. There was a lot of kissing, but no sex. While it was clear that Rudolf wanted to make love, Menia was a virgin, and given his regard for her and the uncertainty of their future, Rudolf did not press her. At the airport, he was inconsolable, sobbing, "I'll never see you again!"

Rudolf's Moscow jaunt, his denunciation of conformity in response to a recitation of the restrictions applying to dancers while on a Vienna tour, and his tendency toward self-promotion in an atmosphere where equality amongst dancers was the shared value, made him the object of malevolent scrutiny by bureaucrats and jealous dancers alike. Menia was in Vienna for the dance festival where Rudolf and Alla performed their *Corsaire* pas de deux before a cheering audience of 17,000. She was with the National Ballet of Cuba delegation. Rudolf broke Soviet rules by insisting on taking the Cuban teacher Alberto Alonso's classes instead of the Kirov's.

When it came to "individualist" tendencies, Nureyev proved incorrigible. In preparing for his Kirov debut as Albrecht in *Giselle*, he demanded that his tunic be shortened to make his lower body appear longer. This exposed his pelvis, covered by just a dance belt and tights. Thanks to Nureyev's pioneering, such costuming is the norm today for men, but in the early 60s, especially in the Soviet Union, it was considered nothing short of obscene to reveal so much—or so little—especially where, in Rudolf's case, he dared to go a step further, insisting on wearing white tights. His innovations—including radical changes in choreography (he substituted *entrechat quatres* for *brisé volés* in *Giselle*, for example)—made him wildly popular with audiences and ushered in an unprecedented wave of balletomania. While his relationships with women were marked by obsession and a kind of passion, the passion wasn't so much sexual as narcissistic. Later in life, his homosexual orientation would assert itself directly, but for audience members of either sex, Rudolf Nureyev exuded libidinal energy, instilling into ballet a level of sexual urgency that its earlier representations had only hinted at.

As he acquired new partners and more repertoire, he remained in the thrall of Dudinskaya, in no small measure because of her connections to the international ballet world. Rudolf began private English lessons in order to speak with foreigners, a practice roundly discouraged by Soviet authorities. He saw every foreign company perform from Ballet Nacional de Cuba to a U.S. touring company of *My Fair Lady*, meeting the performers backstage after the show. He finessed backstage chats into social outings, leading the KGB agents tailing him on more than one wild goose chase. His goal was to tour before international audiences, but his adventures set him at odds with the very bureaucrats who cast such tours.

It seems obvious that the 46-day East German tour Rudolf was sent on a week before ABT opened in Moscow was engineered by the KGB to curb his ecumenical behavior. This was especially frustrating for him, as he had looked forward to seeing Maria Tallchief and Erik Bruhn perform. Learning Bruhn had taken Leningrad by storm increased his curiosity about the Danish dancer.

When casting for the Kirov's Paris and London Spring tour went up, Rudolf's name was not there. A month before the tour, he learned that he had been added thanks to Sergeyev's intervention. Pushkin coached Rudolf for the tour. Before leaving, Rudik visited his parents, and his sister Lilya and her new baby, Alfia. When Rosa, with whom he hadn't been getting along, showed up with her baby at the airport, he shooed her away.

At a Paris reception, where French dancers were arrayed on one side of the foyer of the Palais Garnier and Soviet dancers on the other, Rudolf took the initiative of introducing himself to Claire Motte, Claude Bessy, and Pierre Lacotte. Speaking in tentative English, he said, "I'm not really allowed to talk to you, but I think that's crazy. You're dancers and I would like to know what you think about Kirov company."[12] The dancers invited Rudolf and his tour roommate, Yuri Soloviev, to Claude Bessy's apartment for dinner. Rudolf talked nonstop, mostly criticizing the ways of the French people and cross-examining the dancers on their technique and knowledge of dance repertoire, with Soloviev saying practically nothing. Rudolf looked so sad at the evening's close that Claire Motte handed him a box of chocolates. He saw the films *Ben Hur* and *West Side Story* with his new friends and found Paris entertaining but tastelessly decadent and lacking in substance. The "KGBeshnicks," as Rudolf dubbed them, pounced on him when he returned from his late-night outings, but failed to deter him.

Nureyev left Paris audiences spellbound. *Le Figaro* called him "the jewel in the crown" of the Kirov. *L'Aurore* wrote, "The Leningrad Ballet has its own man in space."

Meanwhile, the "man in space" was doing some very down-to-earth shopping with the help of Simon Virsaladze, the Kirov's lead designer, investing his savings in wigs and fabrics not available at home for future use. Later, when the subject of Nureyev's Paris defection arose, Virsaldze said, "He's a very strange man. He might have a temper and maybe he doesn't know how to behave himself, but he's the first dancer in my experience who ever asked me to go with him to buy fabrics for costumes. Everybody says that Rudik is a boor. But look what he is indeed."[13] The motive for and planning of Nureyev's defection in the Paris airport at the tour's end has since been a subject for debate. Using up his scant $10 per diem to buy items unavailable in the Soviet Union seemed to suggest that he had every intention of returning there, until he learned that because of having broken Paris tour rules he would not go to London. Had he intended not to return all along? The act of defecting was precarious to say the least. Learning that Nureyev was not continuing on to London, Clara Saint arrived at the airport at the last minute and alerted the gendarmerie posted there that he was defecting, as he rushed helter-skelter toward them, declaring, "I want to stay in France!" The likelihood is that he longed for a career of broader scope, without the specific intention of leaving the Soviet Union for good, and when confronted with the London ban, decided to stay. It was not the political decision the anti-communist press conflated it into with headlines about "leaps to freedom" that never occurred, but a career decision, and an impulsive one at that. Baryshnikov, reflecting on it years later, commented,

For other people, including me, there were years of thoughts and plans and doubts and the long business of working up your courage. But Rudolf didn't need courage. He had so much courage that it wasn't even courage anymore...So for him to bolt at that French airport—it was like a bird in a cage, and suddenly the door is open.[14]

Nureyev fell into a post-defection depression because, in spite of having taken Paris by storm, he had nowhere to live and no money. Through his dance connections he was able to find work with the Cuevas Ballet, and thanks to Maria Tallchief's interest in him as a potential partner, to connect with her and Erik Bruhn during a German TV taping in Frankfurt. Tallchief called Erik Bruhn in Copenhagen from a pay phone, telling him: "There's someone here who wants to meet you..."

Nureyev's sexuality seems to stymie his biographers. He was "outed" by what he anticipated would be viewed as an ignominious death from AIDS-related pneumocystic infection at the age of 54, on January 6, 1993. Rumors of his heterosexual liaisons were always circulating in the dance world, but when he moved in with Erik Bruhn, alternate-seeming rumors—that he was gay—were confirmed in a relationship that appeared more problematic than satisfying to both partners. It could be said that Bruhn urged the relationship into crisis mode: when he was unable to dance due to an injury, he proposed that Rudolf replace him in an NBC-TV Bell Telephone Hour Special, partnering Maria Tallchief. Rudolf reluctantly agreed. The exposure catapulted him far beyond even Erik's immense celebrity. Rudolf admired Bruhn for his limpid technique, but Rudolf's offstage temperament and the press hysteria around his defection automatically conferred upon him a star status that eclipsed Bruhn's quieter stature as the ballet world's "danseur noble." Unable to trust the admiration and intimacy offered by Nureyev, Erik was literally sickened with jealousy, yet awed by Rudik's zest for life.

While in Copenhagen, Rudolf received a second phone call that would permanently alter his professional future. It came from Margot Fonteyn, England's most celebrated ballerina. "Would you dance in my gala in London?" she asked. He agreed, and began arranging to go to London, the very city placed off-limits by KGB authorities just two weeks earlier. With the gala began the ballet world's most memorable partnership, an international romance across the proscenium between Fonteyn, Nureyev, and audiences who had never before sought or bought tickets to the ballet. It launched Rudolf's career outside of the Kirov and relaunched the then 42-year-old Fonteyn's.

Rudolf's reception at the gala prompted Ninette de Valois, director of the Royal Ballet, to invite him to dance three performances of the Royal's *Giselle*. Rudolf and Bruhn teamed up with Sonia Arova and Rosella

Hightower to start the first of several pickup companies that Nureyev would initiate, so that he (and in this instance, Bruhn) could experiment with some personal choreography. He accompanied Erik to New York, where he first saw the works of George Balanchine, which he longed to dance. But Balanchine told him, "You don't know how to dance the way we dance, and it would take you too long to learn...Dance your princes, get tired of them, and then when you're tired, come back to me." If he was a prince on stage, in real life Rudolf was becoming "ballet's pop star," as Richard Buckle dubbed him. Arlene Croce wrote: "He connected with the rebellious, hyperbolic spirit of the times, and suddenly ballet was in."

Rudolf Nureyev attracted a retinue of high-toned followers, such as Princess Margaret, Queen Elizabeth, and Jacqueline Kennedy, and he utilized his connections among international high society to feather his nest, socially and financially, so that when he succumbed to AIDS at the age of 54 he had amassed a small fortune. Suffering from pericarditis at the end of his life, he had begun to learn conducting when it became clear that his dancing days were coming to an end, and conducted ABT's Spring gala, with Sylvie Guillem and Laurent Hillaire dancing the Fonteyn and Nureyev *Romeo and Juliet* title roles. While some critics complained of the slow tempo, New York City Ballet dancer Peter Martins said, "I have never seen so much respect for him as I did that night." He then went on to stage *La Bayadére* for Paris Opera.

In his final days, Rudi van Dantzig, Toer van Schayk, and John Taras visited Rudolf. He was tended by "his women, " Douce François, Marika, and Jeannette Etheridge. His remaining family from Ufa, his sister Rosa, niece Gouzel, and nephew Yuri, visited him at Perpetuel Sécours Hospital. Close friends kept a vigil. He died peacefully in his sleep on January 6, 1993. At his funeral, held on January 12, he was laid out in his tuxedo and Missoni cap at the Palais Garnier. Six male dancers, led by Charles Jude, carried the coffin to the top of the grand staircase, with ballet students lining the stairs. Rudolf was eulogized in a civil ceremony, as musicians played excerpts from Bach and Tchaikovsky. The poetry of Pushkin, Byron, Michelangelo, Göethe, and Rimbaud was recited, each in its original language. To strains of Jessye Norman's recorded rendering of *Song of a Wayfarer*, Rudolf's body was carried to the Russian Orthodox Cemetery at Sainte-Geneviève-des-Bois. After his coffin was lowered into its grave, friends tossed in ballet slippers. Over those, mourners scattered white roses.

4

Margot Fonteyn

She is young and lovely to look at, has a technical equipment so strong that she seems to ignore it altogether, moves not only with ease but with an active pleasure in movement and is just about as enchanting a dancer as has come along in a score of years. What she did with the by no means unfamiliar title role of this old ballet [*Sleeping Beauty*] was artistically beautiful and theatrically exciting. Indeed, it is possible to say that we have never seen the famous "Rose Aadagio" really danced before.

—John Rockwell, "Sadler's Wells Makes U.S. Debut," *New York Times*,
October 10, 1949[1]

For the better part of the twentieth century, the Ballerina Assoluta, Dame Margot Fonteyn, was synonymous with the words "prima ballerina." Fifties-era nine-year-olds, still coltish in their first pair of pointe shoes, parted their hair in the middle, marrying the sides in a chignon at the nape of the neck in imitation of Fonteyn's. They studiously copied her gestures, facial expressions, and the inclination of her head. When at seven I confessed to my mother my wish to become a dancer, she stared into my hopeful brown eyes, smiled coyly and said, "But you'd have to marry a diplomat—like Margot Fonteyn!" A diplomat? I met one once, when the Dutch Baron Von Kessenich decorated my father for wartime heroism. When he bounced me on his knee like a toy, I instantly recognized that a dancer's life was not for me.

Peggy Hookham, on the other hand, began contemplating life's banquet of possibilities when her father's employer transferred him from London to Shanghai. Peggy got to go. Felix, three years older, was left behind to attend an English prep school. Margaret Hookham was born on May 18, 1919, to Felix John and Hilda Fontes Hookham. As a toddler,

Margot Fonteyn in *Corsaire*. Photo credit: Henrietta McDowell. Courtesy San Francisco Performing Arts Library & Museum.

she regularly tested the relationship between time and space by attempting to "fly" from the fourth step of her family's small house in Ealing. John Hookham believed that ballet lessons would straighten a slight curvature in Peggy's spine. Her mother enrolled her in Miss Bosustow's Academy in what Fonteyn describes as "a pretty little house just around the corner."[2] Peggy's debut came at the age of four, when she danced the role of Wind with the baby class. Peggy spotted a playbill for a dance performance and asked who the pictured lady was. Mrs. Hookham said, "Anna Pavlova...the greatest dancer in the world." "Then I shall be the second greatest!"[3] Peggy famously responded. Mrs. Hookham took Peggy to see Pavlova perform, but no inspiration resulted from that exposure. Mrs. Hookham made the fatal error of unfavorably comparing Peggy's *retirés* to those of Pavlova, unwittingly inflicting insult. The performance remained a lifelong archive for the sting of the hurtful comparison, and Peggy developed an anxiety about disappointing her parents. Still, her determination was never in question: "I was aware that the stage has its own laws...I treat each encounter as a matter of life and death...I have learnt over the years the difference between taking one's work seriously and taking oneself seriously. The first is imperative and the second disastrous."[4] In November 1927, leaving their son behind, the Hookhams sailed to the United States, making their way to Louisville, Kentucky. They remained in Kentucky, waiting to continue by ship from Seattle to Shanghai, just long enough for Peggy to witness a Ku Klux Klan cross-burning. They moved into the Russian Concession in Tiensin in the spring of 1928, where Peggy studied with Mme Tarakova, who inspired her to make little dance pieces of her own.

In June 1929, Peggy and Hilda returned to England to visit Felix. Peggy returned to Miss Bosustow to qualify for a new level, and continued to choreograph short theme pieces. Back in China, she spent the summer on the beach in Hong Kong, swimming and diving from sunrise to sunset. She made friends with a Norwegian man who was her first partner at tea dances. Later, when she danced in Oslo, Margot Fonteyn received a letter that said, "I wonder if the famous Margot Fonteyn can be the little Peggy I used to know in Hong Kong?" There was a snapshot of the two of them on the beach. On the back it said: "This is Peggy, she swims like a fish and dances like a ballerina."[5]

The family moved to Shanghai, and upon Mrs. Hookham's and Peggy's return from an eight-month sojourn to London, they met the Russian ballet teacher, George Gontcharov, who was giving dance instruction to Peggy's friend, June Brae. He had teamed up with two other Russian teachers; George Toropov from Moscow and the stylish-looking Vera Volkova from Leningrad. Mrs. Brae and June began speaking of returning to London. The discussion posed the question of the girls' future, and at 14, Peggy informed her headmistress that she was returning to England to train for a dance career. Unable to dissuade Peggy, the teacher advised her to read broadly, lest she feel unprepared for the world outside of ballet.

Mrs. Hookham researched Alicia Markova's training, and learned that she had studied with Princess Serafine Astafieva. They found the Astafieva studio in Chelsea. The princess was reluctant to accept Peggy until Mrs. Hookham's flattery helped broker an agreement for a daily lesson. Restraints vanished under Astafieva's tutelage. "Let your breath out before you bend back,"[6] she advised, and then the backbend came easily. Peggy could see where Markova's lightness was learned. Among the former students who showed up was Keith Lester, whom the princess invited to partner Peggy, instructing her to use her breath to help with the lifts. Peggy's tenure with the princess was not to last. Mrs. Hookham had a new plan: enrollment in the Old Vic and Sadler's Wells (Vic-Wells) school. In a lame effort to protest, Peggy brought no dance clothes to the audition, which she took in bare feet and a petticoat, but was accepted anyway. Developing an instant aversion to the snobbery permeating her new surroundings, Peggy sneaked off to Astafieva's studio, breaking the school rule forbidding outside study.

Ninette de Valois, the school's most revered figure, noticed Peggy immediately, turned to her teacher Ursula Moreton, and asked, "Who is the little Chinese girl in the corner?" "She's not Chinese," Moreton responded, as she beat out the counts with a stick. "Where does she come from?" Valois asked. "Shanghai," answered Moreton.[7] This amusing *non sequitur* merits the explanation that Hilda Fontes Hookham was half English and half Brazilian. "Fontes" was her Brazilian father's name, but she was not acknowledged by his wealthy, latifundist family because her mother had been his mistress. It was easy to mistake Peggy's Latin look for Asian.

Vic-Wells proved to be a veritable chamber of horrors. Lillian Baylis, an administor there, asked Peggy, "Do you believe in God, dear?" This was no idle inquiry, as Baylis made it a habit to appeal to God in a rather public way, especially concerning potentially embarrassing or difficult questions. For example, a student request: "May I have more scholarship money?" Baylis: "I'll have to ask God." A pause while she asks. Then: "No! God says 'No.'"[8] Fonteyn's first crush was on her partner William Chappell. They danced *Rio Grande: Day in a Southern Port,* Margot as the Pickup Girl. The role was regarded as a trifle risqué for a girl Peggy's age. Baylis, having approved her costume of a sheer skirt, still insisted that the nude statue on the scrim be painted over.

Not inclined to share the limelight, de Valois worked to extinguish any memory of the Astafieva experience. She corrected Peggy in a raised, exasperated tone of voice that often bordered on rage. Being thrown out of class for arriving late became more of a reprieve than a penalty. Coached in a stage whisper by another student through her first *Nutcracker* Snowflake, Tchaikovsky's music and the sheer joy of dancing onstage made Peggy see that she had, despite the difficulties, "found her place."

The moment came when the student tested the raging waters of day-to-day company life. Fonteyn writes,

> I had thought "nice" was the ideal to which everyone aspired the world over, only to find that here it was more a term of disparagement, while "brilliant," "witty," "eccentric," "glamorous," or, at the very least, "amusing" were the only desirable attributes.[9]

As she laughed along with the dancers at their pleasantries, she often did so without understanding the intended humor. With the girls her age, she still found ways to covertly joke and play onstage.

In her first serious role as the Young Tregennis in *The Haunted Ball-room*, Peggy was startled to discover that she could become a professional dancer. As if to test herself, she inventoried her deficiencies: a low arabesque and elevation, stiff feet, and trouble with pirouettes. But passion triumphed over scrutiny, and she reconciled the two by working hard to master the roles she was given. Ninette de Valois was a force of nature. She was still performing and choreographing at the same time that she directed the company and the school. Though she admitted to preparing for a performance by taking two aspirin, a hot bath, and a glass of sherry, Fonteyn recalls that her brisés looked to be faster than any orchestra could match. Many of the classical ballets would have been lost to the world had she not curated the works of Petipa and Tchaikovsky, and restaged Diaghilev's *Sleeping Beauty*. When Frederic Ashton became artistic director, he set choreography on Peggy. She had never worked with a choreographer before, but Ashton was so deft that he expected even this novice to master his steps instantly. Peggy was overwhelmed, and at first their relationship was uncomfortable. When she caught on to how he worked, her happiest moments onstage were found in dancing Ashton's ballets with complete abandon. Each day, he seemed to channel the spirit of another of his favorite ballerinas—Pavlova, Karsavina, Spessivtzeva, or Lopokova—demanding to know why his students couldn't replicate their signature virtuosity. For Fonteyn, it was as if he translated the language of music perfectly into the language of dance.

It was unclear to Margot when she became a company member. In some ballets, she was cast in the corps, and then in more prominent roles. After her first performance in a 1935 *Les Sylphides*, de Valois settled the question in the car on the way home, "You need not wear student's rehearsal dress any more—you are in the company, you can wear a black tunic."[10] She began giving Peggy soloist roles to develop her feet, and the handsome 17-year-old Michael Somes as a partner. When Alicia Markova left the Vic-Wells Ballet to form her own company with Anton Dolin, Fonteyn found herself cast as Odette in *Swan Lake*; Ruth French was given Odile. Peggy wanted to use her mother's maiden name, Fontes, as a stage name because of its exotic ring. Meredith Daneman, a Fonteyn biographer, explains that the Fontes family objections cited Hilda Fontes Hookham's "illegitimate" claim to the name. A variation on Fontes turned Peggy into "Margot Fonteyn." (In 1956, she would become Dame Margot Fonteyn of the British Empire.) Margot's new status as a company member thrust her into the sophisticated sphere of London Society at the exact moment in adolescence when childhood ways are discarded in favor of adult vanities. She says of this time:

> It was easy for me to step out into the limelight through the plywood door of Giselle's cottage and suffer her shyness, ecstasy, deception and madness as if it was my own life catching me by surprise at each new turn. It was a fresh,

living experience for me at every performance as the drama unfolded.
But when I left the stage door and sought my orientation among real people,
I was in a wilderness of unpredictables in an unchoreographed world.[11]

Margot relied on daily company class to keep fit and prepared, but
also as an emotional anchor in the choppy seas of the ballet world. Her
favorite teacher was Stanislav Idzikowski, whose steadfastness she
admired. She studied secretly with Lydia Kyast, who had trained with
Karsavina. In 1936, after a frustrating dress rehearsal for *Apparitions*,
Ashton took the opportunity of a cab ride home to berate Fonteyn for what
he saw as her inadequacies. Margo had a crush on him and so the sting of
his criticism was felt both professionally and personally. By opening night,
however, she had finessed his corrections into a triumphant showing.

De Valois informed Margot that she had cast her as Giselle for the
1936–37 season. When Margot protested that she wasn't ready, de Valois
silenced her with the words, "That's for me to decide." Margot's ambiva-
lence is evident when she says, "What a beautiful step! I shall never be
able to dance it."[12] She overcame unreadiness by sheer determination
and preparation, putting her obstinacy in the service of her development,
and rejecting it as an instrument of resistance. De Valois happened to see
Margot on a Rosebery Avenue bus, reading a copy of *Ulysses*, and
shrieked, "For God's sake child, don't read that in public; you could be
arrested!"[13]

At a Cambridge party in 1937, Margot noticed two brothers dancing
to Cuban rumba music. Margot awoke the next morning savoring the
memory of the one named "Tito." Tito surveyed her in silence, but made
her feel loved and cared for as he spoke in spare and not always clear
language about who he was and where he came from. He left her with a
souvenir coin from his father's second presidential term in Panama.
Margot gave Tito a photo bearing the inscription, "For my dear Tito from
Margot."[14] She waited for word from him, but none came. When they
met again the next May, she greeted him with some degree of remove.
Guessing that she was wary, he asked, "Are you still mine?" Her "no"
was intended as a reproach, but it failed to deter him.

Margot spent the season dancing Odette/Odile in *Swan Lake*, and
mastering her first set of 32 fouetté turns. She rated her roles on a fear scale:
Swan Lake and *Sleeping Beauty* equaled terror; *Giselle*, dread; *Firebird*, fear;
with *Ondine* actually evoking enjoyment![15] On their breaks, the dancers
would go to Paris to seek out the best Vaganova teachers in their exile
duchies. Olga Preobrajenska was considered fearsome by her students.
Her accompanist was her victim. He was not attuned to her habit of
changing tempo according to whim. Children were admitted midway
through class to do barre during adult "center." Her studio was like a
dance Tower of Babel. During the break between seasons, Margot studied
with Mathilde Kschessinskaya, like Astafieva, a princess without a palace.

Hers had been memorialized in a famous photo, the one with the balcony from which Lenin had chosen to make his appeal to the masses. Lubov Egorova was the most temperate of Fonteyn's Paris teachers. When Margot was cast as Aurora upon her return, she wrote that she imagined it as "climbing to the moon on a ladder woven from sand."[16]

Margot's meetings with Tito were occasional, as she was committed first and forwmost her career. Still, it was not easy to hear rumors that Tito had been living with an American woman in Paris, confirming, for Margot, gossip that he was a womanizer.

With Britain's entrance into World War II in September of 1939, the company was disbanded, but then reconstituted in order to undertake a five-year tour of the military encampments. The male dancers were drafted, and by the time the war ended, the company was significantly weaker for having lost them. De Valois refused to hire men of other nationalities, lest it demoralize the English dancers, so the new crop of male dancers were students, boys just learning to lift and partner. While Ashton served in the Air Force, Robert Helpmann, an Australian who was exempt from the draft, began to choreograph. Performances ran without intermissions so audiences could reach home before the bombing started! During the war years, Fonteyn took Vera Volkova's classes at a studio in Cambridge Circus. Her images—delivered in broken but evocative English—were unforgettable: "Head is like you are smelling violets over right shoulder," and "Leg does not know it is going to arabesque."[17]

In 1946, Sadler's Wells Ballet moved to the Royal Opera House, Covent Garden, and became the first resident ballet company there. For the reopening, *Sleeping Beauty* would be staged by Oliver Messel, and include major elements of the Diaghilev version. In 1947, Léonide Massine traveled to England to dance in two of his own ballets with Margot, *Le Tricorne* and *La Boutique Fantasque*, both originally set on Diaghilev. Fonteyn adored being partnered by Massine in Le Tricorne's Fandango. She seemed to find her mental balance in the studio. Still, it took time for her to absorb corrections. Her teacher Harijs Plučis once commented: "Margot, my dear! Now I understand you. I tell you corrections today and after two years you do perfectly."[18]

When one hears the word "impresario," the name Sol Hurok inevitably comes to mind. A Brooklynite, Hurok traveled the world looking for talent, in Fonteyn's words, "like an old Russian peasant woman going off to the market, basket on her arm, to pick out the best of the produce."[19] In 1949, enchanted by Margot, Hurok arranged a U.S. tour. When *Sleeping Beauty* opened at the Met, Margot had the worst case of stage fright of her career. She and Helpmann made a smashing showing. In Washington, D.C., the performance quite literally fell on its face, as dancer after dancer (including Margot), fell on the slippery stage at Constitution Hall. For the next four years the company toured the United States and Canada, with every kind of attention paid to Margot: flowers, reviews, flattery, photos, interviews, gifts, but at the day's end, she returned to an empty if lavishly appointed hotel room in a city she wouldn't have time to get to know all that intimately.

In the 12 years that she was on tour, Margot heard from Tito Arias once. By telephone, he begged her to meet him at the Atlanta airport. She asked him to call her when he actually arrived. He didn't call, and she didn't meet him. She was involved with the conductor and composer Constant Lambert, whose wife eventually left him, but it was too little too late in the life of the affair, and Lambert moved on to other women.[20]

Her most famous partner was Rudolf Nureyev. She felt a strong sense of fidelity toward the works they danced, and found it difficult to adapt to new partners. Among others that she partnered were Attilio Labis, Egon Madsen, Richard Cragun, Anthony Dowell, David Wall, Donald McLeary, Desmond Kelly, Ivan Nagy, Heinz Bosl, Christopher Gable, Garth Welch, Karl Musil, and Mikifumo Nagata.

In 1952, a bout of diphtheria left Margot unable to feel her feet, as the nerves there had died, and she was unable to dance for five months until they regrew. After the Granada Festival, where the dancers stayed in the home of the famed composer Manuel de Falla, they were off to New York for the 1953 tour, opening with *Sleeping Beauty*.

There, a visitor's card bearing the name "Roberto E. Arias" was delivered to Margot's dressing room. Tito had come to propose marriage. Margot could scarcely recognize the old Tito in his new *gordo* body, nor summon feelings that many years before had led her to expect much more from him than he delivered. He threw a party to honor the Panamanian president, which turned into a celebration of ballet's most famous female dancer. Fonteyn fans puzzle over what moved Fonteyn to marry Tito: he claimed no interest in ballet, had a roving eye, and an oddly impish, yet rotund appearance. A letter from Tito to Margot may help solve the puzzle:

> This letter seems to be more for me than for you—yes, it is a need to confess that I have not recently allowed my better nature to guide my love. Unfortunately, I do not always act as I write, but today my better nature needs to dialogue with you, without seeking promises by innuendo and without recoursing to shallow heroics. But all of Tito, the gentle and the violent, the good and the bad, the relaxedly serene and the emotionally tense, loves you most dearly.[21]

Because Margot had engaged in several affairs, some of Tito's friends voiced skepticism about the marriage. Tito reminded them that "there are some birds in Panama that run through the mud, but when they come out, their feathers are clean and white." The actor John Wayne loaned his sailboat to Arias. Tito invited Margot for a sail. On the sail, Margot let go of her romantic feelings for her previous ballet partners, William Chapell,

Margot Fonteyn in *Gayneh*. **Photo credit: Henrietta McDowell. Courtesy San Francisco Performing Arts Library & Museum.**

Frederick Ashton, Michael Somes, and Roland Petit, and decided to marry Tito.

In the year's interval between her engagement and marriage, Margot learned and performed *The Firebird*. Diaghilev's régisseur Serge Grigorieff and his wife Lubov Tcherneicheva taught it to her, Tamara Karsavina coached her, and Michael Somes partnered her, dancing the role of Ivan Czarevitch. Conductor Ernest Ansermet was in the rare but gracious habit of asking the dancers what tempo they preferred, reminiscent of the famous joke about the conductor who approached a prima ballerina just before a performance and asked, "Madame, shall I play it too fast or too slow this evening?" Fokine had made the ballet as counterintuitive as possible. Where a dancer would feel comfortable turning in one direction, he had her turn in the other. The firebird was drawn as a cipher, devoid of emotion, driven by its narcissism and pride of grandeur. Margot's head was swimming. In spite of the artistic hurdles, the performance soared, and Margot and Michael took multiple curtain calls before dashing off to the dressing room to change for the final act.

Margot and Tito married in Paris on February 6, 1955. She planned for a civil ceremony with 10 witnesses, but over 50 persons, mostly press photographers, crammed into the room, pushing Margot's parents to the rear and out of view. The couple honeymooned aboard a yacht in the Bahamas.

They received an invitation from a wealthy newspaper mogul to tour Brazil, including the country's very first construction of the new capital, Brasilia, and saw São Luis, the town in which Margot's Brazilian grandfather was born.

Just a few days following the triumph of the Cuban revolution, Tito proposed a trip to Havana. Jammed into elevators with young *barbudos* fresh from combat, Margot feared that her feet might be blown off by an accidental discharge of rifles that hung from their shoulders. Instead, Margot and Tito were treated to a tour of the Presidential Palace, meeting Cuban President Manuel Urrutia, and Fidel Castro, who apologized to Margot for his unfamiliarity with her language. She found his voice and bearing attractive, but could not follow the long discussion in Spanish between Tito and him.

The Cuban revolution had inspired a layer of youth throughout Latin America to consider revolutionary solutions to the problems that beset their own nations. Some began to identify with the struggles and aspirations of the urban working class and peasants in the countryside. Others, like Tito, who simply wished for a regime change, believed that guerilla warfare offered an expedient for realizing such goals, and admired what little they understood of the Cuban model. Tito assembled a small group whose aim it became to overturn the Panamanian regime by an adventurist act. Margot, the daughter of an anti-labor, anti-communist, pro-capitalist tobacco company executive, joined them solely in her new capacity as Tito's wife.

In a scheme using Colombian drug planes to secure arms and a small fleet of boats, Tito and his putschists hoped to initiate a "bloodless" coup. Unlike Fidel, Che Guevara, and *Los Barbudos*, they had neither a following nor a program for taking power. Everything that could go wrong did, and all parties were soon captured, questioned, arrested, and in Margot's case, deported to Miami. One participant was shot to death by a National Guardsman. Margot made her way to London, while Tito took refuge in Brazil, and it was two months before they reunited.

En route back to London from Leningrad, Georgina Parkinson learned that the Kirov's best male dancer had defected in Paris. When she reached London, Margot received seemingly related news that Galina

Ulanova would not dance in an upcoming Royal Academy Gala. A gala committee member proposed that they invite the new defector, with "nostrils of a genius,"[22] instead. Vera Volkova became the intermediary who verified that Rudolf Nureyev, then 23, was indeed an extraordinary dancer, and wished to dance with Margot. Margot refused, but Nureyev accepted. He chose Rosella Hightower to partner in the *Swan Lake* pas de deux and asked Ashton to set a solo for him, which Ashton did. To put him at ease and assess him as a possible future partner, Margot invited Rudy to stay with Tito and her. After Rosella and Rudy were mobbed by the post-Gala audience, Ninette de Valois asked Margot if she wanted to reconsider her decision, to which Margot gave the oft-quoted response, "I think it would be like mutton dancing with lamb. Don't you think I'm too old?"[23] But she recognized that Nureyev was going to take the world by storm, and if she wanted to be in the eye of it, had better start dancing with him sooner than later. When they ran into a snag and neither was willing to budge, they would break for tea or have some lunch. Once, when Margot got carried away in a rehearsal of *Romeo and Juliet*, Rudy warned her, "Don't get hysterical."[24] Speculation about their relationship was rendered all the more intriguing by Rudolf making no effort to hide his homosexual orientation. They loved one another, in whatever manner, and despite Margot's devotion to Tito and Rudy's involvement with Erik Bruhn and others. As she put it, "There was a high degree of expectation...generated by...a web of romantic attachment that had very publicly been spun about Rudolf and myself."[25] Unfazed by scandals, Margot and Rudy spent nearly every night out on the town in London. At the evening's end, Rudy would take off in pursuit of other diversions.

In 1964, Tito ran for the Panama National Assembly. Margot some spent time campaigning with him, and then left on a four-week tour of Australia with Rudolf. Her return to London coincided with Election Day in Panama, but it took several weeks before the results became public. In the interim, Alfredo Jimenez, who had run as an alternate on Tito's ticket, asked Tito to register him as his substitute deputy. Tito preferred to wait to learn the vote tallies, but Jimenez couldn't. Armed, he intercepted Tito's car at an intersection and shot him five times at point-blank range. A tracheotomy stabilized Tito's breathing. An archbishop administered last rites to the nonbeliever, who despite his heresy, survived. As he lay sandwiched in a Stryker Bed, his uncle delivered the news that he had won the highest number of votes for Deputy in the history of Panama. Margot was in Bath when she received word of the attempt on Tito's life. On the plane to Panama, she saw the headline, "Paralyzed!" Four weeks later, Tito was transported to England for rehab. Just as Margot was to dance Rudy's new *Raymonda* in Spoleto, she left again to be at Tito's bedside. She found him in a coma, not expected to survive. After recovering, Tito would spend two and a half years in rehabilitation. Upon his return to Pamana, he was sworn in as deputy. By 1968, he was out of office.

Margot and Rudy embarked upon ballet's most celebrated partnership when they agreed to dance Kenneth MacMillan's *Romeo and Juliet*. Then *La Sylphide* toured so extensively that one notice read: "Margot Fonteyn, who has triumphed in many more exotic places, last night conquered Flatbush."[26] In Managua, Margot and Tito dined with the despised dictator Anastasio Somoza. En route, Somoza's son ordered his driver to remove his machine gun from the front seat because there was a lady in the car.

The most publicized scandal occurred in San Francisco's psychedelic Haight-Ashbury. An odd-looking man approached Margot and invited her to a "Freak Out." She suggested to Rudolf that they go. He reluctantly agreed. Once there, and noticing drugs, they headed for the door. The police arrived, they were arrested, and the following day, paparazzi photographed the couple as they were leaving the police station.

In her autobiography, Fonteyn describes as "fanatics" the political activists who picketed her performance in apartheid South Africa and those who urged her not to perform for the murderous generals of the Chilean Allende regime. She expressed sympathy for their causes and assuaged her guilty conscience in the instance of South Africa by demanding that there be a separate performance for nonwhites and a free one for nonwhite school children. She writes that she doesn't believe in "muddling art and politics," as if unaware that the stumping she did for her husband had not impacted his political fortunes.

Imelda Marcos, wife of the notorious then-Filippine dictator Ferdinand Marcos, invited Margot to stay at the Malacañang Palace. Dame Fonteyn's proscription against muddling ballet and politics apparently applied only to the more proletarian causes and political figures. She and Tito became disenchanted with Fidel Castro when the Cuban revolution nationalized the riches of U.S. corporations. Alternatively, Fonteyn expressed admiration for the Marcos' showy acts of charity and noblesse oblige, while she excoriated Castro for acting to secure his country's independence from U.S. interests.

Rudolf and Margot were invited by Martha Graham to dance at a June 19, 1975, gala benefit for her company. Graham set *Lucifer* on Rudolf and Janet Eilber. Margot would dance it at the gala. She had trouble with a fall to the side. As Graham moved to strike it, Rudolf baited Margot, saying, "OK, be comfortable then."[27] Finding courage, she did the fall. Critic Clive Barnes gave the $50-$10,000 per ticket event rave reviews, noting that Margot still had some work to do before she could be a Graham dancer.

Inspired by Graham's concept of space as one's partner, Fonteyn learned Desdemona in Jose Limon's *Moor's Pavane* and danced it with Rudy at the Kennedy Center. When Margot toured, Tito delighted in arranging to meet her, only to alter his plans to throw her off course. When he agreed to meet her in Paris, he went to London instead. Rather than anger Margot, these wild goose chases amused and assured her that Tito's zest for adventure had not been undone by mere paralysis. Tito's servant Buenaventura Medina reveals that, unbeknownst to Margot, Tito would cry when he saw her dance onstage, all the time insisting that ballet held no interest for him.

In spite of Frederick Ashton's promise to Margot that he would cue her when the time had come for her to retire, in the year 1977, he instead choreographed a pas de deux on her and David Wall, which they took to Brazil. She fell, and the audience vigilantly rose to its feet in an act of support. In November 1976, during the *réverence* following their final *Romeo and Juliet*, Rudolf accepted the red rose that Margot plucked from her bouquet, and then knelt at her feet. "To me, she is part of my family. That's all what I have. Only her." In spite of their mutual affection, their life perspectives couldn't have been more divergent. When Margot received a bracelet of precious gems as a "merde" gift from Ferdinand and Imelda Marcos, she protested, "What can I do? I can't give it back!"[28] Unwrapping a pair of diamond cufflinks from the very same benefactors while in a taxi with the actress Monique Van Vooren, Rudy gave them away to the cab driver. Van Vooren asked, "Don't you like them?" to which Rudolf replied, " I like *them*. I don't like the source."[29] In 1976, John Hookham died of a heart attack. Margot's 60th birthday was followed by a May 23rd Royal Gala, featuring a tribute from Ashton, and three-minute ballet danced by Margot and him called "Salut d'Amour." Margot danced the tango from *Façade* with Robert Helpmann. Flowers were tossed onstage from every direction, until Margot was ankle deep in them. They were gathered up by a young boy and presented to Margot, who in turn presented them to Ninette de Valois as "Happy Birthday" was sung. Margot attended the post-performance party in a red chiffon dress, and was named "Ballerina Assoluta" by Princess Margaret and presented with a silver medal. The press dubbed this event her "farewell to the stage," but it was just the first of many.

Fonteyn undertook several projects. She made "The Magic of Dance," a BBC special, and wrote two books: *A Dancer's World* and *Pavlova Impressions*. She declined offers to teach, but did agree to coach only the most promising of dancers. She launched a program to promote a style of South American dance, but when 16 dancers who had been hired to take part in the project died in a plane crash, the project faltered and ended. Margot and Tito bought a farm in Panama, which they named La Quinta Pata. In 1982, Dame Fonteyn was installed as Chancellor of Durham University by Prince Charles. In her acceptance speech, she expressed her belief that every child is born with a talent that should be sought out, encouraged, valued, and respected.

Margot's friends Nora Kaye and Robert Helpmann died in 1987. On January 27, 1988, Margot's mother, "the Black Queen," died at age 93. In August, Frederick Ashton died, and though Margot wrote a tribute comparing him to Shakespeare, she did not fly to England to deliver it. Rumors that illness prevented her from attending are confirmed in a statement by her her gynecologist, Basil Appleby: "In June, 1988...I found that she had a very advanced growth...It was a rogue sort of cancer that one unfortunately sees from time to time."[30]

Declining treatment, Margot spent her remaining days with Tito. Arias had hitched his wagon to the political star of Gen. Manuel Noriega, the drug-dealing admirer of Hitler, who had hitched *his* to the Iran-Contra-tarnished star of the CIA. Noriega lost his usefulness to the CIA, and became a target of the U.S. military. His downfall hurt his cronies in Panama, and Tito and Margot's La Pata Quinta suffered financially. To ensure Margot a modicum of financial security, the Royal Ballet placed her on retainer.

Margot was coaching dancers at Houston Ballet when she learned that the cancer had metastasized to her bones, and sought treatment at Houston's T.C. Anderson Clinic. In 1989, it was Tito's cancer that brought Margot back to Panama. He died moments after she entered the house, but before she was able to say goodbye. His former mistress, and companion when Margot was away, Anabella Vallarino, committed suicide that same day. The funerals were held in tandem, mourners attending Tito's in the morning and Anabella's in the afternoon.

By 1990, Rudolf, himself sick with AIDS, helped with Margot's hospital bills. Margot survived Tito by 27 months. When she knew the end was near, Margot called her brother Felix, and not finding him home, left a farewell message on his answering machine. She died on February 21, 1991, "like a little fish...a fish receiving air," Querube Arias, her devoted stepdaughter recalled.[31] On July 2, a "Service in Thanksgiving for Her Life" was held at Westminster Abbey, with Ninette de Valois delivering a euglogy that emphasized Fonteyn's artistry and inborn musicality. John Lanchbery conducted selections from *Sleeping Beauty* and the *Sarabande* from Horoscope, played by the Orchestra of the Royal Opera House. Two of those closest to Fonteyn were missing from the gathering of international mourners: Rudolf Nureyev, who left a message that said, "Rudolf is afraid of dying and he misses Margot terribly,"[32] and Buenaventura Medina, the servant who had squired Tito and Margot through some of the most difficult moments in their lives. No one had thought to arrange a flight for him. However, he visited Margot's grave at the foot of Tito's in Jardin de la Paz, just outside of Panama City. Inscribed on her gravestone were words spoken to her by Tito when their lives took them in different directions: "Nuestro separacion es solo geografica." [Only geography separates us.][33]

5

Mikhail Baryshnikov

What is perhaps most impressive about Baryshnikov as a technician is his purity of line, both at rest and in motion. Every aspect of ballet form has its archetype of perfect balance and extension, a classical picture of poised weightlessness. But the exigencies of muscular effort—the physical reality from which ballet is the metaphorical escape—usually distort that purity...Classical training struggles to overcome such imperfections, and Baryshnikov manages to do so better than almost anyone within memory.[1]

—John Rockwell, *New York Times*

Mikhail (Misha) Nikolayevich Baryshnikov was born in Riga, Latvia, on January 27, 1948. His parents were Aleksandra and Nikolai Baryshnikov. Nikolai was a high-ranking military topographer in the Soviet army, and Alexandra Kiseleva sewed for a couturier, and had an abiding love of ballet. Both parents had been married previously, and met after World War II, in the Volga River region. Both were lonely, and Aleksandra, responsible for her son and mother, was without a job. In Misha's eyes, practicality and loneliness, not love, forged their bond. In Stalinist Russia, where revolutionary vigor had been supplanted by post-war despair, differences in their backgrounds were irreconcilable. Nikolai's family had owned a factory before the revolution, and he was educated, cultured, but brittle in his military bearing. Alexandra was bright but uneducated— a peasant girl from the countryside. By the time Misha was born, there was a discernible tension between the unloving couple, with Nikolai isolating himself as much as possible. He retreated behind books. Misha became a devotee of the mother he resembled.

Riga, Latvia's capital, was a city of divided allegiances. It sat across the Baltic Sea from Sweden, passed back and forth between Germany

Mikhail Baryshnikov with Carla Fracci in *Medea*. Photo credit: Thomas Victor.

under Hitler and the Soviet Union under Stalin in the years just prior to Misha's birth. As a Soviet republic, it endured the presence of Soviet military personnel and viewed non-Latvians such as Nikolai Baryshnikov as occupiers. Though he spoke Latvian fluently, Misha was sensitive to the anger and resentment of his neighbors, which affected how he chose friends. He cultivated friendships with children who were not quite pariahs, but regarded as different—children of the more bohemian families of artists, musicians, and Jews. Though he sought their company, he did not invite them home because of his father's outright anti-Semitism and contempt for Latvians. Misha therefore led two lives, and it was his "public" life that he preferred, because it offered an opportunity to develop his personality and wit, and take the physical space to distance himself from his stern, hostile father, and all that he represented.

"If you're good in school, do your homework, have decent marks, you could be busy twenty-four hours a day,"[2] says Baryshnikov of this period. Though not a model student, he was on the lookout for a means of self expression. Many were available that had nothing to do with school. The government's attitude was that so long as you were serious and strove for excellence, it would reward your talent, regardless of family position, income, or parental approval. From the age of six, Misha took full advantage of the opportunities. He put his relentless energy into soccer and gymnastics, received high marks in fencing, and ran track.

He swam and managed to sit still long enough to fish. His most pleasant recollections of family life are of outdoor activities: spring picnics and Sunday mushroom hunting in the fall. Even his father relaxed (out of uniform) during the two-week family summer vacations.

Misha joined the children's chorus. He began piano lessons, imagining that he would become a great concert pianist someday, but possibly because he was too antsy to practice, his talent proved unworthy of his ambitions. He had an ally in his mother, who loved going to the ballet, opera, and theater—for her, necessary antidotes to a grim marriage. She occasionally took Misha with her. He enrolled in after-school folk dancing because it offered two advantages: he got to move, and it placed him closer—much closer—to girls. It occurred to him that ballet classes held the promise of more elaborate theatrical stories and intrigues, and unlike giggling schoolgirls, ballet partners seemed either very serious or exuberant. While ballet was a survival of the pre-revolutionary Czarist era, it had become the property of the proletariat, and while much was disfigured to suit the whims of Stalin and his coterie of bureaucrats, at least on its surface, the ballet world seemed inalterable. At 12, Misha took the Riga School of Opera and Ballet Theater entrance exam. This impulsive act was heartily endorsed by his mother, but was met with tepid support from his father, who had hoped that Misha would have a career rebuilding the post-war infrastructure of the Soviet Union as an engineer, or become a pilot. A deep de-politicization occurred in the wake of Stalin and the Khrushchev-led regime that followed him. Young people rejected the *poseur* politics and privileged yet mind-numbing social habitat of the bureaucrats. They embraced the 60s youth culture that had burst on the scene, which gave expression to the worldwide youth radicalization, a brand of politics that felt authentic, in contrast to what the bureaucrats peddled. Youth mobilized in the streets to oppose the Vietnam War, colonial oppression and racism, and challenged notions of women's inferiority. While revisions made the feudal ballets more anachronistically "proletarian," one could still jump as high as one wanted, and imagine dancing in a world much more fantastic than the one at hand.

Misha's decision to begin ballet at the age of 12 issued from a cold calculation of his prospects. He was no good at sitting still. This caused him trouble in school and then at home when his parents learned that he lied and cheated to cover up. A dance career could mean job security, travel, and an array of privileges, which, while detested, were nonetheless valued and validated as the coin of the realm.

The Riga Choreographic Institute was the academy of the Latvia State Opera and Ballet Theater. The theater opened in 1919, two days after the Red Army occupied Latvia.[3] Alexandra Fedorova, a Kirov-trained dancer and sister-in-law of Michel Fokine, started the school, a provenance that brought with it the best of Vaganova pedagogy. In nine years,

Baryshnikov would become an accomplished professional dancer, and the rigors that would ensure his success began on Day One.

He spent half his day in academic classes, and the rest in the studio, learning ballet technique and its lexicon. Academic subjects included Math, Art History, French, Russian literature; in the studio he was learning character dance, piano, music, and fencing. Misha confronted his weaknesses as a dancer: the tendency of his hips to turn in, and a short, dense upper body that made him appear stocky. He directed his limitless energy into reshaping his line. His teachers, seeing his zeal, ambition, and natural affinity for music, responded with great enthusiasm.

During the summer prior to Misha's second year at the Riga Institute, while he was staying with his maternal grandmother near the Volga, he received news of his mother's suicide. Aleksandra had hanged herself. Unable to make sense of her horrible death, Misha told schoolmates that she had run away and abandoned the family. Stunned, Misha's first impulse was to flee Riga. It felt like too confining a place for him to both cope with his shock and commit himself fully to his career. When he returned to Riga, he was assigned to an intermediate class taught by Yuris Kapralis. Kapralis' analytic approach struck a chord with Misha, who learned how to learn from him. Soon he was receiving fives—the highest grade possible. By his third year, he had been promoted to the advanced level, and was dancing student parts in *The Sleeping Beauty* and *The Nutcracker*. It was intoxicating. Misha knew instantly that he wanted to spend his life with "the orchestra, the lights, the smell of makeup and powder."[4]

At 14, his teacher Bella Kovarskaya set a solo tarantella on him to music by Rossini, to give him something that would develop a stage presence to equal his technical level. He danced with two young ballerinas, and it was a great success. Kovarskaya also taught at the Vaganova Institute in what was then Leningrad (now St. Petersburg), and spoke of her "charming, talented student" to Alexander Pushkin, who had been Nureyev's teacher there, and was considered the best of the Soviet dance educators.

Just before he turned 16, Misha was given his next solo, the Young Boy with the Bow in *Shakuntala*, as part of a tour with the Latvian Opera and Ballet Theater Company that would take him to Leningrad. His teacher strongly suggested that he stop in and see Pushkin while he was there. Leningrad TV knew that Misha was on his way to their city before he did! They had received orders to do close-ups of the new outstanding boy.[5]

Built by Peter the Great, Leningrad was proclaimed "the bridge to the West," a monumental reproach to the rural idiocy that characterized the Russian countryside. With its classical design, all marble and gold rising out of the snow to meet the winter skies, it was a dream destination for many who lived in cities even as beautiful as Riga. With an absence of fanfare, Pushkin asked Misha to jump, felt the muscles in his calves, and then sent him to the school's doctor for a more thorough checkup. Misha was admitted to Level Seven, taught by Pushkin himself. The school was a shrine to excellence, and included a museum of ballet history, a studio with a stage raked at the same angle as the theater's, and a staff of cleaners who kept everything spotless. It was a state-supported school, and its students were held to the highest standard on that account.

"Leningrad was a shock.," says Misha. " I had to work from eight in the morning until eleven at night, and pass all exams: French, geometry, piano lessons."[6] Misha was skeptical that he could acclimate himself to the discipline and rigors of such a life. It is instructive to see how a simple change of venue affected Misha's attitude. In the United States or any other major industrial, capitalist country, his restlessness might have been diagnosed as hyperactivity and medicated. At the Vaganova Institute, the antidote was hard work in the service of the high academic standards of the school, poised to match the high standards in the studio. Misha worked hard to do well in his "sitting subjects," developing a special fondness for literature, languages, and dance history. His dance history teacher, Maria-Marietta Frangiopolo, was a former Kirov dancer of French extraction, and put herself completely at the disposal of her students, larding the course with personal vignettes about her experiences as a contemporary of Balanchine, and providing difficult-to-find ballet magazines, and materials that included accounts of what was happening in Western dance, in spite of the fact that the school's policy makers deemed them contraband: bourgeois, degenerate, and devoid of redeeming social value.

Character class was of the utmost importance in the Vaganova Institute curriculum. The dancers learned mime, acting, and the subtle gesturing that gives a character an identity. The character teacher was the incomparable Igor Belsky.[7]

The class that meant the most to Misha was Batterie with Alexander Pushkin. He and Pushkin understood the responsibilities their talent and ambitions conferred, and avoided the petty politics that saturated the school, strangely united by their outsider status in cliquish Leningrad dance circles. Pushkin, whose world crumbled when his protégé Nureyev defected, was thrilled with the prospect of a new challenge. Pushkin's talent was in coaching the student to become his own best teacher. Misha's previous teachers believed that because of his build and impish face, he would be relegated to character roles. Pushkin thought differently: "Keep going, keep going," he advised, confident that Misha could become a successful *danseur noble*.

Barbara Aria, the author of "Misha: the Mikhail Baryshnikov Story," describes Pushkin's batterie class:

Pushkin's warm-up period was perfect. The timing was perfect, the pacing was perfect, and as Baryshnikov remembers, "then suddenly the pressure

starts and the combinations get harder and harder, harder and harder."
The second part of the class grew naturally, seamlessly, out of the first, and
Pushkin's endlessly varied combinations of steps were such that the dancers
had to exert themselves in gradually increasing increments, never straining
or jarring, until they had reached the very limits of their capacity. Through
Pushkin's method, Misha trained the muscles of his body to work effortlessly,
almost automatically in any combination of steps.[8]

It was under Pushkin's eye that Misha developed what Clive Barnes
described as his "pantherine" leap.

Misha lived in an austere dormitory on Pravda Street, in a room that
housed 10 other students. It might have been tempting to embrace the
school as home, but his attitude was professional, and the emotional
distance he maintained made it impossible for the school to substitute
for a traditional family in his life. Instead, as happened with Nureyev,
Pushkin and his wife Ksenia Losifovna Lurgenson a former dancer, took
on the role of Misha's surrogate parents, and their home became his
refuge, and that of several other students. In keeping with Leningrad's
reputation for offering solace and hospitality, the couple's cramped apartment was very much a full-time salon, where meals were available, along
with discussions about music, art, film, literature, and dance. It was there
that Misha quietly resolved to assume a cultured profile worthy of his
host city that was both an avant-garde and classical window on the West.
He made an effort to speak a better Russian than the version he had
grown up with in Latvia, convinced that respect for one's language "is
respect for yourself."[9]

Misha won the Gold Medal at the 1966 Varna competition. He was in
his final year at the Vaganova Institute, when every student is scrutinizing
the competition for the one or two corps de ballet openings at the Kirov.
Final exams counted, political conduct counted, a cooperative spirit
counted, and Misha had succeeded in each category. The White Nights
Festival graduating students' performance was an annual dance tradition.
It was a celebratory event for the dancers' friends and families, and a
ritual attraction for critics and hangers-on. The students were wracked
by pre-performance jitters in anticipation of who would end up with
contracts and nice apartments.

Of Misha, critic Gennady Smakov wrote, "Baryshnikov created
the rare impression of a body dancing by itself, without instructions,"
recalling afterwards that "The cries of 'Bravo!' seemed to shake the
painted vaults of the theater, threatening to fell the chandeliers and crack
the layers of gilding."

The Kirov made a rare exception to its longstanding hierarchical tradition and hired Misha as a soloist, allowing him to bypass the corps de
ballet. The very few precedents included such dance legends as Nijinksy,
Pavlova, and Nureyev. The Maryinsky Theater became the home of the
Kirov in 1860, and in pre- and post-revolutionary times alike, the theater

has occupied a place of honor in the national patrimony. Rampant starvation, massive numbers of executions by the Stalin-led government, and tens of thousands of war dead left the Soviet Union in tatters after World War II, but restoration of the Maryinsky was nonetheless a priority, and the stage Misha stepped onto has remained his favorite throughout his life.

He took full advantage of his time off to read Russian literature and absorb the Leningrad ambience, making friends with its resident intelligentsia. He also began a tentative relationship with a student named Tatyana Koltsova.

Misha longed to dance the classical roles, but his boyishness seemed to work against him, and he ended up dancing the heroes in crude socialist realist ballet stories. He entered the 1969 Moscow International Dance Competition with a very short work by Leonid Yacobson called *Vestris*, consisting of one-minute vignettes about the life of the dancer Auguste Vestris. Maya Plisetskaya, who sat on the panel along with Galina Ulanova and Agnes DeMille, gave Misha 13 out of 12 points! He won the Gold Medal, with Helgi Tomasson, representing the United States, winning the Silver. Yacobson's piece was modern, and provided Misha with the opportunity to showcase his mime and character talents. The Soviet bureaucrats hated it. Misha nonetheless received a small salary increase because of having won the Gold. At 20, having seen the larger world of international ballet represented at the competition, Misha was beginning to strain against the strictures of even the generous Kirov. He longed to dance exactly the kind of modern work that was looked upon with disfavor by the politburo chiefs.

Baryshnikov also won the Paris prize that year, and was cast in the Kirov's *Don Quixote* and immediately hailed as the best Basilio in Leningrad. He danced Mercutio in Igor Tchernichov's *Romeo and Juliet*. The role of Juliet was to be danced by Natalia Makarova. Misha, then 21, was swept off his feet by the 30-year-old ballerina, whose unhappy marriage had just ended. *Romeo and Juliet* wasn't part of the Kirov season that year, and the dancers worked on it voluntarily, without pay, and on their own time. They rehearsed it for six months, but censors banned the production, labeling it an example of bourgeois decadence, owing to the manifest eroticism and "Western"-style arabesques. Maria-Marietta Frangiopolo sealed its fate when she said, "This flower of evil must never be permitted to blossom."[10] Makarova would not be permitted to dance Juliet again. Neither Misha nor Valery Panov, cast as Tybalt, danced the ballet again, and the choreographer, Tchernichov, was exiled to a remote region of the Soviet Union.

Under the cover of the grotesque 1968 invasion of Czechoslovakia by Soviet troops to suppress dissident protests there, there was a renewed campaign on the part of the Soviet Stalinists to "tidy up" at home. For the ballet, this took the form of a new generation of political police, and in the post-Nureyev-defection frenzy, the administrative director job was given to Petr Rachinsky, known as "The Fireman," who was expressly charged with eradicating decadence and deviance, artistic as well as political. Tours outside the country took on special significance because they were where temptations to adapt to Western decadence and deviance were unrestrained. Never knowing when a tour was imminent, eager dancers would snitch on colleagues at whim to assure that they themselves would be reliable risks for the tour roster.

Misha's beloved teacher Alexander Pushkin died suddenly of a heart attack in March 1970. Bereft at the loss of the person who took over where his father had never really even begun, Misha at 22 decided to honor Pushkin's memory by teaching his classes. The studio was a haven in which to teach and otherwise keep one's counsel.

While on tour in London with Sergeyev's *Hamlet*, Misha learned what he could about life in the West and visited Nureyev's luxurious house, where the two dancers spoke of Pushkin and just about everything except Nureyev's defection 10 years earlier. Misha even took the risk of befriending a North American, Christina Berlin, who worked as Margot Fonteyn's assistant. Her infatuation with Baryshnikov led her to study Russian and visit Leningrad a short time later, but by then the dancer was on his guard, worried that any association with Westerners might compromise his career. A surprise during the London tour was Makarova's absence onstage during the final performance, where flowers were strewn at Misha's feet during the curtain call. She was having dinner with some British friends, and with a little prompting from her host, decided in an instant to defect. Misha was aghast—and the other dancers joined in the chorus of condemnation that ensued, with Sergeyev soon dismissed following charges of embezzlement. Misha basically decided to go along with the denouncing of all things Sergeyev, winning him favor with Irina Kolpakova, who along with her husband assumed the directorship of the company. He was rewarded with the role of Adam in *Creation of the World*, in which the maturation of Adam was a metaphor for Misha's own development into an international ballet star, and danced in the film *Fiesta*, based on Hemingway's *The Sun Also Rises*.

After an investigation, including the questioning of Valery Panov, Misha was cleared to go on tour to Japan. When he returned, he was given Albrecht in *Giselle*. He was 24 and dancing the role of his dreams. His interpretation dispensed with the character's aristocratic icy remove, guilty for having seduced a peasant girl. Instead, he danced it as he felt it, with the passion of a young man taken by a girl who is off limits because of her social class. It was a huge success. Misha was given his own apartment, and Tanya Koltsova, by then a corps de ballet member, moved in with him. They were quite serious, and everything seemed perfect.

Mikhail Baryshnikov in *Largo*. **Photo credit: Asya Verzhbinsky.**

Soon, Misha's requirements exceeded what the Kirov could deliver by way of new works and well-suited partners. As his celebrity grew, the challenges diminished. He began drinking, broke up with Tanya, and perhaps the last straw was when a "creative evening" he was permitted to choreograph and cast was denounced for its "modernity" by the Kirov chiefs. As Misha thanked the dancers who performed it, he broke down in tears, feeling chafed by the golden handcuffs that shackled him to the Kirov. The only other opportunity inside the Soviet Union would have been with the Bolshoi. It was that—or defect—or both! He wasn't a political dissident—he hated politics. He was a celebrity, and deeply troubled by the prospect of trading his homeland and the privilege of dancing at the Maryinsky for an uncertain career in the West. Misha was added to a

Bolshoi tour of Canada in June of 1974. While there, and helped by his friends Sasha Minz and Dina Makarova, dance critics John Fraser and Clive and Patricia Barnes, dancers Gelsey Kirkland and Peter Martins, and a lawyer, Misha gave up all that was familiar to him to take a chance on the West. When it became clear that Baryshnikov hadn't defected in order to become rich, nor because he had a political axe to grind, the international press seized upon his goal of gaining "artistic freedom." Many Western dancers could cite that same motive for simply changing companies *within* their native countries without going to the extreme of defecting, but the transparently anti-communist cry "artistic freedom" conferred upon Misha the ungainly title of the "next" defector, read "ballet star."

After making his Western debut in a Canadian television production of *La Sylphide*, Misha accepted guest roles in *Giselle*, partnering Makarova, and "Kingdom of the Shades" from *La Bayadere*, staged by her for ABT, and danced the *Don Quixote* pas de deux in Washington, D.C. The *Giselle* reviews were ebullient. It was said that a violinist in the orchestra almost lost his grip on his instrument as Misha's Albrecht soared above the stage in the second act. Another critic compared him to an astronaut taking leave of the earth. He was the Albrecht who shared Giselle's torment, rather than the guilty Albrecht delivered to audiences a week earlier by Nureyev. With the help of Dina Makarova, Misha made contact with Gelsey Kirkland, whose relationship with Peter Martins was over, and whose desire to "defect" from New York City Ballet was more urgent and less tentative than Misha's had been to leave the Kirov and the Soviet Union. As they were negotiating their contracts with ABT, Misha and Gelsey began a personal relationship. In private, according to Kirkland, he was passionate, yet unattainable emotionally. In public, he withheld affection. Acclimating to the United States and the rigors of celebrity became one and the same experience for Misha, who relied heavily on a circle of Russian émigré intellectuals for emotional support. He missed the quiet dignity of Leningrad, and could make no sense of the shallow, course ways of New Yorkers and their noisy city, which he mistook as typical of the United States. He told reporters that America was spoiling him, and that he could not imagine living anywhere else.[11] In spite of comments such as these, he savored occasional long-distance telephone conversations with Russian friends, during which he spoke of missing the Kirov and life in the Soviet Union. His relationship with Gelsey mostly consisted of late-night visits that bespoke an urgent need for comfort. They began working on the next season's repertoire, attempting to school each other in the techniques in which they had been trained. Their relationship made progress in fits and starts. Misha hoped to overcome his homesickness by throwing himself into whatever dance opportunity—modern, classical, or whatever—came his way.

The couple's ABT debut in Washington, D.C., was received with lavish praise. In "he said, she said" interviews, Misha compared Gelsey to a well-cut diamond who could fit into any setting, and she said he was the best dancer she'd ever seen. Clive Barnes wrote, "[They danced] as if they'd grown up together. Perhaps they had."[12] Their public image reflected the pet notion of the press that they were bursting free of their respective bindings. In private, something different was taking place. Gelsey, under the pressure of her new shared stardom, patterned her interpretation of their relationship after the story ballets they were dancing. Misha wanted nothing more than to leave behind the old classics and devote his energies to new experimental dance works. His initial steps in that direction came with his role in Roland Petit's 1946 piece, *Le Jeune Homme et la Mort*, featuring a libretto by Jean Cocteau, which he danced in January 1975. The ballet was nihilistic; the protagonist lost his bearings and hanged himself. The next experiment was to dance George Balanchine's very demanding *Theme and Variations*, where repetitions pound the same set of calf muscles over and over. While dancing *Don Quixote*, Misha felt and heard his ankle shatter, but continued on by reversing the direction of his pirouettes, taking weight off the injured ankle. As the curtain closed, he collapsed onto the floor, passed out, with Makarova shrieking as if *she* had been felled.

During the first heady weeks after his arrival in the United States, Misha met Howard Gilman, the wealthy owner of a paper company. Gilman owned a 5500-acre estate in Florida called White Oak, which he made available to Baryshnikov for his recuperation. Time for reflection and healing allowed Misha to draw a balance sheet of his gains and losses since defecting. He longed for the peace and dignity of his former life. He was disappointed in the lack of support for dancers in the United States, the crass bottom-line, box office-driven conditions under which he had to work, the agnostic attitude toward preparation of dancers, and the sense that his celebrity was more important than his artistry. Of that phenomenon, former ABT dancer Bruce Marks remarked, "There were no ballet stars, only defectors."[13] Other dancers at ABT were beginning to experience Misha's celebrity in a rather unpleasant way. They felt that they were being sidelined in favor of the star-defector, and some worried that if the defection craze grew, they might all be out of work before long. Baryshnikov was earning $3,000 per performance, while soloists who had stuck with the company through thick and thin for over a decade were lucky to be grossing $400 a week. His partners were complaining that ballets such as *Giselle* were becoming "all about" Misha, who had carved out a mad scene of his own for Albrecht and disdained to rehearse with his partners because he was so familiar with *his* role. Makarova decided to split her time between ABT and the Royal Ballet. Kirkland scheduled *extra* rehearsal time. This worked to alienate him from her on a personal level, though he favored continuing their professional partnership. Misha's partnerships were suffering meltdowns in quick succession.

Viewed objectively, he hadn't come to the United States to dance the same roles under worse conditions than those that prompted his defection from the Kirov. He came to dance newer, edgier works, but he had to go to Spoleto to find what and who he was looking for. He saw Twyla Tharp perform there, and wanted to take a chance on changing his profile to dance her work. Tharp leaned on the North American idiom, pop culture specifically, to create a signature style of off-balance work that skidded into the music, as if the bodies were arriving on the heels of the steps. Oddly, this had a lot in common with the look of Vaganova, but Tharp's oeuvre was not ballet-derivative. She seemed to be finishing Martha Graham's and Merce Cunningham's sentences for them.

Push Comes to Shove was set by Tharp on Baryshnikov, and the title captured the flavor of the collaboration it represented. Tharp worked long hours to achieve exactly what she wanted, and making it happen with a classically trained Russian dancer required more than her usual unflinching rigor. Baryshnikov described the preparation of the piece as "a cross between a perfect vacation and being in church."[14] Misha's head was turned by all the opportunities and successes, and he found himself unable to limit his commitments—both professional and personal. The off-again/on-again relationship with Kirkland was interrupted by Misha's brief sexual forays into the ABT corps de ballet. The biggest problem Misha had was deciding whether to dance five Giselles in Germany or two galas for Prince Ranier in Monaco, at the same time that he was accepting invitations to dance works by Tudor, Robbins, Ailey and play a major role in the 1977 film *The Turning Point*. While appreciative that the film would offer ballet access to a wider audience, Misha disagreed with many of the editing choices, and deplored the way his acting "read" in English. The film received mixed reviews, some critics finding it slight, and others delighting in its candor about the real lives of dancers. It was a huge box office success and, in tandem with the defections, assured ballet a permanent visa on U.S. shores. In 1978, Baryshnikov was nominated for an Oscar as best supporting actor for his performance. At a party given for him and his co-star Leslie Browne, he arrived with actress Jessica Lange. Recently divorced, Lange had studied painting at the University of Minnesota and mime in Paris, and had just finished shooting the movie *King Kong*. Actor Jack Nicholson described Lange as a "fawn crossed with a Buick."[15] After having met Misha, she returned to New York to resume acting classes and research the life of the actress Frances Farmer, whom she would eventually portray on screen. While apparently very much in love, the lives of the new couple were separate and distinct, with Misha committed to taking on the restaging of what would prove to be a very successful *Nutcracker* for ABT, in which Kirkland would return to the stage in the role of Clara. Then he restaged *Don Quixote* for a tour calculated to keep *The Turning Point* audiences in the thrall of ABT.

Misha found himself revisiting his decision to defect as he continued to hold dear the basic values that guided Soviet ballet pedagogy, performance, and support of the arts. He could not shake the guilty belief that leaving the Soviet Union represented a betrayal of those values and the investment in his career that his government, with all of its obvious defects, had made in him. The suicide of his contemporary, Yuri Soloviev, prompted Misha to reflect upon his motives. Curiously, this train of thought led him to Balanchine, whom he began to view as the continuator of the Russian tradition on U.S. soil. Fearful of approaching Balanchine directly, Misha disclosed his wish to work with him to Peter Martins and Jerome Robbins. It was not long before Misha received a call inviting him "to talk." Misha joined NYCB at union scale. In the spirit of what can only have been viewed as some cosmic joke in the midst of Baryshnikov's self-doubts, the fast food clown Ronald McDonald introduced him to an audience of mothers and children on the lawn of the company's summer venue at Saratoga Springs. After that surreal introduction, he made his company debut partnering Patricia McBride in *Coppélia*. Over the year that he spent at City Ballet, Baryshnikov worked very hard to become a Balanchine dancer, incurring injuries and tendonitis that were near-crippling. He enjoyed the "pure dance" experience of performing *Rubies*. Balanchine had suffered a heart attack, and while he worked tirelessly with Baryshnikov, did not make any new ballets, and so Misha did not have the experience of having work set on him by Mr. B. When ABT offered him the Artistic Director post vacated by Lucia Chase, Balanchine advised Misha to take it. Misha then learned that Jessica Lange was pregnant. He took a year off to rest and recover from his injuries before assuming the ABT directorship. Aleksandra Baryshnikov, who would be called Shura for short, was born on March 5, 1981, and promptly became her father's emotional raison d'être.

Once at ABT, Baryshnikov worked to instill in the company the kind of work ethic and discipline that he learned at the Kirov, making an effort to eliminate the star system and bring young dancers forward from the corps to dance principal roles. These changes, and Misha's habit of being present everywhere on the one hand, yet terse and incommunicado on the other, fueled company gossip, resentment, and dire predictions. As Misha danced less, he took on more and more projects: his own small dance troupe, Baryshnikov and Company, and film projects that he found more taxing than dance productions. After a massive number of script changes, which Misha roundly protested, *White Nights*, in which he starred with tap dancer Gregory Hines, morphed into an anti-Soviet propaganda piece. Still, he continued to accept roles that fans saw as unworthy, such as the frosty womanizer in the HBO series *Sex and the City*.

    Approximately a year after Aleksandra's birth, Jessica Lange began
seeing the actor and playwright Sam Shepard, and she and Misha parted.
ABT's ebbs and flows tended to mimic Misha's mercurial need to recon-
cile the stability and discipline of his Soviet life with a tendency to skitter
from one project to the next. The film *Dancers* was extremely taxing
for Baryshnikov, and in 1990, after his assistant Charles France was fired
by the ABT board, Misha quit, and Jane Hermann and Oliver Smith
succeeded him as co-Artistic Directors, with Kevin McKenzie assuming
the directorship in 1992.

    In a September 9, 2004, item in telegraph.co.uk, Ismene Brown
updates readers on Baryshikov's activities since the 1990 White Oak
Dance Project, which commissioned 43 works in its 12 year life. Baryshnikov tells her, "I can't stand authority. I like to make my own mistakes."
In that spirit, he has opened The Baryshnikov Center for the Arts in
New York's Hell's Kitchen, where mid-career dancers and their companies enjoy residencies and performance opportunities. The ambitious
project represents Misha's atavistic effort to defy the anarchy of capital-
ism on its own turf:

> I think I got disappointed over the years, about New York, about the States.
> You know, sometimes you go and visit Europe and see good old socialism
> in its good part! You see public concern about art, and young people's partici-
> pation and young faces in the audience. Then you arrive in the States and it is
> $150 to go to an opera. Ridiculous. We have so much young talent on the
> streets, but because everything is commercial, they finally drift away from
> their dream of their life.[16]

    How does Misha spend his leisure time now that his dream center
has opened, and he is free to make his own decisions as well as mistakes?
He is married to former ABT dancer Lisa Rinehart, and they have three
children, Anna Katerina, born May 22, 1992, Sofia-Luisa, born May 24,
1994, and Peter, born in 1989, the year Misha won a Tony for his performance in "Metamorphosis." His eldest daughter Aleksandra made Misha
a grandfather in 2003 with the birth of her daughter. Misha fishes, plays
golf, and has written a children's book.

    In the December 12, 2005, *New Yorker*, dance critic Joan Acocella
quotes Baryshnikov:

> When a dancer comes onstage, he is not just a blank slate that the choreogra-
> pher has written on. Behind him he has all the decisions he has made in his
> life...Each time he has chosen, and in what he is onstage you see the result
> of those choices. You are looking at the person he is, the person who, at this
> point, he cannot help but be.... Exceptional dancers, in my experience, are
> also exceptional people, people with an attitude toward life, a kind of quest,
> and an internal quality. They know who they are, and they show this to you
> willingly.[17]

6

Anna Pavlova

The object of talent is to create. That of theory is to study the things created, and to provide elements for their appreciation. Consequently, theory can refer only to things already created. Her travels have yielded Pavlova a wealth of resources for her imagination to work upon. Those resources could not have been found at home, where the official repertory and time-honoured tradition would have imposed limits upon her eager activity. Russia was for her a preliminary stage. Like a chrysalis, she gradually assumed shape and stored the power to break from her bonds: and when the time had come, she soared freely in the light of day, a lovely, resplendent butterfly.

—V. Svetloff[1]

An obituary in *La Russie Illustré* gave Pavlova's year of birth as 1885, but it is possible that she was born as early as February 16, 1881, in St. Petersburg, making her between 46 and 51 when she died. Her birth was two months premature, and her father died when she was two years old.

"Nura," as she was called, felt as if some giant hand had come along and "pulled down the sky"[2] when a boy caught and crushed a butterfly she was dancing with one day outside the family's country dacha. To celebrate Christmas when she was eight years old, Nura's mother took her little butterfly dancer to the Maryinksy Theatre to see Tchaikovsky's "Sleeping Beauty" in four acts. When the curtain rose on the golden hall of a grand palace, the child shouted in delight. As the corps de ballet danced a waltz, her mother asked Nura whether she would like to dance like that. Nura answered, "Oh, I should prefer to dance as the pretty lady does who plays the part of the Princess."[3] She sat riveted, memorizing as much as she could so as to be able to recreate it the very next day. She predicted that she would dance the title role in the ballet some day, and when

**Anna Pavlova in *Dragonfly*. Courtesy San Francisco Peforming Arts Library &
Museum.**

she learned during an interview that the ballet school would not admit
her for another two years, she kept up her campaign for the duration.
At the age of 10, her mother enrolled her. She intended to become a ballerina as soon as she could.

Peter the Great took an active part in the tradition of ballet that he
initiated when Russia embraced the new courtly dance from France
called "Ballet," where dancers trained in the Italian style performed on
the Versailles palace lawn. French dance masters such as Didlot continued
to train new generations of dancers in the art. Peter's daughter Elizabeth
maintained an even greater interest in the school than he did. Russia
infused the classical forms with its own Eastern mystical romance, of
which Diaghilev's choreography was a prime example. It is claimed that
the discipline at the ballet school was more intractable than the military
academy's and produced not only the finest dancers, but dancers with a
strong academic background.

Here is a description of the school by Mr. Rothay Reynolds that appeared in J.E. Flitch's *Modern Dancing and Dancers*:

> Here one may see a class of merry boys instructed in their art. A master, usually one of the best dancers in the theatre, shows them the steps and movements to be learned, and half a dozen do their best to copy him. After ten minutes they go and rest, and a second batch comes forward. The boys seem to enjoy the work, and even when they are supposed to be resting some of them will continue to practice and give each other friendly hints. In another and similar room is the girls' class, where the method is the same. Then there is a room with many toilet-tables on which grease-paints are set out, and with mirrors and electric lights arranged exactly as at the theatre. Here the pupils assemble for lessons in make-up. A boy has to learn to transform himself into a Chinese or an old man or a beautiful young Greek, and he has to pass examinations at different points of his school career in this art.[4]

Anna's day began in a large room, a well lit salon with a high ceiling and a huge mirror, in which there was no furniture except for a few benches and a piano. The walls bore portraits of the members of the ruling Russian dynasty. Beginner students had their lesson first and when they vacated the studio the older students filed in for their class. At noon, a lunch bell rang, and after lunch the students went for a walk. They returned to dance classes, continuing until four in the afternoon, and then had dinner and enjoyed some leisure time. After dinner, there were fencing and music lessons, and rehearsals of pieces that would be performed on the stage of the Maryinsky Theatre. On feast days the students were taken to the Theatre Michel to see French plays performed by French actors who belonged to the Imperial Company.

The early roles in which Pavlova excelled were Frost in *The Season of the Year*, Zulmé in *Giselle*, Aurore in *The Awakening of Flora*, the Fairy Candide in *The Sleeping Beauty*, and Fleur de Lys in *Esmeralda*. After dancing Lisa in *The Magic Flute*, Juanita in *Don Quixote*, Pierrette in *Harlequinade*, and the Chief Naiad in *Sylvia*, she was given the title role in *Giselle*. She was taught by Gerdt and Marius Petipa. Senior dancers and ballerine assolute were Kschesinskaya, Legnani, and Preobrajenska. Anna traveled to Milan to study with Cecchetti. Later, when she came to Milan on tour, Cecchetti was present at all her performances and would give her corrections afterward. Pavlova never stopped studying, even after she completed her courses at the Imperial School. Among the teachers she continued to study with were Oblakof, Ivanof, Johansen, Gerdt, Cecchetti, Baretta, Vasem, and Sokolova. The ballet was such an exclusive institution in Imperial Russia that when one of the balletomanes died, there would be a plethora of applications for the vacated seat. Each ballerina had her own followers, who would literally follow her from city to city to see her perform, a tradition which continued into the mid-twentieth century.

When Legnani, a very strong and muscular Italian ballerina, visited St. Petersburg, she amazed the Russian dancers by performing 32 fouettés. Anna was so envious that she practiced until she could do 32, and showed her teachers and classmates her new skill. Gerdt, her teacher, reprimanded her for taxing her muscles and delicate feet, saying,

> Now you have shown us that you can do the most difficult acrobatic feats. I beg you never to try again to imitate those who are stronger than you in their muscles. You must realize that your daintiness and fragility are your greatest assets. You should always do the kind of dancing which brings out your own rare qualities instead of trying to win praise by mere acrobatic tricks.[5]

She mastered the particular technique favored by each of her teachers, but Pavlova was not a cultist, and did not blindly follow one singular ballet doctrine. She followed advice that made sense to her and that helped her to articulate her natural sensibilities, believing that only those without artistry faultlessly reproduce what the teacher holds out as the ideal. Her goal was not to imitate, but transform. It was because of the early recognition of her capacity for innovation that she was not relegated to bringing up the rear of the corps de ballet, but entrusted with small solos, and then greater ones. She danced Hulnare in *Le Corsair*, Sister Anna in *Blue Beard*, La Fée des Canaries, and Princess Florine in *The Sleeping Beauty*, Henriette in *Raymonda*, Ephemeride in *The Brook*, and the Spanish Girl in *La Fée des Poupées*.

Czar Alexander and Czarina Maria paid frequent visits to the school. Nura cried when the Czar appeared at one of the school's performances and chose another girl, Stanislava Belinskaya, to pick up and kiss. Her distress was so convincing that the Czar then picked her up, too, and when she continued to weep, demanding to be kissed, he kissed her. But in the year 1905, when student demonstrators were being shot in the streets, Anna wasn't looking for kisses from the Czar. Instead, she, along with the famous Father Gapon and Michael Fokine, met in Fokine's apartment to organize the participation of dancers in a strike against the Imperial Ballet. They demanded higher pay and improved working conditions, and Pavlova regarded with disdain those who wanted to reap the benefits of activism without themselves stepping forward. Her speeches were so impassioned and persuasive that the Ballet wanted to fire her, but in the wake of the uprisings, the government backed off, and no action was taken against her.

The dance iconoclast Isadora Duncan visited Russia in 1907 and amused audiences there by appearing nude, choosing the more revered music of Schumann and Chopin over that of Minkus and Drigo. Fokine took to her immediately and voiced the wish to Marius Petipa that there could be "a dancer with the sensibility of Isadora Duncan and the technique of Kschesinskaya." Petipa was no fan of what he called

"Duncanism," but was quick to point out that "There is one of our dancers who has all the feeling of Duncan and all the technique of Kschesinkaya. You know whom I mean—Anna Pavlova."[6]

Possibly inspired by "Duncanism," Diaghilev began experimenting with a maverick style that gave the world *Les Noces* just as Pavlova was advancing to the highest ranks in the company, and the position of Ballerina Assoluta was being vacated by Preobrajenska. In 1899 there were 100 members of the corps de ballet, and *Le Corsair*, accompanied by an orchestra of 120 musicians, was staged at a cost of 500,000 rubles, but Pavlova decided to forfeit the opulence of the Maryinsky, as well as the handsome pension that would have been hers at the approximate age of 35 had she stayed. Having rejected Diaghilev's first offer to join his International Ballet, she eagerly accepted his second. Her radical departure was vindicated in the spring of 1909, when her invitation performances in Paris for the company won her recognition throughout Europe. She was able to return to the Maryinsky as a guest, delighting those who had seen her move gradually from the rear of the corps to the front, with an exquisite Giselle. In her new company, instead of dancing six times a week for the Russian aristocracy whose lucre allowed them to maintain a virtual monopoly over all house seats, she was able to perform eight to ten times a week for all in the world who wished and were able to see her. Over an obscure retirement, she chose to dance to her death.

In April 1909, Pavlova took a month's leave of absence from the company before being promoted to the top rank, in order to form her own company, with the goal of seeking a broader audience. In April 1908, she took a dozen female dancers and eight men to Helsingfors, and then went on to Stockholm, Copenhagen, Prague, Vienna, and Berlin before returning to St. Petersburg. Uncomprehending that the near-riotous crowd assembled beneath her hotel window was there because of her and not the company as a whole, it was her maid who explained it to her. It then occurred to her that the time to share her gifts with the world had arrived.

She reprised her earlier European tour, returning to Stockholm, Copenhagen, Berlin, and Vienna. Following a second appearance in Stockholm, fans removed the horse from the carriage in which she was riding, and personally drew it back to her hotel. Later, she was given a medal by the King of Sweden, and the Swedish Order of "Litteris et Artibus" (Arts and Letters) was conferred upon her. By May-June, the company had arrived in Paris, and she danced principal roles in *Les Sylphides*, *Spectre de la Rose* (partnered by Nijinsky), *Cleopatra*, and *Pavillon d'Armide* at the Théâtre du Châtelet. Parisians were enchanted by the sets, the costumes by Bakst, and the radical experimentation with classical ballet that, before Pavlova's appearance, only Diaghilev had come to represent.

In 1910, Pavlova ventured to London on her own to give a private performance at the invitation of King Edward. Then she left Diaghilev in order to dance with Mikhail Mordkin's tiny company in a vaudeville act at the Palace Theatre in May 1910, against the advice of friends who thought it undignified to appear in such a venue. Dancing *Bacchanale*, a lusty but athletic work set to the music of Gazounov's "Seasons" (and even slapping Mordkin during one contentious performance), Pavlova became the talk of London, was celebrated everywhere, and never for a moment regretted her decision to dance at the Palace Theatre. During her second season, Laurent Novikoff partnered her (as she had refused to ever dance again with Mordkin), and she added *La Fille Mal Gardée* and *The* [Dying] *Swan* to her London repertoire. The last was so moving that audiences held their applause for 10 seconds after its dramatic finish, and then tossed so many bouquets that tiers of flowers blanketed the stage.

Pavlova's next stop was the Metropolitan Opera House in New York, where audiences were primed for her Giselle, local newspapers having published reams about her, including images of her, essays on the art of dance, and strictly speculative material about her tastes, ideas, and adventures. She returned to the United States several times during her career. Of the many countries her company toured, the United States was possibly most appreciative. In 1911 and 1912, she danced two seasons in London, and a command performance before the King and Queen. In 1913, she danced for Kaiser Wilhelm, who, when the audience fell silent, stood up and applauded her himself, whereupon "the theatre thundered with a tempest of cheers."[7] After a return to Russia to rest for a brief time, she took up touring again, this time to Russian cities, and during a performance before the Tsar, he called her to his box and congratulated her for having toured Russian artistry abroad to such good effect, adding, "I have but one fear, and that is that other countries may some day take you away from Russia for good and all."[8] He might have done better to find a more historically substantial object for his fears, and worry that his own subjects might some day "take" *him* (and his dynasty) "away from Russia for good and all"!

Pavlova traveled to London via Germany, where in the days leading up to World War I her personal effects were confiscated. She returned to the United States in September of 1914, dancing a winter season in New York at the Hippodrome, and then traveling to California for a rest in May of 1915. She returned to New York in 1916, where she danced at the Century Theatre. In March, she toured Cuba, Panama, Chile, Peru, Argentina, and Brazil, spending Christmas of 1916 in Puerto Rico, insisting that a traditional Russian Christmas tree be mounted in her hotel—amidst a heat wave. It wasn't until March of 1917, while she was in Costa Rica, that news reached her of the October Revolution in Russia. She continued on to Panama, Ecuador, and Peru, where she was presented with a gold engraved plate, and then to Chile, Uruguay, and Argentina. She gave several performances in Venezuela and Puerto Rico, with a brief rest before touring Brazil. While retracing her steps through Buenos Aires, she decided to board a French freighter carrying saltpeter to Santiago de Cuba. No accommodations except the deck were available, so that is where the 65-member company camped out, braving the elements.

When she concluded her South American tour in 1918, she had a season in Mexico, where she was honored with the most elegant reception of her entire tour. She extended her two-week stay to eight weeks. She danced for an audience of 36,000 people each Sunday in the Bull Ring and in what were known as the middle class theatres, where families attended performances of her popular *Mexican Dances*, with choreography that leaned heavily on the traditional dances of the Mexican countryside. The history of Latin American ballet is rich with legends of how during the October Revolution, Russian dancers who were stranded in countries throughout the Caribbean decided to remain in those countries, teaching ballet and starting their own dance academies, which gave rise to a number ballet companies throughout Latin America. While Pavlova was not among them, the impact of her company's tours left a definite imprint. She returned to Buenos Aires, and then to Europe in October of 1918, where she visited Lisbon, Madrid, and Paris.

After a 1921 performance at London's Drury Lane, she left for a 140-town tour of the United States, on a specially outfitted train which housed the company between performances.

In 1922, Pavlova traveled to Japan, where she danced in both Western-style and authentic Japanese theaters in the cities and the countryside. She began taking notes for a piece she would name *Oriental Impressions*. She continued on from Japan to India, where she witnessed a policeman beating an Untouchable on the head until he passed out, and declined to ever visit the country again, giving away articles of clothing she had bought so that she would indeed have no mementos of caste-bound India, except for the notes she took for *Oriental Impressions*. Her next tour stop was of Cairo, and then Alexandria. After a vacation in Italy, she spent the 1923 season in London at Covent Garden. She returned to New York, California, and Mexico the following year, and then in 1925 danced seasons in Paris and Germany before traveling to South Africa and then on to Australia, touring thousands of miles of what was then a fairly rough-and-tumble terrain. She continued on to New Zealand, returning to Germany by the end of 1926. In 1927, she gave 80 performances in more than 50 theaters throughout Great Britain, and then danced in Holland, Germany, Italy, Switzerland, and France before returning to South America in June of 1928.

After a brief stop in London, Pavlova then toured Egypt, India (in spite of her earlier vow not to), Burma, the Straits Settlements, Java, and Australia, returning home for a vacation in August 1929, after which she

Anna Pavlova. Courtesy San Francisco Peforming Arts Library & Museum.

toured Spain, Switzerland, Czechoslovakia, Denmark, Sweden, Norway, Hamburg, and Paris. The last tour she took began in 1930. In spite of an injured patella, she danced in the English provinces, appearing for the last time on December 12, 1930, at the Golders Green Hippodrome just a few steps from her home, Ivy House. Her intention had been to seek treatment in the South of France before touring Holland, but when she reached Holland en route from the south of France, she contracted a chill after having washed her hair and gone out in the cold, and she died after reaching The Hague.

Pavlova had lived at Ivy House, at Hampstead. The house was surrounded by lovely gardens, a lake designed by Pavlova, and on the lake were the swans that Pavlova adored. In spite of her habit of throwing her arms around them with great affection, they never did her any harm.

She would roughhouse with them, and they would "get in the game," stroking her face with their beaks. There were also peacocks and flamingoes, and Anna's adoration of them was unmitigated. Her greatest desire was to live in a country cottage and escape the din of city life. From the beginning, there was a dance studio at the house. There Anna taught young girls whom she would groom to join her touring company as members of the corps de ballet. While she preferred Russian-trained dancers, the girls came from all over Europe, and were Danish, English, German, Polish, Italian, and Czech, but she gave them Russian surnames, as was the style in that era. Many of the girls came from schools in Paris that had been established by Russian émigrés, such as Egorova, Tefilova, and Preobrajenskaya. About 300 dancers performed with Anna during her 20-year career outside of Russia.

What were the tours like? When Pavlova took her multi-national company on tour, there were 22 female dancers, 12 men, two principal dancers, one of whom was a character dancer, and the other, Pavlova. Of the two men, one would be Pavlova's partner, and the other the ballet master. A small orchestra also went along. When the theaters could not provide accompaniment, the Cherniavsky Trio traveled with the company to provide it. Then there was a stage manager, an electrician, a librarian, a wig custodian, three stage hands and a number of supernumeraries, Pavlova's maid, and five wardrobe mistresses. Victor Dandré was Pavlova's husband, and he acted as the company's general manager. All final decisions—artistic and administrative—were made by Pavlova. It was not unusual to play seven towns in six days, requiring a degree of efficiency and organization on a par with military maneuvers.

A strategic approach failed Pavlova when it came to managing the company's finances. While very generous personally, often giving substantial gifts to departing dancers or insisting on the best medical treatment for company members and then rewarding hospital staffs additionally, she was considered a tightwad when it came to wages. On tour, dancers were forced to pay their own per diem expenses, including hotel bills, taxi fares, and for shoes and tights. She would allow only principal dancers to travel first class, which in certain countries and elite social circles was regarded as shocking. She was to have said, "Why should I pay these girls at all? They should pay me for the privilege of belonging to my company!"[9] She spoke of the company as "one big family," which tended to obscure the fact that she was becoming immensely wealthy on the backs of corps de ballet members whose wages were meager. It was not unusual for her to haggle over sixpence, and then agree to spend 200 pounds on a whim. Though it did not appear that she deliberately set out to exploit, she easily fell into the practice of doing so. While the dancers harbored a thousand resentments and jealousies as rivals for roles, incredibly, there was no complaint among them regarding low wages.

In spite of her pettiness in matters of finance, she exuded a charisma that held international audiences in her thrall. Her power issued from a genuine affection for her audiences and fellow company members. Acts of arrogance left her aghast. While in Milan, a company member briefly left his seat on a train. Two passengers came aboard. One of them took the company member's vacated seat, refusing to relinquish it to him when he returned. A guard was called, who arrested the company member for "insulting fascism." The dancer was held by the police and interrogated for several hours, and set free only after having it made clear to him that he was obligated to give his seat to "an Italian" whenever requested to do so. Pavlova took the incident personally and thought it merited an international protest, outraged that she should have been insulted as a foreigner in Milan, the birthplace of ballet of all places, and home to Cecchetti and Legnani, who were that very evening expected to come see her dance. The Milan incident typified Pavlova's response to injustice; it was, however, not at all typical of the way in which she comported herself while traveling when she wasn't going toe to toe with fascist *carbinieri*. In most other instances she sought out—to the point of embarrassing traveling companions—the most extensive guidance in understanding and experiencing the culture of the host country, exemplified by her visit to Agra, where she meditated in the temples and stood outside all night long gazing at the moonlit Taj Mahal in the bitter cold. Her inclination to become thoroughly conversant with the appropriate culture was best expressed in her own malapropism, "I like to talk to everybody *man to man*."[10]

She was especially generous in sharing her artistic views with the press:

> And I can quite truthfully say that my successes are due firstly to my ceaseless labour and to the merits of my teachers. Marius Petipa was the first to guide my steps. In that respect, I must say that I have been particularly fortunate.
>
> I have the greatest appreciation for Fokin, and believe that of all the reformers of dancing he is the most gifted. He and I followed the same path during the whole of my career in Russia. We made our debut together in Drigo's *Harlequinade*. He used me as "material" for his creations. We were uniformly in agreement, and in quest of new revelations in an art of which we had the same conception.
>
> It is our duty to accept all that is beautiful in new artistic departures. But at the same time, we should never lack the courage to stick to all that is excellent in the older forms of art...what Marius Petipa has done is in many respects marvelous. The only misfortune is, that in his days the Ballet was considered, so to speak, a second-rate art....It is only at a later time that great composers, such as Tchaikovsky and Glazunof, began to take an interest in Ballet music. And is not music the very soul of Ballet? Art should not, and cannot remain immovable. Progressive evolution is its law. We owe an immense debt of gratitude to Fokin, who succeeded in introducing

innovations in the becalmed regime of our choreography. But Fokin's advent was heralded and made possible by Petipa, who was the first to create our school of classical dancing. In order to do well in the new ballets, it is necessary to have been fully trained according to the principles of that school.[11]

She also commented:

The American's nature is more demonstrative [than the British]: but they too are discriminating, and capable of keeping their appreciation for things which really deserve it. Both the British and Americans arrive at their judgments in full independence—a fact which I greatly appreciate. They never start with preconceived notions. Suggestions made by the Press, and judgments emanating from small groups of artists, do not seem to carry with them the importance which, as I seemed to guess, they carry at times in France...

I have sometimes heard people say that England and America had inadequate notions as regards the art of choreography. That is entirely untrue. They are highly cultured people...I should even incline to say that they sometimes display more expert knowledge than others.

I have danced in the greatest theatres of the United States, beginning with Boston. I have never seen a bigger one; nor have I encountered in the United States a finer and more cultured audience.

But the taste of the Americans differs to a degree from that of their British cousins. In the United States, the most successful ballet was *Giselle*.[12]

Pavlova's biographer Walford Hyden was her accompanist and the company's orchestra conductor. They visited and revisited every disagreement between dancer and musician that has ever arisen, and sometimes scores were thrown onto the stage (Hyden), or demands to eliminate an entire instrument which meant also striking 20 bars of music were tendered (Pavlova). Regardless of their cross-training, dancers tend to jealously guard the idée fixe that *they* should determine the tempo, while musicians are inclined alternatively to believe that the dancer should adapt to the composer's directions. Hyden expresses his frustration about Pavlova's tendency to hold an arabesque *en pointe* long after any other mortal would have let it go, requiring that the music be held as well, to the delight of the audience and utter consternation of the orchestra! After music, stage floors often posed the greatest challenges to the company while on tour. Each stage was examined for the most minute weakness or defect, and planks were hammered over it, or the stage itself was resurfaced. The routine was to examine the stage, then wet it just enough to dampen it so that the pulverized rosin could be sprinkled onto it to achieve exactly the right traction to minimize the chances of the dancers slipping. After one long afternoon "seasoning" the floor, a stage manager who observed all the attention the floor was receiving, though not having been let in on the nature of the concerns, ordered the stage waxed and polished to a high gloss, in order to please the visiting company. When Pavlova returned for the performance and saw the glistening yet menacing result of the stage crew's efforts, she ordered every speck of wax and polish sanded off of the surface, and the curtain held 20 minutes in order to carry out those orders to her satisfaction.

It would come as no surprise if Pavlova's gravestone bore the inscription, "The devil is in the details," because it was her unstinting and inexhaustible attention to them that drove the company. She would lead by example, rehearsing a 30-second phrase for an hour and a half until it met or surpassed her expectations.

Pavlova's personal rituals and habits were, unlike some others of her rank, completely in the service of her art, rather than acts of rebellion against it or a means of letting off steam. Hyden describes the moment just before her entrance:

> She seemed to nerve herself for an effort as she listened for the music to accompany her entry. At the last moment, she would draw herself up to her full height, take a quick deep breath, moisten her lips, at the same time smoothing her waist inwards with the palms of her hands on her hips. This gesture was involuntary and she never failed to make it. It was as though she was gathering herself together spiritually...The gesture always ended with a quick backward movement of the right hand, as though she were pushing at something unseen behind her, an invisible force which gave her momentum for the whole of her dance.[13]

While she enjoyed applause, she didn't "mug" for it in her dancing. She seemed to dance purely to please her audiences, and was never at ease at the end of an evening until after she had received visitors in her dressing room following the performance. She enjoyed a hearty midnight meal, but eschewed after-theater parties, and drank only an occasional glass of wine. Her body was her instrument, and she treated it with appropriate care and respect.

It is therefore the greatest irony that it should have betrayed her mortally at such a young age, when she had accomplished so many of her plans that suggested other more elaborate pursuits. Like the chrysanthemum she danced in *Autumn Leaves*, a fearsome force of nature overtook and ravaged a more subtle force that embodied everything that was splendid about the natural world.

Pavlova died at 12:20 A.M. on January 23, 1931. Having completed a very taxing tour in December, she was left with a knee inflammation that required rest and treatment. She took only a few weeks' rest in the South of France, and then set out on another demanding tour, which began in Holland. Her plan had been to then travel through Germany to Riga and Reval, and then on to Poland, Rumania, Serbia, Italy, and France, before beginning another world tour.

En route to Holland from the South of France by train, she contracted a chill following an accident in which many of the train's windows shattered. Passengers had to leave the train and wait along the right of way in the cold night air. By the time Pavlova reached Paris, she was ill but would not admit it. Friends advised her to cancel the tour and seek medical treatment, but she dismissed their concerns, saying, "I cannot allow myself to be ill. I must take myself in hand. I must work. I can stand any kind of physical pain. But if my nerves go, I am finished."[14]

By the time she reached the Hague, she had acute pneumonia. She collapsed. Doctors were called, and said that she could be saved by means of a "trepanning" (drilling) operation on her ribs, which would have meant that she could never dance again. She refused. On January 22, at 6 P.M., the doctors announced that she was beyond saving. Pavlova was gasping for air, and said, "I am dying. Ease my pain." The doctors' injections offered no relief. Around midnight, she became delirious and began asking for her Swan dress. Her voice became weaker, as her arms fluttered for the last time. Her lungs failed, and Anna Pavlova died.

Pianowsky, the company's ballet master, arranged her body in its coffin. A shroud was made by her wardrobe mistress, Manya. Her coffin was sent aboard ship in a theatrical crate, on which the letters "A.P." were painted. Her remains, draped with the Czar's flag, were taken to the Russian Orthodox Church on Buckingham Palace Road. A Russian choir chanted while thousands of mourners filed through the church and placed flowers on her coffin until it was no longer visible. These included great wreaths and tiny threepenny bunches of violets and lilies. She was then taken, accompanied by only a few close friends to the crematorium at Golders Green.

When a great composer dies, his or her music lives on. When a great dancer is cut down too soon by injury or death, her performing genius is extinguished forever.

7

Li Cunxin

Among those to watch is Li Cunxin...He dances with extraordinary elegance, using his torso and arms with wonderful grace and he is a whiz of a turner as well.

—Anna Kisselgoff, "Dance: A Surprising Houston Ballet,"
New York Times, April 8, 1981[1]

On a snowy day in 1971, in the city of Qingdao, in the People's Republic of China, as children sat in a frosty classroom singing songs that praised Chairman Mao, they were interrupted by visiting cultural workers from Beijing, sent by Mao's wife, Jiang Qing, on a very particular, if unusual, mission. They were looking for suitable students for the newly re-opened Beijing Dance Academy. It had been closed during the Cultural Revolution, but Madame Mao, Jiang Qing, loved ballet, and utilized her influence to rehabilitate it. The Cultural Revolution, then winding down, was actually its opposite: a reactionary purge of cultural innovators and political opponents. Launched to end the cultural imbalance between the countryside and the city, it proved a menacing projection onto the masses of the worst conceits, vanities, and pecadillos of the Chinese Communist Party's middle class leadership.

The visitors selected one of the girls, and as they were leaving Teacher Song pointed to a waif-like little boy: "What about him?" Song says she doesn't know what made her point him out at the time. Her question changed the boy's life forever. His name was Li Cunxin. Inside of 10 years, he would be one of the world's top 10 male dancers.

The visitors measured the children's body parts—down to their toes. One turned Li's legs outward. Another straightened the boy's lower back with his knee, pressing Li's knees back to assess his hip flexibility. It hurt,

Li Cunxin in Red Guard Uniform. Courtesy Li Cunxin.

but losing face by crying out would have hurt more. One girl and one boy were chosen. Li heard the word "ballet," and had seen a ballet on screen where the dancers performed on tiptoe. He feared ending up crippled like his grandmother, whose feet had been bound. In another round of auditions, two teachers held Li's standing leg as another lifted his other one, asking whether it hurt. It hurt a lot, but Cunxin denied that it did, even as his hamstrings tore. What made him lie?

Li's parents lived with his six uncles and aunts and their children—20 people in a six-room house. Li's mother, a highly skilled seamstress, had to prove her mettle through tireless sewing, washing, cleaning, cooking, and tending to the children, including her seven sons. His father worked two jobs—on the collective farm, and carting building materials. There was no electricity, and meals were eaten by candlelight.

As more children were born, new rooms were built onto the dirt-floor house. Li's parents had four of the rooms. There was no refrigeration or running water at the time, and a big clay jug held drinking water, while two built-in woks and a kind of bellows served as the stove. The family fetched water from the nearby village. Bathwater was heated in woks. The toilet was a hole in the ground in the courtyard. With no sewers, a laborer carted away the foul contents of the hole each day in a wheelbarrow.

The Li family farmed corn and yams on one twentieth of an acre. The government appropriated most of the crop and the rest was divided among those who worked the land, based on a point system. The maximum number was the rough equivalent of 17 cents.

Li Cunxin, his parents' sixth son, was born on January 26, 1961. When he was 15 days old, his mother was preparing for New Year celebrations. She left Li tightly swaddled in a quilt on the earth bed while she steamed bread buns. His arm got free and was severely burned and became infected. After several painful treatments, it finally healed, leaving a scar that the cultural workers noticed on the day of the auditions.

The boys foraged in the fields behind their house for yams that hadn't been harvested. One year, the collective experimented with growing peanuts. Rats stored the peanuts in burrows. Li and his friends dug in the burrows to retrieve the peanuts. Li's paternal grandmother helped look after the children, and Li grew very attached to her. She took the blame for Li when he tried to please his parents by cooking a meal, then slipped and knocked over precious plates, which broke. When she died, Li felt her loss deeply.

In his autobiography, *Mao's Last Dancer*,[2] Li recounts a lesson learned about stealing. When he was five, Li was playing at a friend's house with a new toy car that the boy's uncle had brought from the city. Li took the car and ran home with it. His mother knew that such toys did not just materialize in their impoverished neighborhood. She asked Li who he had been playing with. He said, "Sien Yu." His mother took him back to Sien Yu's, and asked his mother if the car was her son's. When she nodded, Li's mother apologized and returned the car. Sien Yu's mother politely excused Li for being too young to understand stealing. Li recounts being filled with hatred for his mother for embarrassing him, as he kicked and screamed all the way home, yelling, "I want a car!" His mother held him as she sobbed, apologizing for being too poor to buy him one. Li remembers pledging to himself to make sure that some day there would be enough food for his family. Still, life wasn't always bitter: The boys invented their own entertainment, playing word-finding games with newspaper wall coverings in the evening, or kicking up a ruckus at school, and in one instance, a frazzled teacher visited their parents. The boys "created chaos" during the teacher's visit, Cunxin knocking her teacup over in her lap. When she finally gave up and left, their father went after them with a broomstick—and beat them while their mother continually stuck her head into the doorway to egg him on. This was unusual behavior for Li's father. A quiet man who worked hard, he often diverted morsels of meat or cabbage to the plates of his hungry sons. He enjoyed telling a parable about a frog who lived at the bottom of a well.

> There was a frog that lived in a small, deep well. He knew nothing but the world he lived in. His well and the sky he could see above it were his entire universe. One day he met a frog who lived in the world above. "Why don't you come down and play with me? It's fun down here." "What's down there?" The frog above asked. "We have everything down here. You name it. The streams, the undercurrent, the stars, the occasional moon, and we even get flying objects coming down from the sky sometimes," the frog in the well answered. The frog on the land sighed. "My friend, you live in a confined world. You haven't seen what's out here in the bigger world." The frog below was very annoyed. "Don't tell me that you have a bigger world than ours! My world is big. We see and experience everything the world has to offer," the well frog said. 'No, my friend. You can only see the world above you. The world up here is enormous. I wish I could show you how big it is,' the frog above replied. The frog in the well was angry now. "I don't believe you! You are telling me lies! I'm going to ask my dia." He told his dia about his conversation with the frog on the land. "My son," he said with a saddened heart, "your friend is right. I heard there is a much bigger world up there, with many more stars than we can see from here." "Why didn't you tell me about it earlier?" the little frog asked. "What's the use? Your destiny is down here in the well. There is no way you can get out of here," the father frog replied. The little frog said, "I can, I can get out of here. Let me show you!" He jumped and hopped, but the well was too deep and the land was too far above. "No use, my son. I've tried all my life and so did your forefathers. Forget the world above. Be satisfied with what you have, or it will cause you such misery in life." "I want to get out, I want to see the big world above!" the little frog cried determinedly. "No, my son. Accept fate. Learn to live with what is given," his dia replied. So the poor little frog spent his life trying to escape the dark, cold well. But he couldn't. The big world above remained only a dream.[3]

Li asked whether they lived in a well. His father explained that it depended on how you viewed it. Looking down from heaven, yes, it would seem that they were living in a well. Looking up from below, no, they were not in a well, but neither could you call where they were "heaven." The only taste of heaven the boys got was during the Lunar New Year, when jellyfish with garlic sauces, *siu bao*, and pork dumplings piled up in the small kitchen. As the Cultural Revolution gathered steam, they were in some ways impervious, leading the same life that poor children in capitalist countries do, except that they attended school every day and were not subject to the rigors of child labor. Still, they did not escape witnessing the brutality of Mao's purges, and in one instance, the children looked on as 15 men accused by Red Guards of being landlords, factory owners, and counterrevolutionaries were executed by firing squad.

Just after his ninth birthday, Li began school. Li's family prepared him for his new identity with a new cotton quilted winter jacket, and schoolbag made by his mother. His father bought him one notebook for math and another for calligraphy, and made him a wood pencil box. Among his school supplies was Mao's Little Red Book. His instructions were to be a good student and make his family proud.

The letters he learned to write looked to Li like a pile of grass. He joked that peasants must have invented them. His teacher was patient as he struggled with calligraphy. Li was elected a Little Red Scarf Guard, an honor conferred on those who fulfilled Chairman Mao's "Three Goods": good study, good work, and good health. Li excelled at sports and became co-captain of the rope-hopping and track and field teams.

The Li children reenacted operas and ballets based on storybooks the older boys received at school, making up dialogue and sharing the role of hero. The Qingdao Propaganda Bureau toured such movies as *The Red Lantern*, and the ballet *The Red Detachment of Women*. The village set up an outdoor viewing area with a screen hung from a wooden frame. Movies inspired Li's desire to become a revolutionary hero. He became engrossed in the dancing, fighting, and acrobatics that made the Beijing Opera famous the world over. Li preferred opera over ballet, believing that dancing on toes was a strange way to get around. Li's dream of one day being able to perform movie feats was only that—a dream—until the cultural workers chose him for Jiang Qing's new project.

There were audition "callbacks" on city, county, and provincial levels. During the county audition, a teacher noticed Li's burn scar and referred him to a doctor, who expressed concern that the scar would grow as Li did. After verifying that he had no relatives who weren't workers, peasants, or soldiers, he was told that his family would receive a visit. Weeks passed, and the deflated Li was sure his scar had disqualified him. Then one day, as Li's father was returning to work after lunch, a delegation of smiling public officials appeared. One asked which child was Li Cunxin. "Your lucky son has been chosen for Madame Mao's Beijing Dance Academy." Everyone drank tea, and Li's mother declared it the happiest day of her life. Taking leave of Cunxin was like pushing a bear cub up the tree. He was reluctant to leave, but she convinced him that the alternative would be a life in the fields, subsisting on yams. She reminded him to come home to help her push the wind box, his chore since he was a toddler.

An official acceptance letter informed Li that he had won a full scholarship. He was 11 years old in February 1972, when he left for Beijing. The village turned out to congratulate him and his family. As they celebrated, a quiet anxiety gradually grew in Li. He hadn't yet left and was already feeling homesick for his mother. He surreptitiously left his little brother the black corduroy jacket she had made for Li. Li visited his grandmother's grave. His oldest brother, Cuncia, accompanied him to Qingdao City on the village's only tractor as his brothers ran behind it shouting goodbye, covered with the dust it kicked up. The students took a bus to the train that would take them to Beijing. Li had never seen a train up close.

In Beijing, the students saw thousands of people rushing in all directions. Li struggled to keep up, dragging his heavy bags along. After a time, he no longer saw a single familiar face, and sat down against a wall. A soldier approached to offer help. Li explained that he was lost, and the soldier helped him to the exit with his bags. Li spotted one of the Beijing Dance Academy teachers in front of a bus filled with Shanghai students. He tried to close the door of the bus as he boarded it, but the driver had closed it automatically. The door shut, causing Li to fall to the floor— providing amusement for the others. He realized that he had left the countryside behind for good.

In the capitalist world, male dancers tend to come from relatively humble backgrounds, and female dancers from homes of privilege. Because there are few boys, they are given scholarships and receive royal treatment compared with girls, who must buy expensive pointe shoes, pay high tuition, and stay well-groomed to compete for the rare company contract. Boys enter a glamorous world they would otherwise never get to glimpse. Tasting the good life enjoyed by the Chinese officialdom began when the bus passed Zhongnanhai where Chairman Mao, Jian Qing, and the top government officials lived. Guards armed with machine guns lined the high barbed wire-fringed red and gold walls. To be so near the cult leader was thrilling beyond belief. For a boy who had never even seen traffic lights, the flow of thousands of bicycles and the men and women in their neat Mao jackets was like a pageant. The date of October 1, 1949, the founding of the People's Republic, was no longer just a figure on a chalkboard, but a living reality.

Over the ballet academy gate were the words "Central 5-7 Performing and Arts University" in bright red letters. May 7th is the date on which Jiang Qing gave a celebrated speech encouraging intellectuals to participate in the revolution, and not except themselves from the labor and discussions involving workers, soldiers, and peasants. Li was assigned to the younger boys' class. He had running water and a bed of his own for the first time. The quilt sewn by his mother offered comfort.

Dance clothes included cloth ballet slippers, with replaceable leather strips around the toes and heels, and blue shorts. Chiu Ho, the head ballet mistress, considered the country's foremost expert on ballet, had trained with Soviet teachers. After the boys chose the tightest-fitting shoes possible, Ho dismissed them. Li spoke up and asked whether they had to try on pointe shoes. "No, only girls wear pointe shoes!" Ho said, as she and the shoemaker convulsed with laughter. This was great relief for Li, who had dreaded having to wear them ever since he learned of his acceptance into the school.

The schedule was Ballet, Folk Dance, and Beijing Opera movement, lunch, nap, then Math, Chinese, History, Geography, Politics, and Art Philosophy according to Jiang Qing, dinner, study, or ballet practice. Li's first teacher was Chen Lueng, who had auditioned him for the school. The beginner two-year Vaganova syllabus was considered crucial. The students would learn positions, combinations, and the French terms that comprise the international ballet lexicon. Jiang Qing expected students to also learn them in Chinese. Li devised pneumonic tricks for mastering the French. For *tendú*, there was *ton jiu*, meaning "nine candies," and for *penchée, pong xie*, meaning "crab." Li wrote the words phonetically in a diary. When calligraphy failed him, he drew pictures!

There were strange rituals, such as sprinkling the floor with water to prevent slipping. There were odd stances: legs turned out in the five basic ballet positions. As his teacher taught the boys to strengthen their arms and corrected their alignment, Li wondered when the fun of leaping and skipping would begin. The preparation was agonizing. He invented ways of managing pain, counting through the stretches. Beijing Opera class was taught by a brutal teacher, Gao Dakun, who pushed the boys or glared and called them names. He called Li Brainless Big Head.

Chen Yuen taught Chinese Folk Dance class, and that was the most fun because students danced to the accompaniment of musicians playing traditional instruments, such as Li's favorite, the Yanqin. His favorite dance was the Mongolian Horse Riders' Dance. The music helped him visualize the horses and the riders wandering the deserts.

Though being away from home was a hardship, Li made friends, did his own washing and sewing, and discovered the small campus library. While he was not happy, neither did he want to besmirch his family's reputation by doing poorly. His goal was to be average—neither a failure nor a striver. He longed to return to the countryside, and so enjoyed the three-week agricultural work brigades. There were year-end exams in ballet, acrobatics, folk dance, and Beijing Opera Movement. Li had a horrible case of stage fright at the prospect of dancing before an audience of 50. He forgot his combinations, and afterwards took refuge in a weeping willow tree. His highest grades were in Math and Chinese. He was rated average in ballet and below average in Beijing Opera Movement. He expected to be expelled.

The school's director, Dr. Wang, wished Li a safe vacation, with no mention of the feared dismissal. Cunyuan met him at the station, listening as Li recounted meeting Jiang Qing, seeing the Great Wall and where Mao lived and worked, and tasting delicacies. When he realized that he was provoking his brother's envy, he switched sides and began complaining about mean teachers and plugged toilets. His brother begged him not to complain so that their parents would not think him ungrateful for the opportunity to become a dancer.

Li Cunxin. Photo credit: Jim Caldwell.

Life had improved some for the Li family. With Cunyuan working on the commune, Cunsang in the navy, and Cunxin at school, some of the burden had been lifted. Li shared his Beijing candy and gave his father the three yuan he managed to save. No mention was made of his grades. On the last night of his stay, Li's father handed him an envelope. Inside was a very expensive fountain pen. His father said advised him to use the pen every day and in doing so remember his parents and their expectations that their son would return home with better grades the following year and make them proud.[4]

Returning was easier because Li now knew Mandarin. The students performed before Jiang Qing, who assessed them students as deficient in technique, and assigned two star pupils from the Beijing Martial Arts School and the acrobatics school to join the ballet students. Their back flips and other tricks astounded their classmates, but one of the acrobats, Wang Lujun, who could do 32 "butterflies" in a row, had difficulty with ballet. He and Li became blood brothers. Lujun's nickname was "the bandit." The students spent summer break working in a garment factory. While they were away, a school new director was appointed, and a new teacher named Xiao.

Xiao, a small man, whose nickname "Woa Woa" meant "baby," shared his immense enthusiasm for ballet with the students, promising to be both friend and teacher. He began by admitting he did terrible pirouettes, and proved that those who do not make good dancers can be among the best teachers. He urged the students to keep a journal of their highs and lows, discoveries of new methods, and combinations that went well or badly. He had a mercurial personality, and was easily angered when the students forgot combinations, but just as forthcoming with praise when they acquitted themselves well. He displayed amazing elevation, demonstrating that a small build was no handicap if a dancer was physically fit. He told a fable about a poor scholar, who ran out of money on his way to the capital to the emperor's annual scholars' competition. Still far from Beijing, he had no money to rent a horse. Hungry and tired, he passed a shabby house from which one could detect a wonderful fragrance. A knock at the door drew the attention of an old lady. All she could offer him was millet soup, for which he thanked her as he sat resting while the soup cooked. He fell asleep and dreamed that he had won the competition and would live a prosperous life, and awoke believing what he had dreamed, until he noticed the millet soup cooking in the wok, and recalled that he was just an ordinary man and his dream had been too good to be true.

While those who teach poorly sometimes tender friendship to compensate for their weaknesses, that was not true of Xiao. His friendship never deluded students into thinking that he had low expectations of them. The fable's lesson was that good things don't come to dreamers. Only hard work brings achievement and self-realization. For over a year, the students worked on just three consecutive turns, focusing on achieving perfect balance on demi-pointe, with correct arms, hands, backs, and shoulders, clean spotting, and turnout. Xiao took interest when he noticed how intently Li concentrated and listened, quickly seeing that while Li had not responded well to the other teachers' shouting, he could be transported by gentle words. He remarked on every hint of Li's progress, gradually moving him from the back of the class to the front.

In history and political geography class, nothing was said about the world outside of China. The shallowness of the regime's claim to communism was registered in its refusal to teach the ideas of Marx, Engels, Lenin, or Trotsky in deference to drilling the thoughts of Chairman Mao. The folk dance teacher Chen Yuen was a favorite of the students. He told jokes and took students out to search for frogs and cicadas at night, which they would cook. He shared his photography hobby with them. Then he became withdrawn, and finally disappeared. He had been caught having homosexual relations, and was relocated to the countryside for "re-education." He returned as a handyman, accidentally sawed off three fingers, and ended up a janitor. Ma Lixie replaced him, daring the students to dance better than he did, as he chanted,

"Qing chu yu lan er sheng yu lan." ["Green from blue is the stronger of the two."]

Li made friends with Chong Xiongjun, who came from right outside Beijing. Chong invited Li home, where he was treated as one of the family. Chong's parents worked at a glass factory, and the atmosphere in their apartment reminded him of home. Chong's father took Li on a tour of the glass factory, where he saw machines heating the glass into molten threads. He saw hundreds of beautiful marbles. Chong 's father suggested that Li take a pocketful for his brothers. On his next visit home, Li brought back improved grades, and gifts for everyone, including marbles. He also brought a different perspective, and a developing family conflict began to fuel that point of view. His parents had chosen a wife for his brother, Cunyuan. Cunyuan was in love with a different woman, but his parents opposed him marrying her. During Li's visit, his brother ran away, returning just in time to take Li to the bus station, where he advised Li to make the most of his opportunity to escape the "rural idiocy" of village life. For the first time, Li realized that the countryside that he missed no longer fit who he had become. There was only one direction for him: forward to a dance career. Shortly after his return, Li joined the Communist Party. While sharing in the overall fervor for Mao, he questioned the party's "Red versus Expert" efforts to make crops grow on rocky terrain that every peasant knew would never produce anything. He took his membership seriously, hoping to make an important contribution. By 1974, the head of a rival Communist Party clique, Deng Xiaoping, was gaining ground based on his criticisms of Mao's economic policies. At the academy, however, it was still Jiang Qing who held sway. Unhappy with the students' technique, she hired Zhang Ce, a retired principal from the Central Ballet, to head up the school, who brought with him Zhang Shu, one of his former teachers, to head up ballet instruction.

In his third year, Li improved under the tutelage of Xiao. He spent more time on tricks, *tours en l'air*, triple pirouettes, and acrobatics. Only one nemesis remained: Gao! After a long wait for the bathroom one day, Li was late for Gao's class. Gao stopped the music and said, "Here comes my prized student with the brainless big head! Why are you late?" While Li had intended to apologize, instead he said: "I'm not a brainless big head. I do have a brain!" Gao shouted, "Get out of my class! Get out! Never come to my class again!"

Blind with anger, Li sought out Xiao. Xiao advised him to tell Gao that name-calling offended Li. He told him a story about an emperor's guard who asked his teacher to teach him to become the best marksman in the land. The teacher asked him to leave, but the guard returned every day for a year and begged the man to teach him. The teacher was finally won over by the guard's singlemindedness and agreed to teach him. The teacher directed the guard to lift a heavy bow and hold it up. Within minutes the guard's arms began to shake from the strain. Each day the teacher had him carry increasingly heavy loads. Then when he lifted the bow again, it felt as light as a feather. When he asked how to shoot an arrow, the teacher asked him if he could see any objects in the distant sky. He looked as far as he could see, but could see no objects. The teacher directed his gaze to a tiny spider in a tree so distant that he could barely make it out. He practiced focusing on the spider one eye at a time. In time he saw the spider in more detail, and with both of his eyes, the faraway spider might as well have been the same size as his shield. The guard became the best bow shooter in the land.[5]

Li apologized to Gao. He also told him that he didn't like being called names, and asked Gao how he would feel if Li called him the teacher with the brainless big head. Li admitted that he hadn't been the best student in the days when he was homesick. He said that his attitude had changed, and that he hoped to become a good dancer. He asked his teacher to give him a chance and judge him by his future efforts.

After a dumbstruck silence, Gao said, "I'm sorry that I called you something I shouldn't have. I won't in the future, as long as you work hard." Then he asked, "Cunxin, are you going to be able to do your split jumps in the exam?"

"I will," Li replied. He ran down the stairs three at a time, feeling completely unburdened for the first time since his arrival at the academy. He headed off to the studio to practice his split jumps. To Gao's shock, Li scored a triumph in the afternoon exam.

When Xiao was threatened with dismissal, Li spoke to his head-master, and Xiao was retained. Xiao challenged Li to go from four to five pirouettes, and before long Li was getting first cast roles. Despite (or among!) the numerous tyrannies of the Maoist regime, students were allowed to grade their teachers. When a student accused Xiao of showing favoritism toward Li and another student, he came to his own defense by praising the two students' progress, and recommended that the others emulate them. It was around this time that the factionalism in the Chinese Communist Party was at its worst. Deng Xiaoping was arrested by the Mao group. Jiang Qing was arrested as part of "The Gang of Four." The pro-Mao political directors of the academy were removed. Hua Guofeng became head of state after Mao's death. Li became the favorite of the academy's vice director, Zhang Ce. He stayed through the holidays in his sixth year, realizing that his future depended mostly on his willing-ness to go the last mile. He used the time to practice, perfect his pirou-ettes, delighting in having the shower all to himself! Inspired by tapes of Baryshnikov, Li worked harder, waking at five A.M., strapping sandbags onto his ankles, and spotting his turns to candlelight in the dark studio.

In 1978, Deng Xiaoping assumed the "helm" vacated by Mao. The Cultural Revolution was denounced, and reforms opened up access to Western films, books, and the performers who arrived in China. By graduation—an extra year had been added by the new director——Li was up to 10 pirouettes, had mastered the double cabriole, and, having been assigned third cast in the role of Prince Siegfried in *Swan Lake*, was moved up to first cast for opening night. Shortly after that successful performance, visitors were again to change the life of Li Cunxin, this time from the West. Ben Stevenson, director of Houston Ballet, taught two master classes at Beijing Academy. Stevenson offered scholarships for Houston's summer program to two of the students who took his classes. Zhang Weiqiang and Li Cunxin were chosen.

Barbara Bush, the future U.S. "First Lady," was a member of Houston Ballet's board. On her authority, bureaucratic obstacles were set aside so that the boys could participate. Li and Zhang took a crash course in English, learning the alphabet and a few greetings. Li spoke with his family by phone, which he would not do again for many years. His mother cautioned him that Americans were wild, and to take care.

The boys were treated to a life that the majority of American dance students never enjoy. They stayed at Stevenson's luxurious home and dined at the best restaurants with Houston's wealthiest arts patrons, while the other boys might have been lucky to grab a bagel and coffee before class. Did Li and Zhang question whether this was the typical life of the American dance student? They certainly were suspicious of the opulence. They had expected a dreary city festering with crime and poverty. The Ballet bought them two pair of everything: tights, dance belts, slippers—items that their classmates purchased at the own expense. Li describes his visit to board member Louisa Sarofim's house:

> I couldn't believe her wealth. When I saw her garden, pool and the surroundings, I thought I had just walked into a well-maintained park. She took us inside, and I saw some of the most beautiful paintings I had ever seen. Ben told me later that some of the paintings were worth millions of dollars. A million dollars? The number was too enormous for a Chinese peasant boy to comprehend...The amount of wealth surrounding ballet in America seemed amazing to me. There was money everywhere... The financial and cultural gaps were simply too great to comprehend.[6]

There were no visits to Houston's barrios or trailer parks. The American panorama gleamed nearly flawlessly. At the term's end, Stevenson invited the boys to return at the season start and stay for a year, but China's Ministry of Culture denied Li a passport based on his age. Desperate, he sneaked out of the academy three times to petition the Minister of Culture at his home, but was rebuffed by guards. He phoned Ben Stevenson, and in Pidgin English, explained that his "big leader" had said no. The Minister of Culture was in South America. With the school's help, Li lobbied the Minister of Education. Xiao and Zhang Shu succeeded in convincing Lin Muhan, who convinced the remaining four ministers to act affirmatively in the Minister of Culture's absence. At a goodbye party at Xaio's house, the teacher toasted all the students:

To Chairman and Madame Mao's last generation of dancers, who've studied under the strictest and most disciplined rules imaginable, giving you an edge over the others...My second toast is to Cunxin's American trip. I hope you will respect your past and charge toward the future. Perfect your art form. Make all of China proud. *Gan bei.*[7]

When he saw Ben Stevenson spend $5,000 on Christmas presents, Li calculated that the amount equaled his father's wages for 65 years! Did Li think that the average American could spend so much? Shown capitalism from the perspective of the richest, most privileged Americans, Li was comparing it to the mendaciously-termed "socialism" in the deformed workers' state of China. Dancing solos in Stevenson's *Nutcracker*, learning English, making friends, and meeting his first girlfriend, Elizabeth Mackey, filled Li's first year in the United States with lush and unique experiences. At the last minute, Li partnered Suzanne Langley in the Houston Grand Opera's *Die Fledermaus*. It wasn't capitalism that calmed his nerves, but knowing that his reputation as a Chinese dancer trained under Jiang Qing, the honor of his family, his teacher Xiao, and his best friend Bandit, were all "present." The audience shouted its approval, and the reviews lauded the new star as being "from China, of all places!" Li realized that he would have to choose between being a ballet star in his own country near his family, or remaining in the United States and becoming an international ballet figure. Li had worked so hard that he ended up with multiple injuries—the most serious being to his shoulder, posing a problem for an upcoming *Corsaire*. He took Xaio's advice to heart—when you see a mango for the first time, don't gobble it up all at once, but taste it slowly, layer by delicious layer—and also the story of the bow shooter. He worked patiently to master the double tours. His performance was hugely successful, and was celebrated by Chinese Senior Consul Zhang Zongshu, seated in the audience, who promised to "do anything" in his power to extend Li's stay. As the audience demanded an encore, Ben Stevenson announced that China had granted Li five more months with Houston Ballet. He announced Li's promotion to soloist with the union's full support. During a New York tour, Li met George Balanchine and Jerome Robbins, and saw Baryshnikov, Makarova, and Kirkland in class. He had reached a crossroads. If he failed to return to China, he would jeopardize his parents' reputations, Xiao and Zhang's careers, and Ben Stevenson's credibility there—all people to whom he was greatly indebted. He decided to go back to China. Then, in a sudden reversal, he married Elizabeth.

"Li, I can't *believe* this! You are destroying everybody's lives. I won't be allowed back to China!"[8] Ben shouted in response to Li's phone call to inform Stevenson of his plans. Ben urged Li to meet with the Chinese Consul. The Consul maneuvered to meet with him alone, and Li was locked in a room big enough for just two single beds and a bureau. As Ben and Li's friends waited, Li was interrogated by Chinese officials.

Word of his detention reached others. A small demonstration was organized, and then-Vice President George Bush and President Ronald Reagan interceded to secure Li's release.

In spite of the harm done to Stevenson's relationship with China, he welcomed Li into the company. The decision to defect was not without its dark side, and Li began to have nightmares about his family. The stresses of ballet life and Li's expectations of how a wife should behave contributed to the failure of Li and Elizabeth's marriage. She found a job with a company in Oklahoma, and they decided to divorce.

If Li had caused Ben Stevenson considerable angst, he and Houston Ballet were repaid handsomely by all that Li Cunxin's legendary dancing brought them. In his partnership with Janie Parker, Li built his own reputation as a world-class dancer, and Houston Ballet's as a world-class company.

After a time, the Chinese government forgave Li's decision to leave, and permitted his parents several visits to Houston. Li was able to visit China and dance there with the Houston Ballet, helping to mend fences between Ben Stevenson and the Chinese regime. Li toured the world with the company, and entered the Jackson, Mississippi, dance competition, where he won a silver medal, the highest awarded to the competing male dancers. Li was promoted to Principal. In 1983, he met Mary McKendry, an Australian principal dancer performing with London Festival Ballet. Eighteen months later, Ben Stevenson brought McKendry to Houston Ballet. During Li's hospitalization for a severe back injury, Mary encouraged him to read English-language books. As they danced together and became friends, their relationship deepened into a romance, and they married. They traveled to China and built a relationship with Li's family, and Li visited his teacher Xiao. In 1989, Li and Mary's first child, Sophie, was born. Mary made the difficult decision to give up her performing career in order to work with Sophie, who was deaf. In 1992, Thomas was born, and Bridie in 1997. In 1995, Li joined the Australian National Ballet. As he approached the age of 36, he continued to dance as a principal, while preparing for a career in finance. He danced his last role—Basilio in *Don Quixote*—at the age of 38. Ben Stevenson came to see it. During an interview, while on a tour to promote his memoir, *Mao's Last Dancer*, Li confessed that he has contemplated returning to ballet as an artistic director of a major ballet company.[9] Like the bow shooter and the frog in the well, Li Cunxin's life is a parable that continues to unfold, hastened by the man who, as a boy, helped push the wind box for his mother.

8

Gelsey Kirkland

Miss Kirkland tore into the choreography with enthusiasm and a sense of fun. At times she tossed the role about like a kitten flicking a ball of wool from side to side, and at other moments she streaked along radiating flirtatious innocence. The part demands a soubrette who can move like the wind, and Miss Kirkland has the quickness as well as the elastic vivacity to carry her easily from one involvement to the other.

—Don McDonagh, reviewing Jacques D'Amboise's *Irish Fantasy*[1]

Gelsey Kirkland was born on December 29, 1952, in Bethlehem, Pennsylvania, in rural Bucks County, where many of New York's artists and writers gravitated in the years following World War II. Her father, Jack Kirkland, who adapted scripts for Broadway and Hollywood, was several decades older than her mother, Nancy Hoadley, who had been an actress when she met Jack and became his fifth wife. Jack was "getting work," and so the Kirklands purchased some farmland in upstate New York. Gelsey grew up there with her older sister Johnna and younger brother Marshall. She engaged in what is today trendily referred to as "magical thinking," imagining that monsters were real creatures, for example. Having once noticed her mother at the side of a lake on their property, Gelsey contended that her image was made sparkling by Hoadley being immersed in the water, even though she was on land. Gelsey declined to talk until she had passed the age of two, and in her first effort begged a departing visitor not to go. While very much a creature of the rarified environment cultivated by her parents, she was also privy to a view of the adult world brought into focus when her usually adoring father acted out his torments in episodes of drunken didacticism. These were staged to inculcate exemplary behavior in his children, even as he showed himself an unfit model.

Gelsey Kirkland with Anthony Dowell in *Romeo and Juliet.* **Photo credit: Dina Makarova.**

Too concerned about maintaining his family's upper-middle-class standing to truly qualify as a bohemian, Jack Kirkland was compulsive about perfection, a word he taught Gelsey to spell before she could read, and sought to combine the free-ranging prerogatives of the artist with comforts and luxuries underwritten by a hefty income. Conquering this paradox became his greatest aspiration, and being unable to his most vexing frustration, which he nursed side by side with a glass of whatever he was drinking. When the farm failed, the Kirklands took an apartment on Manhattan's West Side. Gelsey and Johnna—two years apart—shared a bedroom, *and* a relentless sibling rivalry, the seeds of which germinated at the nearby School of American Ballet.

Gelsey relented and accepted her sister's view that Johnna was the better dancer of the two. Johnna staged a series of episodes at what was then called "The American" (now "SAB"), aimed at publicly humiliating her sister. Gelsey decided that besting Johnna at ballet would provide a most satisfying means of making her pay for ridiculing how Gelsey dressed, and in one instance holding her upside down and dropping her on her face. Her mission was made easier by having attracted the attention of George Balanchine, Artistic Director of the New York City Ballet. Gelsey was an apt pupil, and easily adopted the dance style taught at the school. That style is a shorthand version of the Russian technique Balanchine learned, which he modified to exaggerate hyperextension of the knees and swaybacked placement of the torso to better serve his radical choreography. Gelsey was adept at the quick, complex steps, derivative of the frenetic pace of the American Century. She had no reason to question Balanchine's departure from the classical techniques of Cecchetti or Vaganova because she did not know what they were. While she heard rumors about Balanchine's seemingly-avuncular groping of girls he favored, she was happy that his interest in her was less tactile than aesthetic. She was willing, at first, to make the sacrifices demanded to contort her body into the mold of the former New York City Ballet dancers who taught her, even as she came more and more to regard them as sycophants.

There was no need for Gelsey to engage in second-guessing her artistic director, a harmlessly decadent, if vain preoccupation of her classmates. When at 17, she learned from the stage manager that Mr. Balanchine had decided to use her to set a new version of the old Fokine ballet *The Firebird*, she surmised that her future with the company was assured. Had she known that this guarantee would exact a high price, she might have anticipated the collateral damage attendant to stardom in Balanchine's "no stars" company.

During their initial collaboration, the very young dancer began to experience the deliberate depersonalization which Balanchine instilled. At first it mystified and puzzled her, but as Firebird rehearsals continued and what she regarded as an impossibly ungainly costume was built for her, confusion straitened into anger. When she asked Balanchine what to do with her arms, his response was, "You know, dear, normal. Like canary."[2] Though she was only 17, and the product of Balanchine training, Gelsey knew the difference between Fokine's mythic firebird and a canary.

At the same time that she revered Balanchine, Gelsey was deeply troubled by the determinist view of female dancers on which his oeuvre rested. She wanted more substance, and sought coaching help from the renowned teacher, Maggie Black, who had studied with the British choreographer Antony Tudor. It was not simply a matter of artistic discontent that sent Gelsey in search of remedial instruction; she was suffering from crippling tendonitis. Under Black's tutelage, she was able to begin the arduous process of realigning and reconditioning her stressed body, which gave it the kinetic impulse to infuse her Firebird with passion. Balanchine tolerated her rebellion, suppressing his anger, but when the time was right, he took the role away from Kirkland, though not before she had received laudatory words such as these Byron Belt: "In the handsome new 'Firebird,' Gelsey Kirkland's third performance was warmer and more effective, particularly in the 'Dying Swan' use of her lovely arms."[3]

Maggie Black was not the only secret Gelsey kept. After desperate measures, including breast enhancement surgery, Gelsey failed to seduce her partner, Fernando Bujones, and tipped the scales in a more radical direction by stealing her close friend's husband. She dubs him "Jules" in her autobiography, *Dancing on my Grave*. "Jules" played in a rock band that accompanied the Joffrey Ballet, and introduced Gelsey to Eastern religion, method acting, and youth culture.

Kirkland saw Makarova dance *Giselle* in 1970, and Nureyev and Fonteyn dance *Romeo and Juliet* in 1971, and was enthralled by their interpretations of the two classics. Regarding Makarova, Balanchine remarked that only the Russian ballerina Olga Spessivtseva could dance *Giselle*, because she herself went mad. Of Nureyev, he said that he "always tries to be prince," and of Fonteyn that she had "hands like spoons."

These pronouncements made it clear to Kirkland that Balanchine left no room for interpretations other than his own. She found that she could no longer tolerate the Balanchine strait jacket, and stopped taking his class. Refusal to take the artistic director's company class is an act of rebellion in any company; at New York City Ballet, it was tantamount to heresy. Soon Gelsey's mother received a letter from a friend who was a friend of Balanchine's former wife, Tamara Geva. In the letter, she wrote:

> Danilova told her [Geva] Balanchine was angry because Gelsey was studying outside with Maggie Black. Danilova also said she's talked to Gelsey, telling her about Balanchine's anger and his deep capacity for vengeance. He swore Gelsey wouldn't be given anything important until she stopped the outside studying.[4]

By 1972, Kirkland had become a principal, and while not cast in any of Balanchine's new works, other resident choreographers—John Clifford, John Taras, Jacques D'Amboise, and Jerome Robbins—cast her in theirs. Working with Robbins on *Scherzo Fantastique* reprised the difficulties she had had with Balanchine. She describes how she was expected to raise her leg into a slow arabesque while all around her dancers were performing very quick steps. To achieve a high arabesque, the Balanchine dancer is encouraged to "cheat" and raise the hip of the working leg. During rehearsal, Gelsey raised her leg without cheating to achieve a more classical line at the expense of elevation. Robbins' voice came over the theater microphone: "Miss Kirkland, will you take that goddamn tiara off your head!"[5] The "tiara" was Kirkland's insistence on correct placement. She ran offstage in tears. Robbins' idea of an apology was a hug and a suggestion that she relax. Kirkland found that she could not relax in either of the Robbins pieces, *Dances at a Gathering* or *Goldberg Variations*.

Kirkland's collaboration with D'Amboise was aided by an image she received from Maggie Black. Black proposed that Gelsey imagine a shaft of light across the stage, and rather than strike the flirtatious poses D'Amboise wanted, respond to the shaft of light to evoke something authentic and personal. Gelsey convinced D'Amboise that this worked for her, and to let her to keep it. As a result, she enjoyed a more respectful and egalitarian relationship with him than the other NYCB choreographers.

Back in the fold, albeit by a circuitous route, Kirkland was once again cast in Balanchine works, and listened to his advice about how to dance, but actually heeded instructions from Maggie Black. Her anxieties about the duplicity began to build, and home was no haven from it, as "Jules" was more manipulative than Balanchine. He questioned her about her comings and goings, at the same time warning her not to question his. Gelsey took to sleeping on the sofa when in the aftermath of an argument he threatened to call the police. Added to her mental discomforts were physical ones. Inflammation at the site of an earlier breast incision meant she would need more surgery.

During the company's 1972 tour of the Soviet Union, Gelsey investigated the classical traditions George Balanchine had abandoned, as she performed his works without the benefit of Black's coaching. She continued to absent herself from company class, and used a tape recording of Black's exercises to prepare for performances. Put off by sparse accommodations, horrified by the raked stage upon which she was expected to dance, and having pared down her diet to candy bars and coffee, Gelsey found herself on the brink of a nervous breakdown. Still, while in Leningrad, she arranged to visit the Vaganova Institute, and saw a notice posted inviting NYCB dancers to observe company class at the Kirov. A bus was waiting for the dancers to take them to the class, but Gelsey found that she was its only passenger. In the Kirov lobby, she noticed a male dancer with dark blond hair. In the class she observed, he was called upon to run a variation from *Don Quixote*. It was the most astounding men's work Kirkland had ever seen, and she writes that she made "the snap judgment that he was the greatest male dancer on the planet."[6] Gelsey learned that he was Mikhail Baryshnikov, "Misha." What she did not learn until later was that he had seen her perform *Scherzo Fantastique* in Leningrad on that same tour.

Gelsey became ill in Moscow but was prodded to dance anyway. Just before the curtain, Balanchine knocked on her dressing room door. According to Kirkland, he pushed a pill into her hand, which he said was Vitamin C. It had a salutary effect on her dancing, and she felt better instantly. She said that he suggested that she ask for it any time she wasn't feeling well. When she continued to feel sick the next day, an assistant to Balanchine warned her off taking any more of the pills. Kirkland believes that the pill Balanchine gave her was an amphetamine. Perhaps coincidentally, he chose to tell the New York Times that the triumph in Moscow occurred because, "They are overwhelmed by our ability to manipulate time. We have our special speed..."[7]

After the 1972 Nutcracker season, Balanchine remarked to dancer Cathy Haigney that Gelsey's only problem was that she wasn't a defector, a wry joke prompted by the sensationalism generated around Baryshni-kov, Makarova, and Nureyev. Shortly thereafter, Ivan Nagy and his wife Marilyn attempted to convince Gelsey to consider joining ABT, where Nagy danced and partnered Natalia Makarova. She had hesitations, believing that her training had not adequately prepared her for classical ballet, which in her mind comprised a conglomeration of all non-Balanchine styles. She knew that if she changed companies, she would become even more dependent upon Maggie Black.

Black's taking a vacation gave Gelsey an opportunity to resume class with her former teacher, Stanley Williams. She became convinced her that she ought not to rely on just one teacher, and upon Maggie's return, Gelsey shared those conclusions with her. Maggie called Gelsey ungrateful and asked her not to return. Gelsey sought out David Howard as a teacher. He gave a barre that moved through rotational exercises rather than discreet steps. When Gelsey pursued him after class for an assessment of her work, he suggested that she bend her elbows. She bent them, and waited for his approval. He suggested that she release them rather than bend them, and added that in order to release her elbows she would need to release her shoulders. Gelsey wanted to know what to do with the rest of her body as she released her arms, and Howard told her to resist, resist with her entire body, thus introducing her to the inter-penetration of opposites, which would lead her to more investigation of the dialectics of kinesiology.

Howard agreed to take Gelsey on as a student. He emphasized that their relationship would be very different than the one she had shared with Maggie Black. He would not be her best friend, nor permit her to attach herself to him as a surrogate parent.

In her earliest days as a student at The School of American Ballet, the teacher had written the names of steps and positions on the blackboard for the children to memorize, offering no explanation to help them understand what those steps were. If a philosophy was at work, it was that of pragmatism: learning the meaning of the steps and positions would come with doing them. From David Howard, however, Gelsey learned a whole new lexicon, the key to which was "the compositional circle," where the dancer opposed, resisted, released, rebounded, rotated, spiraled, and steps became movement along coordinates. She began to experiment with these concepts as she rehearsed with Helgi Tomasson for Jerome Robbins' *An Evening with Waltzes*. The new frame of reference, and her partnership with Tomasson, made her feel as if she were dancing weightlessly. Then Helgi injured his back, and John Clifford was put in for him. Kirkland describes the experience as "looking up in the middle of a conversation to discover that you were no longer talking to the same person."[8] Robbins wanted John to lift Gelsey up and then straight down before she went into a slide. Gelsey objected, explaining that to go into the slide, Clifford would have to place her on an angle when he brought her down to the floor. Robbins insisted that Clifford try it his way, and the second it hit the floor, Gelsey's foot broke. To avoid atrophy of the muscles, the doctor advised against a cast, and the foot healed all wrong.

Balanchine's remedy for the broken foot was to send Gelsey on a company tour of Europe on crutches. While there, she managed to find a doctor willing to inject her with cortisone, but the shots failed to alleviate the pain, and Gelsey returned early. Upon arriving home, she ended her relationship with "Jules," whose aggressive pursuit of other women invited the breakup. The healing she needed was provided by David Howard, who taught her to utilize her torso and the center of her body as a springboard for recovering her strength. It was as if she were beginning her dance education anew. She describes the process as "pushing through a medium in order to reveal my inner world."[9] As she learned to appreciate Howard's method, she felt the need to devalue and discount what she brought to the four-hour sessions with him. She made odious comparisons between herself and Makarova, whose long neck was an obsession for Gelsey: Howard patiently explained that each dancer has a different body, and while she could never have Makarova's neck, she could work on how to manage the weight of her head so as to lengthen her own. Gelsey decided to have her earlobes trimmed, silicone injected into her lips, and her teeth realigned. None of this "work" would ever be noticed by anyone in the audience no matter what they paid for their seats, so the resulting mutilations can only be viewed as sacrificial offerings to a faltering self-image.

Gelsey returned to Balanchine in a much different frame of mind. Working with David Howard gave her an entirely new vocabulary, and when she danced the Dew Drop in Nutcracker's "Waltz of the Flowers," she was able to visualize an actual drop of dew on her cheek, and understand for the first time that her character's name meant that she was the most tantalizing piece of candy in the entire Kingdom of the Sweets: So tantalizing, in fact, that she attracted the attention of Peter Martins, one of the rising male non-stars in the Balanchine non-galaxy. They began to work together as partners in *A Great Night for Dancing*, which was performed at Avery Fisher Hall, and then the relationship became something else—a romance, partially grounded in their shared eagerness to disengage themselves from what they considered to be the yoke of the New York City Ballet. Their adventures together included a 1974 trip to Montreal to see Baryshnikov dance the pas de deux from *Don Quixote*. They dined with him after the show, Misha paying special attention to Gelsey. He expressed his opinion to her that she would be "a perfect partner" for him.[10]

The Kirkland-Martins relationship incurred little attacks by Martins' previous companion, Heather Watts. After a particularly ugly scene at a party, words were exchanged that could not credibly be retracted, and

Gelsey and Peter broke up. Shortly afterwards, Gelsey received a phone call from Dina Makarova, whom she knew from Maggie Black's connection to the Eglevksy Ballet School. Dina told Gelsey that Baryshnikov had defected, was in Canada, and wished to know whether Gelsey would dance with him. Gelsey's reply was "Yes." Martins encouraged Gelsey to use the opportunity of Misha's interest to leave New York City Ballet. It wasn't clear to her whether his advice was tendered with her best interests at heart, or to take advantage of an opportunity to spirit her out of his life on a positive note. The answer came years later, when they performed the *Tchaikovsky Pas de Deux* together, and he told her that he hated seeing her again because it reminded him of everything he didn't do with his life.

Danilova's coaching of Gelsey for the role of Swanilda in *Coppélia* convinced Kirkland to take herself out of what struck her as a doll pageant version. During a lull in the company's Saratoga Springs, New York, season, she informed Balanchine that she had decided to leave the company. He took this to mean that she was going off on some sort of personal spiritual quest, and gave her an understanding pat on the back, which he annotated with the words, "If you ever want to come back, you can," and then, "if there is room."[11] Later, when he realized that Kirkland's departure was tied to her desire to dance with Baryshnikov, he told *Newsweek* that "every dancer secretly wants to be Giselle."[12] Surely, he meant to say every *female* dancer.

When Misha arrived in New York from Canada, it was rumored that he had broken up with Christina Berlin, the daughter of a U.S. industrialist whom he had met while on tour. Berlin had allegedly managed to conduct a secret affair with Misha and then visit him in Leningrad, and she was present in Canada when he defected. Misha signed a contract with ABT, and recommended that the company hire Gelsey. ABT hired her at $600 per week (double her NYCB salary), and her contract stipulated that she would be Baryshnikov's partner in at least half of his performances. After Gelsey observed a rehearsal, Misha scooped her up in the hallway, and the two of them took a cab to Natalia Makarova's house, where Dina was a dinner guest along with them. It appeared to Gelsey that she was being used by Baryshnikov to signal to Makarova, the former partner and lover who had jilted him, that he had found a new partner who would soon be his lover as well. After a second evening at a party where Christina was present and, according to Kirkland, took a last desperate stab at simultaneously exposing Baryshnikov's caddishness to Gelsey and re-recruiting him as a boyfriend, Gelsey took Misha home to bed with her. They had not yet danced a single step together, and their communication was limited to the few English words that he had learned. The world's two most famous dancers' initial lovemaking was clumsy and, according to Gelsey, absent of passion. It was as if they had gone to bed on cue. Even the most one-dimensional characters in any story ballet are supported by orchestration and the choreographer's coaching. Gelsey and Misha cast themselves in their shallow roles unsupported.

Gelsey describes their romance as a string of nocturnal visits by Misha to her place. If Misha kept his feelings about the relationship from Gelsey, she may have misinterpreted his secrecy as a wish to hide it. Fortunately, their best moments occurred onstage and in the studio. Misha selected the ballets they would perform: Kingdom of the Shades from *La Bayadère*, the pas de deux from *Don Quixote* as well as *Coppélia*, and *Theme and Variations*. Their trial run as partners in Winnipeg received this perspicacious review from Marcia B. Siegel in the *Soho Weekly News*:

> I was prepared for Baryshnikov to be astonishing, but Kirkland matched him. In a way, hers was the greater achievement; the publicity hypes Baryshnikov, plays her as an unknown Cinderella, yet she's as virtuosic as he is...
>
> I suspect Baryshnikov has a tendency to be too serious, and Kirkland's playful streak relieves that heaviness. Her delicacy complements his driving strength. Her exceptional control covers for his moments of recklessness.[13]

In 1974, after a Washington, D.C. tour, Kirkland became nervous about the New York *Nutcracker* performances. In private, Misha used tenderness to calm her, but then lampooned her concerns in public. He shared with her his plans to tour with ABT in the coming season. She read this as a dispatch that he considered their romance moribund. After a scene at their friends', the Gilmans, Gelsey walked out on Misha. This proved to be a dress rehearsal for a more dramatic future breakup, as she equivocated and returned to him when he performed well, then took her distance in reaction to him taking his distance—like the chase in a cha-cha sequence. Their difficulties resumed during Giselle rehearsals, as they differed on interpretations and how to do lifts. ABT staff mounted a "show must go on" intervention, and it did, and quite well! Feeling the need for a respite, Baryshnikov invited French dancer Noëlla Pontois to be his partner in *Raymonda*. Gelsey invited Nureyev to be hers, and relied on mime coaching from Pilar Garcia to better understand how to use the piece's signature scarf prop to her advantage. Antony Tudor cast her in three ABT 1975 season works, *Jardin aux Lilas*, *Shadowplay*, and *The Leaves are Fading*. She began to prepare for the role of Emilia in the 1977 film, *The Turning Point*, but displeased with the shallow personality of her character, rebelled passively. Marrying anorectic with bulimic practices, Gelsey succeeded in reducing her weight to 98 pounds. SAB student Leslie Browne replaced her. After a tumultuous run in *Sleeping Beauty*, Gelsey sought psychiatric help. Therapy resulted in a decision to have more breast surgery to attempt to eliminate scars from the previous ones and a date with the past-middle-aged attending plastic surgeon. He supplied Gelsey with her first line of cocaine and a sob story about his dissolving marriage. Soon afterwards, she started dating Richard Shafer, an ABT corps dancer.

She began working with Misha on his version of *Don Quixote*, smuggling in Pilar Garcia's mimetic advice, which she dispensed to all the principals and soloists! After a highly successful run, Misha disclosed that he was leaving ABT for NYCB. This was taken as the worst of all possible reproaches by Gelsey: that she would no longer be his partner because he was abandoning her for the company she had abandoned in order to dance with him! The ensuing confusion sent Gelsey into a downward spiral. Patrick Bissell, Peter Schaufuss, and Richard Shafer became her partners. None of them was well-suited to her, and in Shafer's case, the partnership resulted in the breakup of their relationship. Gelsey resigned from ABT in January 1980. In Lucia Chase's words, "She did not break down with me this time. She broke up with me!"[14] Gelsey accepted guest engagements with the Stuttgart and Royal Ballets. By the time she returned to New York, Misha had left NYCB to become ABT's artistic director. He began a campaign to win Gelsey back to the company by any means necessary, including seduction.

In the meanwhile, Gelsey's Juliet was a great success in London. She was partnered by Anthony Dowell, and *Ballet Review*'s Dale Harris wrote that she possessed "The gift of bodily eloquence, the ability to communicate the essence of any dramatic situation simply through the mimetic quality which she invests in all her movements."[15]

Gelsey returned to New York with the British dancer Georgina Parkinson and her son Tobias, and all three shared an apartment. Soon after their arrival, Gelsey heard from her former partner Patrick Bissell, who was eager to see her. On a visit to their apartment, he offered Gelsey and Georgina cocaine. Georgina refused, and said that as long as he had illegal drugs on his person, Patrick would not be welcome to stay. Gelsey and Patrick later shared a hotel room, and some of Patrick's cocaine. Gelsey loved the effects of the drug: the "consciousness-expanding" she experienced, and a new feeling of freedom, including from the need to question or analyze what happened in the studio or onstage. She stopped questioning many things in her life, except when Patrick showed signs of paranoia and began carrying weapons, and she became worried about certain non-existent threats. She made the acquaintance of Patrick's dealer, an artist whose loft housed her drug supply. The drugs immediately took a toll on Gelsey's health and career, suppressing her appetite, causing a seizure, and undermining her work discipline. During a Washington, D.C., company tour, she and Patrick showed up late and were fired. By the time of her birthday on December 29, 1980, she was entirely in the clutches of paranoia, imagining that Misha and the company were out to get her. Needing cash for her habit, Gelsey engaged Patrick's agent to find her guest jobs. She danced in a television special, and then with Eglevsky Ballet in a performance reviewed by the Arlene Croce, who on February 23, 1981, wrote: "It was the saddest exhibition given by a dancer whose artistry is increasingly placed at the service of a gift for mimicry. She's dancing the idea of the public's idea of Gelsey Kirkland as a star.[16]

Gelsey and Patrick toured together. Patrick was arrested after smashing a liquor bottle in a hotel lobby. When her stash of drugs mysteriously disappeared prior to a Goucher College performance, Gelsey refused to dance, believing Patrick had stolen or hidden it. Her manager successfully negotiated their reinstatement at ABT in April, but at the end of the season, her contract was not renewed. After another seizure that resulted in a hospitalization, she was convinced to enter a mental institution, expecting it to be an opportunity for rehabilitation. Instead, she was confronted with the chief psychiatrist's morbid prediction that she was a hopeless case. He did nonetheless agree to an arrangement that permitted her to leave the facility to dance in New York (in order to pay her hospital bill!) and return in the evening to the Westchester mental hospital. With the help of her agent, a lawyer he found, and the medical staff at New York University Medical Center, Gelsey fled the hospital and began dancing again. She took up with a patient she had known at the hospital named Mickey, who introduced her to the crack houses he frequented in Harlem.

Tired of touring, Kirkland met with George Balanchine to ask to return to NYCB. He turned her down. Misha rehired her in November 1982. By that time, she was fantasizing about her funeral. She worked hard to be obedient, while continuing to do drugs. She moved in with her mother and stepfather, who, because Gelsey had begun stealing from them to support her $600 a week habit, ended up placing their silverware under lock and key. On a quest for drugs near Hell's Kitchen, Gelsey met Greg Lawrence. Lawrence and Kirkland became well-enough acquainted to return to his place to share drugs when his girlfriend was out of town. Lawrence worked reading books that were under consideration for adaptation into TV screenplays. Both of them were ready to overcome their addiction, and they built a long-term relationship around that goal. Lawrence introduced her to Helga Zepp LaRouche, wife of Lyndon LaRouche, chief ideologue of the U.S. Labor Party. Kirkland wrote:

> A critical answer was provided by Helga Zepp LaRouche, German-born founder of the Schiller Institute. Her polemical writings contained a moving study of Schiller. In spite of her extreme point of view, her unyielding radicalism, this woman provided a crucial turning point for me. Her zealous devotion to the classics and her political war against drugs emboldened me to act, yet in my own way. Her scathing criticism of modern art gave me a clue about the relation between imitation and addiction.[17]

By "extreme point of view" and "unyielding radicalism," Kirkland was referring, albeit euphemistically, to what is widely held to be the fascist point of view advocated by LaRouche. Given the chaos in Kirkland's life, and the upper-middle-class imperatives of perfectionism that were inculcated in her from infancy, it should come as no surprise that Kirkland was rotten ripe for LaRouche's right-wing indictment of the drug culture and critique of experimental art.

After recovering from drug addiction, she and Lawrence traveled to London, where Kirkland had accepted guest engagements with the Royal Ballet to again dance Juliet, and Aurora in *Sleeping Beauty*. Having finished writing Kirkland's autobiography, *Dancing on My Grave*, the couple collaborated on its sequel, *The Shape of Love*, which details Kirkland's fascinating analysis of the roles she danced during that engagement, including her efforts to coach the then-18-year-old Spanish dancer Trinidad Sevillano in the role of Giselle.

Her description in the book of how she approached the scene in which Paris is literally and figuratively "brought home" to her in *Romeo and Juliet* is a masterpiece of character analysis. Describing the part of the scene where she must remain sitting bolt upright for an entire minute, "where most ballerinas died in the role," she writes the following:

> I imagined myself sitting there and felt a jolt of fear. The audience would be asleep before I was able to retrieve the cape, get it over my shoulders, and make my exit—unless I were to lure that audience inside Juliet's mind. But how could a body that was motionless do such a thing? How could I put them on the edge of their seats if I were frozen on the foot of that bed like some pathetic little girl?[18]

She decided to "talk through" the subtext with the dancers, Monica Mason, cast as Lady Capulet, and Derek Rencher, cast as Lord Capulet.

"I don't even know where I'm going," says Kirkland.

> I see the cape out of the corner of my eye...stop...and pick it up. It reminds me of something. I gather it close to my breast, and then it comes to me, like you say—this is the same cloak I was wearing when I married Romeo! So there's a glimmer of hope entering here.[19]

Mason says that this is where Juliet breaks down, but Kirkland disagrees, pointing out that she can't break down because to do so would indicate that Juliet has given up.

"I haven't given up, have I?"[20] Kirkland asks. Mason concurs that no, she hasn't, but reminds Kirkland that the audience must see the character's vulnerability. Kirkland parries with, "I don't have to break for you to see I'm vulnerable!" She had caught her own fire and went on,

> The cape reminds me of him, but it also makes me think of my family. It's the same shawl the Nurse has wrapped around me since I was a child...Oh, the last person who touched it! I can feel despair coming up in my throat, but I'm not going to let go of the hope—it's all I have left. That's what carries me to the bed.[21]

When Mason objects that the motivations are becoming too complicated, Kirkland sums it all up,

> The scene has to move from rage to hope...and we have to see her make a
> choice when she sits on that bed. Otherwise, may as well give the audience
> a refund and go home!...She realizes...she's willing to face death in order
> not to betray love. It's that simple.[22]

All dancers owe it to themselves to read the chapter "To Make a
Juliet" in *The Shape of Love*, from which the foregoing dialogue has been
excerpted. It is indispensable to learning how to set aside the odious
melodramatic practice of "indicating" and instead work from the inside
out to achieve a truthful and believable rendering of the character.

In a 2005 interview in *Dance Magazine*, conducted by Kate Lydon, in
which Kirkland discusses the work she is doing to come to terms with
the Vaganova style, she takes the opportunity to apologize to those whom
she may have offended in her published writings, such as Peter Martins
and Mikhail Baryshnikov. She has been a guest teacher at Dance Theatre
of Harlem and other dance academies in the United States and abroad.
Kirkland's current husband is the dancer-choreographer Michael
Chernov. They live in New York, where Kirkland teaches at ABT.

9

Lázaro Carreño

The choreography in both pieces is full of ingenious lifts and catches that draw gasps of amazement from onlookers. In one instance Mr. Carreño drew Miss Llorente up from the floor and pressed her straight overhead with the ease of a man hefting a familiar weight. At another point, she reclined on his back and suddenly rolled her body up like a furling window shade to perch on his shoulder.

—Don McDonagh in "Dance: Ailey's Cuban Encore," *New York Times*, May 13, 1967[1]

I am watching a documentary film about the life of the Cuban dancer Alicia Alonso, but right now she is not on the screen. Instead, there is a compact, dashing male dancer with a genial, symmetrical face. He is performing the men's solo in George Balanchine's famous *Theme and Variations*. The short but demanding variation requires pristine technique and the masterful strength and stamina to execute fast, high jumps, and multiple sets of double tours, pirouettes, and à la séconde turns. This dancer, who I am seeing for the first time, is surely more technically adroit and stronger than Rudolf Nureyev, and certainly as schooled in Russian technique as Mikhail Baryshnikov. The film's voiceover announces his name: Lázaro Carreño. I make a mental note to find out more about him. I learn that this Cuban-born, Soviet-trained stick of dynamite who had been Baryshnikov's roommate at the Vaganova Academy is the senior member of a famous internationally-recognized ballet family, and has received at least a dozen prestigious international awards.

A few years after I had become a dance writer and my son was dancing his first season with Houston Ballet, the phone rang late one evening. It was James calling.

Lázaro Carreño with Natalia Makarova. Courtesy Lázaro Carreño.

"Mom" he began a little too mischievously, "How's your Spanish?"
I could hear lounge music and lively conversation in the background.
"My Spanish? It's fine..." I answered groggily. "Good!" he shouted in a
"gotcha" tone of voice; the joke is about to be on me this time. The next
voice bore a Cuban accent that boomed amiably over the background
chaos, "Hola, Toba, ¿Que tál? ¡ Es Lázaro!" ["Hi, Toba. How's it going?
It's Lázaro!"] I had wanted to meet and interview Lazaro Carreño for
years. Here I was talking to him by phone thanks to the friendship that
he and my son had developed , both of them new to Houston Ballet—
my son as a corps de ballet member, and Carreño the company's senior
Ballet Master and teacher. The conversation was brief—mostly me
launching salvos of Spanish adjectives, hoping for one that would capture
my deep appreciation of Carreño's artistry, and him agreeing to be interviewed for an article on his teaching technique that would appear later
that year in *Dance Magazine*.[2]

Cuba, before its 1959 revolution, grew sugar for the Coca-Cola company and the Bacardi rum distillery. It was known to tourists for its
cigars, gambling, and prostitution. That reputation changed dramatically after 1959. The revolution there that altered the power relationship
between capital and labor was led by a small dedicated cadre that
organized the peasants in the Sierra Maestra, and linked up with the
trade unions that mobilized thousands of sugar refinery and other
industrial and service workers in the cities. This new generation of
Cubans expelled the landlords and the capitalists, nationalized the oil

and sugar refineries, sent brigades of young teachers to the countryside to teach the illiterate how to read, and did so in the name of reclaiming Cuba's national patrimony. In search of friends, they made a strategic if ungainly alliance with the United States' nemesis, the Soviet Union, and committed their slender resources to international campaigns to provide doctors and teachers to neocolonial countries in Africa struggling for independence. It wasn't long before the island's former landlords in the United States began to regard the revolutionary Cuban government as a threat to prerogatives of private property and the pursuit of profit. They brought pressure to bear that led in 1961 to the unsuccessful CIA-led Bay of Pigs invasion, and what became known as "The Cuban Missile Crisis." Then-President John F. Kennedy declared an embargo against Cuba: No U.S. citizens could go there unless they were visiting relatives or traveling in a professional capacity. No goods or services could be exchanged between the two nations. A secondary embargo was the unofficial one, where U.S. corporations refused to do business with companies abroad that traded with Cuba. The impact on the small island was felt instantly. Cuba was forced to diversify its economy and carefully choose the arenas in which it would engage internationally. Because ballet had an established history in Cuba, thanks to the efforts of Nikolai Yavorksy and his pupils, Alicia, Fernando, and Alberto Alonso, and others, it was soon regarded and prized by the large majority of Cubans as a national treasure.

Lázaro Carreño was born on June 20, 1950, to Delia Vines and Jose Manuel Carreño in the Cuban hamlet of Jomencas, in the central province of Las Villas. His mother's pregnancy was a difficult one, and doctors feared that the baby would not live. Because he survived, his mother named him after Lazarus, the Biblical character who rises from the dead. There were 11 children, and Carreño describes it as a happy, close family, in which he and his sisters and brothers applied themselves to their studies. Their father, Jose Manuel, worked every spare moment at the town's sugar distribution center, and their mother, Delia, took seasonal jobs to help sustain the growing family. Each child was encouraged to become independent. When the 1959 revolution took place, Lázaro was nine years old. To satisfy his appetite for the extras that were beyond the family's means, such as visits to the candy shop or trips to the movies, he delivered newspapers, shined shoes, and ran errands.

One morning, a member of the family noticed an advertisement in the local newspaper. A school of dance was holding a contest, and the prize was a full scholarship to the school. "I filled out the application portion of the ad," explains Carreño, smiling. "There was an audition in Havana, to which 500 kids showed up—about 100 of whom were boys." The children were asked to demonstrate popular dances, such as the rumba and the cha-cha-cha. Of the 500, eight girls and five boys were chosen, and of the eight boys, three were Lázaro and two of his brothers.

His sister also auditioned, but was not selected. "You can imagine how happy my mother was when I started at the National Ballet School in September of 1961!"[3]

During his first two years, Carreño studied Classical Ballet and Dance History, and observed Cuban National Ballet performances. After his first year there, the school announced that a special scholarship would be awarded to the best, most disciplined, and hard-working student. The winner would go to the Soviet Union to study at the Vaganova School in Leningrad (now St. Petersburg). Lázaro did not win the scholarship at the end of his first year. However, it became a temptation and goal to work for, and after his second year he was awarded the scholarship and went to Russia to study with several of the very best teachers in the world. Among them were Alexander Pushkin and Konstantin Sergeyev, who had taught all the best dancers, including Mikhail Baryshnikov, who was to become a friend and roommate of Carreño's.

Training at the Vaganova Institute for five years was the defining experience in Carreño's life. He threw himself into his classes with utter determination. This required mastering the Russian language. He was very young, and his Cuban identity had not yet been fully formed. He left what there was of that persona at the door of the studio. So intense was his transformation that when he returned to Cuba five years later at the age of 16, he had to take classes to relearn the Spanish language. He had not used it in five years! He had, however, learned a language of the body that he would never forget: how to dance, perform, and share key elements of studio teaching with those willing to work hard.

Carreño began his professional career with the Ballet de Camgüey in 1969. The first director of Ballet de Camgüey was Guillermo Nuñez. By the time Carreño joined, its director was Fernando Alonso. It took seven months for Carreño to actually dance with the company because Fermando and Alicia Alonso requested that he go to Havana to participate in the international ballet competition there. He won first place in the youth division. He then prepared for the 1970 Varna competition, where he also placed first in the junior division. These were the first in an impressive series of competitions that Carreño would enter and win, and included the senior competition at Varna in 1972, in which he won second place, and the 1973 Moscow International Dance Competition, where he and Amparo Brito won a gold medal. By this time, he had been promoted to the rank of Soloist with the Cuban National Ballet Company.

Describing the artistic process taking place during this period, Alicia Alonso said, "The Cuban style comes from deep within the Cuban spirit, from our joys and from our sadness. Some people are turned inward. The Cuban people are always overtly sensual. ...What looks natural on the Soviets, would have looked mimetic, like a mannerism on us. We had a hard time explaining that to our Soviet friends."

"When Lázaro Carreño did go study in Moscow," Alonso's current husband, husband, Pedro Simon adds, "we had to spend months after he returned just getting him to dance like a Cuban again. It was a constant fight with Alicia."[4]

In spite of Alonso's hesitations about sending students such as Carreño to Moscow, she encouraged him to train to become a qualified teacher with the Cuban academy. He began teaching at the Ballet Nacional de Cuba in 1972, receiving the title of Special Artistic Master in 1973 and Ballet Master in 1976. In 1974, he was made a principal dancer with the company. Among the dancers he partnered in this period were Loipa Araujo, Josefina Mendes (who had been his first teacher there), Marta García, Marielena Llorente, Aurora Bosch, Amparo Brito, Ofélia González, and Rosaria Suárez. His wife, Dania González, also a former partner, now teaches at Houston Ballet's Ben Stevenson Academy. Lazaro and Dania have a daughter, Dayana, who teaches Economics and lives in Madrid.

While competitions were very much a highlight of Carreño's performing career, he danced numerous principal roles in coveted venues, including with the Alvin Ailey American Dance Theater, American Ballet Theatre, and Ballet Nacional de Caracas. His career became more international as he participated in dance festivals in Panama, Mexico, Venezuela, Canada, and in the UNESCO gala in Paris. The Cubans brought the largest contingent of any country to this last event, including four each of the company's best male and female dancers, as well as Alicia Alonso. They made a big impression, and it was there that Carreño was introduced to the French dancer Paul Goubé's daughter Jennifer, by her mother. She invited Carreño to partner Jennifer at an upcoming competition in Osaka, Japan. The Osaka competition is notoriously difficult, as prizes are awarded on the basis of the couple's performance, not the work of each individual partner. If one partner is eliminated, the couple is disqualified. Carreño accepted the invitation and went to Japan with Jennifer Goubé.

As a couple, they placed fourth. The judges then made the unprecedented decision to create a special prize for the male partner, and awarded that prize to Carreño.

The preparation for the competitions had already taken a toll on the young Carreño, and he had to take a break from his work to have knee surgery. His doctor, Dr. Alvarez-Camba, advised a long recuperation, but against his doctor's orders, he was back dancing within a month. The doctor was so amazed at the speed of Carreño's recovery that he attended his first post-surgical performance, fearing that his services might be required.

In 1983, Carreño placed first in the Concurso Latino Americano in Rio de Janeiro. In protest of the repressive character of the Brazilian government, Cuba had not participated in this event over the previous 25 years. Just a week or two before the competition, the dancers in the

Lázaro Carreño rehearses men; author's son James Gotesky, left, looks on. Photo credit: Bruce Bennett. Courtesy Houston Ballet.

company discussed Cuba's *de facto* boycott, and concluded that it had represented a political error. They decided that they would compete, but by that time had only a week to prepare. The company chose Carreño to represent it in the competition. His competition repertoire included the men's variations and pas de deux from *Don Quixote*, *The Tchaikovsky Pas de Deux*, and *La Bayadère*. Carreño took first prize (gold) for his pas de deux with Amparo Brito and won the Aldo Lotufo Men's Prize as well. This would be his final competition, but not his last visit to Brazil.

Over the years he returned, dancing at the Teatro Municipal in Rio, and sharing the stage with such luminaries as Fernando Bujones and other international stars of the dance world.

In 1989, the National Ballet School of Cuba proposed to Lázaro that he teach a special men's class for boys in their graduation year. In this class, the boys would work to increase their technical skills and polish their artistry to prepare for professional dance careers. Among his students during this period were the finest Cuban dancers in the world today: Carlos Acosta, Jose Manuel Carreño, Joan Boada, Luis Serrano, Jesus Corales, and the women they partnered: Lorena Feijoo, Lorna Feijoo, Alihaydee Carreño, and others.

For many years, Alicia Alonso had journeyed to Spain in the summer to teach what had become the world-renowned *Catedra de Danza Alicia Alonso* in classical ballet at the Universidad Complutense de Madrid. Among the Spanish dancers she taught were Laura Hormigon and her husband Oscar Torrado, who eventually joined the Cuban National Ballet Company. In 1993, she invited Lázaro to take on a professorship teaching the Madrid catedra. It was at this juncture that Carreño's teaching reputation became international, as students from all over the world came to study with him. He began teaching classes at the Teatro Real in Madrid for Victor Ullate, for Nacho Duato at the Ballet Nacional, and for Maria de Avila in Zaragoza. He taught the catedra for three years, until 1996.

During Carreño's tenure, a new company was forming in Barcelona. It called itself E.T. Ballet, and Carreño was invited four months in advance of the company's debut to prepare its members for it. E.T. Ballet's founder was Catherine Béjart, who had danced with Nacho Duato and was eager to have a company of her own. E.T.'s mission was to give students an opportunity to work for two years, preparing and dancing professional works. Carreño's relationship with E.T. stretched out over two years, after which he began to explore relationships with other international companies. In 1996, he worked with Ballet de Rhin, and the Polish Opera Ballet in Lodz, as well as the Royal Ballet in London. He crossed the Atlantic to work with American Ballet Theatre, National Ballet of Canada and its school, and the Royal Winnipeg Ballet. He taught at the National Ballet of Mexico, and returned to the Teatro Municipal in Rio. He then traveled to Europe for a stint with the Paris Opera Ballet.

The public face of the 33-year-old Houston Ballet Company was undergoing a change in the Fall of 2003. Its artistic director, Ben Stevenson, was leaving to direct the financially faltering Forth Worth-Dallas Ballet Company, which was renamed Texas Ballet Theatre that year. Born in Portsmouth, England, Stevenson received his dance training at the Arts Educational School in London, where he received the coveted Adeline Genée Gold Medal, the most prestigious award conferred by the Royal Academy of Dancing. He performed as a principal dancer with the

Sadler's Wells Ballet and the English National Ballet. In 1968, Rebekah Harkness invited him to New York to direct the newly formed Harkness Youth Dancers. After choreographing *Cinderella* in 1970 for the National Ballet in Washington, D.C., he assumed that company's co-directorship in 1971 with Frederic Franklin. In 1976, Stevenson was appointed Artistic Director of Houston Ballet. Over the succeeding 27 years, his distinguished versions of such works as *Swan Lake*, *Romeo and Juliet*, *Cinderella*, *The Nutcracker*, *The Sleeping Beauty*, *Coppélia*, *Don Quixote*, and original works such as *Peer Gynt*, *Dracula*, *The Snow Maiden*, and *Cleopatra* contributed immensely to elevating Houston Ballet to a top-ranking U.S. company. Side by side with his choreographic sensibility, Stevenson demonstrated a gift for discovering and developing dance protégés. Among those whose careers blossomed and matured under his watchful eye were Li Cunxin, Carlos Acosta, Lauren Anderson, Janey Parker, Martha Butler, Tiekka Prieve, and Dawn Scannell.

Houston Ballet was faced with a considerable challenge when the time came to replace Stevenson. Stanton Welch was appointed Artistic Director in July 2003. The Melbourne-born choreographer was in his early thirties, the son of two Australian ballet luminaries, Marilyn Jones and Garth Welch. He had been hired to dance with Australian National Ballet in 1989, where he rose to the rank of leading soloist, having danced a number of principal roles. Determined to cut his own swathe in the dance world, Welch's growing reputation as one of a new generation of contemporary ballet choreographers placed him in a favorable position to continue building Houston Ballet's leading-edge repertoire. Though very much a prodigy as a choreographer, there were still some ways in which Welch was a novice, and he judiciously and carefully constructed an artistic team to curate the company and steward its prestigious academy.

Welch hired Maina Gielgud as Artistic Associate. Gielgud had been Artistic Director of Australian National Ballet from 1983 to 1996 and the Royal Danish Ballet from 1997 to 1999, but her tenure as Artistic Director of Boston Ballet had been aborted in embryo when financial missteps there undercut her effort to bring in world class guest choreographers to broaden the company's scope and direction. In November 2003, Welch hired Lázaro Carreño as one of four ballet masters, and to teach upper level students at the Ben Stevenson Academy. This was in the period during which President George W. Bush coined the term "shock and awe" to describe a sabre-rattling tactic aimed at gaining support for the U.S. invasion of Iraq. It could be said that Carreño's arrival at Houston Ballet "shocked and awed" the new iteration of the company on a much higher and more civilized level than what Bush had projected for people of Iraq. Students first approached his classes in absolute terror of the challenges he posed each day. Then, as they began to meet them and show themselves that they were equal to them, Carreño's class, especially his men's class, became the favored one, with several female dancers taking it to increase their strength and stamina.

Carreño was generous in giving me interview time over the course of the second half of the 2003 season. Since his classes so faithfully embraced the Vaganova method, I was interested in discussing his approach to teaching. It is often the case that the best teachers are not necessarily the best performers, but here was an example of someone who excelled at both, having won an impressive number of first place prizes for his artistry, and having been rewarded for his teaching with the satisfaction of seeing his students taking *their* places in the first ranks of international world class companies. I wanted very much to observe him teaching. *Dance Magazine* gave me that opportunity. I pitched the idea of doing a piece on Carreño for the magazine's "Teacher's Wisdom" column to DM's then-Education Editor, Karen Hildebrand, and she agreed.

The men's class I was invited to observe was given in the studio at Houston's sumptuous Wortham Theater. The pre-class tension was palpable, with male company members either nervously isolating themselves as they stretched and warmed up or practiced a combination in preparation for the performance that evening. Carreño, dressed in a blue and white spandex unitard, quietly entered the studio. He responded to the greetings of some of the dancers with spurts of conversation in a mixture of Spanish and basic English. It was easy to see that he was more at home when speaking with the Eastern European dancers in Russian.

He took a place at the center barre very much in the ritual manner that a surgeon might use to scrub in for a procedure. The men's tension was converted to focused energy as they followed the increasingly rigorous combinations or *entraînements* aimed at preparing them for the second part of the class, called "Center." The dancers' preliminary jocularity was now over. Each dancer was in his own space, deeply focused and working hard, some with more tension than others. Those who had learned to relax and work hard at the same time were rewarded with a "second wind" during the Center and closing Grand Allegro. It is fascinating to observe the work of teachers who have only limited familiarity with the native language of the country in which they happen to be teaching. It's almost an asset to have only basic words at one's disposal. The teaching and learning is in the *tempi* and structure, the teacher's and accompanist's ability to collaborate instinctively yet fully, and the progressively more demanding level of virtuosity demanded over the course of a given week's classes, such that the dancers are able to feel and see their improvement. These relationships of timing, structure, collaboration, and mastery were the salient elements that made watching Carreño's class an education in itself. In most classes, teachers wear street clothes and jazz shoes or even street shoes when they teach. Carreño's choice to wear dance clothes is a conscious one. He actively and fully demonstrates throughout the class, including the exhaustive combinations in the Grand Allegro that demand tremendous elevation, *ballon*, and skill at sustaining multiple turns and landing cleanly. He is the embodiment of a challenge to his students, at the same time that he coaxes them onto the path to victory. At our next interview over lunch, he will tell me with an impish smile, "A dancer's career is hard and [a burst of laughter] very short!" It is clear that he trains his students how to make the most of it.

Karen Hildebrand has asked me to zero in on Carreño's teaching philosophy, getting into specifics. Curiously, he has spoken mostly in abstract terms up to this point, referring to the general lessons he gained from his career, using phrases like "technical challenges," and "quality of dancers," and I am frustrated. My editor and I have worked up questions designed to squeeze the specifics out of him and dig into the pedagogy of his classes: "Your classes are difficult, but students feel invigorated after them. How do you maintain morale? What do you do when a student falls behind? How do you teach jumps? How did the Vaganova training that you brought back to Cuba strengthen the Cuban system? What were the specifics of Vaganova that the Alonsos wanted? How do you meld the strong points of the Cuban training with Vaganova? When you find that you have a student who has attended many schools (unlike in Cuba, where there is a national curriculum followed by all the schools), what are the most common problems the student has to unlearn? Explain, please, how your barre differs from the typical 'Balanchine' barre. Are there elements of Vaganova training that have fallen out of favor that you continue to teach because you view them as essential? Please compare the so-called tricks that are often seen in competitions with the artistry needed to dance in a company." I pressed him for answers, and when he spoke again in generalities, I interrupted, protesting, "No, no, that is too general, give me *la herramienta*, the set of tools you use."

He hesitated, and you could see him make a decision to entrust me with a few secrets while maintaining his characteristically Cuban air of revolutionary diplomacy and tact. When I asked him about the continuity in Cuban training versus the chaos of U.S. training and how he approached that problem here, his answer was:

> In Cuba, students also change schools, but less frequently than in other places. In general, they complete the elementary level in one school, and the advanced level in another. Even though there is a different system of teaching ballet in Cuba, it is regulated throughout the country, which means that all students reach the advanced level having completed similar training. This is something that doesn't occur in other countries, as for example, in the United States, where each school has its own teaching methods, however good or bad they may be. That can mean that by the end of a child's training, he or she may have studied in as many as 10 schools, each one having taught something different.[5]

He had not answered my question about his approach to the problem. Now he knew I needed more. In all of our discussions up to this point, his manner had been somewhat facile, sweetened by a beguiling charm that made it possible to dodge and weave through questions that called for definitive answers. He suddenly became very serious, as if we were both finally looking at the same specimen under the same microscope. The change was as detectable as a breakthrough in physical therapy when scar tissue gives way and a joint opens up, or in dance class when an extension goes higher than ever before and stays there, or a dancer finds a level of attack that surpasses anything he or she has been able to achieve. He is preparing to tell me what he thinks of the so-called Balanchine class. He clears his throat, and sits back for a second, and then leans forward in his chair.

> My barre is based fundamentally on the warmup a dancer requires for the entire body. It is progressive and rhythmically balanced so that at the end, the entire body and all the dancers are fully prepared to confront whatever technical demands they may face. A logical, progressive sequence is followed in accordance with how I was trained in the Vaganova school. Most importantly, I rely on my experience over the course of a 30-year career, during which my own body required the full-body warm up I give, and it has been my main instrument in developing my teaching method. Just like the men, the women also have specific technical goals that they must master. That is the purpose of the second half of the class, and the warm up must thoroughly enable them to perfect and master any and all technical challenges.
>
> Balanchine created a school of dance that was executed in a stylized manner. I think that he accomplished the objectives of his teaching method insofar as they served his style of choreography. Balanchine students achieve very light, fast use of their feet, for example. But personally, I think that dance has evolved a great deal in the last number of years, and the technique that was utilized by him would be insufficient for the dance world of today. For that reason, my barre may appear quite different than a Balanchine barre, but then my students are prepared to dance any style of dance that is required of them. I don't think that is the case with students trained exclusively in the so-called Balanchine method.[6]

Very few teachers have as solid a phalanx of support among their students as does Carreño. He sees them in class, and socializes with them, at times the only gray-haired guest at student parties. I am curious about the psychological dynamic in the studio that allows him to play the role of taskmaster and coach, as well as friend, mentor, and confidante to so many students. I ask him how he maintains such high morale among those he teaches, both company members and students.

His response took me by surprise. I expected a more complex explanation, but what he said was direct, practical and to the point.

A teacher of mine at the Vaganova Institute once said that a class must always be oriented toward the best student in it, and in that way, the others are required to overcome their deficiencies so as not to fall behind. Ballet is very rigorous, and discipline must prevail in the studio during class. The ballet teacher must master several pedagogical aspects in order to integrate the different requirements his class will place on the students. This is especially the case when it comes to teaching the less capable students. For example, psychologically, it is best to avoid always giving corrections to the least promising student—better to use the best student as an example, and give the corrections in a general sense. In this way, all the students feel more equal, and gain more self confidence at their own pace. By the same token, good teaching practice would demand that special attention be paid to students, taking into account the individual's personality or character. For example, there are students to whom one can yell out a correction and they will react positively. The opposite would be a student who is shy at best [where yelling might prove discouraging]. Said another way, *le doy tres gritos y el cuarto es un elogio* (I yell three times, and then the fourth is a cry of praise), even though in reality he hasn't completely overcome his deficiency. The student recovers or discovers his morale and doesn't become dispirited. [7]

10

Natalia Makarova

The performance was special. I had never seen her dance *Giselle* with such freedom and simple elegance. From the outset, and throughout the entire ballet, Makarova was not merely an exemplary Giselle in terms of style and romantic technique. She seemed to have found the golden mean in her interpretation. She made the ballet not only an aesthetic joy but a revelation of human experience magically transfigured by art...[with] so much natural abandon that it might seem as if she were inventing [the steps] herself on stage at that very moment—a kind of artistic freedom reminiscent in a way of Ulanova.

–Gennady Smakov[1]

On a visit to investigate what the Vaganova Institute might have to offer her, the 13-year-old Natalia Makarova found herself wondering why the sign on that building's third floor read "Medical Section." She soon had her answer, as Mr. Shelkov, the school's director, commenced to lift and stretch the young visitor's legs into à la séconde. Then he weighed her! Somewhat in shock when asked for her phone number, she gave the school administrators a fake one. Luckily for the future of ballet, she supplied the correct last name, and so Mr. Shelkov was able to locate the girl with the amazing extensions who was not additionally burdened by having to take the school's entrance exam.

Natalia Makarova was born on November 21, 1940, into a family of Soviet intelligentsia. Her father disappeared during the early years of World War II. The war and his absence transformed her childhood into a fragmented, nomadic, yet unexciting search for reliable sources of food and shelter, stewarded by her mother and grandmother. Under different conditions, she might have become a linguist, a doctor, or an architect, as her grandfather had been. Her own intellectual life was limned by her

Natalia Makarova in *Voluntaries.* © **Martha Swope.**

dogged perfectionism and the gnawing suspicion that she would never be good, pretty, or capable enough. These frustrations made for frequent temper tantrums, which ultimately, in the case of her wish to attend the Kirov School (as the Vaganova Institute was also called), resulted in her prevailing over family objections.

Because she was four years older than the average first-year student, Natasha was fast-tracked into a program that condensed nine years' training into six. In contradiction to the tenets of the Vaganova Method, based on the slow development of the musculature and gradual accumulation of appropriate technique, Natasha was put on pointe in her first year, before her muscles had become stretched, adept, and strong enough to support it. Consequently, she had to pay close attention to care of her leg muscles for her entire career. The school became the centerpiece of her otherwise precarious life. Its appealing stability issued from traditions that arose and remained in place to serve the arts. While persecution of non-Socialist Realist artists such as the directo Vsevolod Meyerhold was *de rigeur* under Stalin in the 1950s, the school's traditions remained intact, even as its artistic life suffered in direct proportion to the government's bureaucratic degeneration. As Makarova put it, "Certain things had been damaged, spoiled here and there, but nothing had been destroyed utterly."[2]

Makarova's Kirov teachers, Mikhail Mikhailov and Nikolai Ivanovsky, were direct descendents of the St. Petersburg aristocracy, schooled in the classics at the Smolny Institute. They somehow slipped through the cracks when Stalin's purges sent others like them off to die in the Gulag along with tens of thousands of workers and peasants. The Kirov teachers exuded refinement and were uniquely reliable agents for transmission of the old style, manners, and education. When Ivanovsky met students on the street, he would tip his hat and offer his respects. His comportment took root in Natasha more than any of the many "sermons" on Communist Morality. Ivanovsky taught traditional dances, enlivened by historical anecdotes, so that a pavanne or gavotte became more of an enactment than a derivation.

Mikhailovich instructed students in the revolutionary work of Stanislavsky:

> Learn to walk like Juliet or Giselle, and then you'll find the key to their plastic movement, to infusing it with precise emotion. This will emerge when you find the proper, the true, natural inner state. The body and the soul will then be in equilibrium, and the role will 'fit' you like a well-made dress in which you are free and comfortable.[3]

Creating a character in motion prompted Makarova to wonder about how to engage in that same process with a character that is motion*less*. Mikhailovich suggested that the dancer locate the "inner state" by seizing some aspect of, for example, Odette's diffidence, dignity, or compassion, and find contentment in it. She learned to resist walking or running onstage doing so in a theatrical manner to avoid affectation. The energy of her passion sends Juliet's cloak streaming out parallel to the floor when she flies to meet Romeo! A potential Juliet must possess enough fire to fuel that run.

The faculty included Elena Vasilievna Shiripina, a former Kirov dancer. Only of middling dance talent, she shined as a teacher, and Vaganova had set the exacting pedant to work training the new generation of dancers. When Makarova's chaîné turns went slightly off course, Shiripina directed her to continue out the door, and then closed it, leaving her in the corridor musing over her error. Makarova cites absent-mindedness as her greatest weakness. She was so often lost in thought that she did not hear instructions or pay heed to which arm was raised or lowered, and would find herself ending a combination facing the opposite direction of her classmates. While she understood the impact of her talent, she was less certain of her *overall* heft, and oscillated between meekness in the face of adolescent cruelty (which reaches its nadir in ballet school dressing rooms), and a counter-phobic strutting among the front ranks of girls who smoked and flirted with boys. Having experimented with her own Odette/Odile issues, Makarova finally withdrew from the adolescent power struggles to channel her energies into the career that awaited her.

The aim of the progressively more complex algebra of Vaganova training is to elicit from children what is truly their own interpretation of movement, so that as they grow into adulthood, they don't manufacture an unnecessary and detrimental mental schism between technique and artistry. For her graduation exam, Natalia danced the second act adagio from *Giselle* with Nikita Dolgushin, whose romantic refinement and willingness to discuss the role made for an expressive performance that surpassed all expectations and met with great critical acclaim. It took only a highly successful "first time out" to establish Makarova as a romantic ballerina, inviting comparisons to Carlotta Grisi and Maria Taglioni. Where others would have been elated to be invited to join the Kirov, for Natalia, the contract was anticlimactic, too easily won. Was her insouciance then a tactic to ward off an overwhelming fear of the career that was in the offing?

After dancing a swan in *Swan Lake* and in *Les Sylphides*, Natalia was cast in the title role of her first full-length *Giselle*. She was 19, a scant two years older than her character. A critic described her interpretation as that of "a young girl from the big city, trembling under a protective covering of independence,"[4] in contrast to a tragic romantic heroine. Unable to gauge the distance between herself and her character, she danced the "Natasha," who found herself in Giselle's shoes: coquettish and artful. It was in keeping with the romantic style of the Kirov, redolent of the history, manners, literature, language, culture, and even the architecture of its St. Petersburg home.

Newer, less classical works challenged Natasha. She found their choreography static, primitive, and melodramatic. As she rehearsed a version of Juliet's role choreographed by Lavrovsky and coached by Tatiana Mikhailovna Vecheslova, the decisions they made one day would fly out of her head the next, because she could not connect emotionally with the choreography. To make it interesting for herself, she would change some small element each time she danced it, hearing praise for this or that evening's work, but never grasping why it was better than another evening's. She had similar problems with *Swan Lake* because she saw the Ivanov-Petipa version as leaving no room for spontaneity. The prospect of dancing Odile terrified her almost as much as the expected 32 fouettés in the finale. She was coached by Vecheslova and Dudinkskaya, the former working on her artistry; the latter, on her endurance and stamina. Thirty-two fouettés should be executed in place and not travel. Rarely succeeding, most dancers trend downstage. In one performance, Makarova ended her last fouetté exiting through the rear back curtain! After a lengthy discussion of the roles of Odette and Odile with Igor Tchernishov, she changed everything, instantly reaping the benefits. After the next show, Sergeyev commented to her about how inventive she was, adding a bit menacingly that she was a "real decadent."[5] Makarova became famous for the twin roles.

Makarova's most difficult moments issued from a lack of stamina and her signature absent-mindedness. During the coda of the flower girls in *Don Quixote*, she began retching onstage, and ran off to the bathroom, leaving her partner to finish alone, then returning in time for the curtain call. Once, she underestimated the bulk of her costume's petticoats during an *en dedans* turn, and ended up and remained in the prompter's box until her partner pulled her out, pretending that her trajectory was intentional. Terror stricken by the prospect of the final Czar Maiden variation in the *Humpbacked Horse*, she became hysterical backstage, refusing to go back out, and had to be pushed onstage. Her performance was so good that it succeeded in defeating her stamina demons. Makarova also attributes her fortification to Natalia Dudinskaya, who insisted that she finish combinations when she felt she could not, to prove to herself that she could.

Makarova learned about partnering from Konstantin Sergeyev, who partnered Galina Ulanova, and directed the Kirov in the 1960s. His strength was in his ability to guide rather than contain his partner. She could count on his support, even as he left her free to move. She explained to his successors that partnering was mostly a function of coordination rather than brute strength. She cites Erik Bruhn, Donald MacLeary, and Anthony Dowell as examples of others who mastered this method. Sergeyev's talents resided in his professionalism and traditional approach to the classics. At the same time that he revered the old ballets and the choreography of Ivanov-Petipa, he was able to excise material that was stale, and discard what seemed dated. Though he staged the requisite Socialist Realist ballets about space travel and peasants surpassing agricultural quotas, and choreographed new, if uninspired works himself, his artistic loyalty was to the old order. This was somewhat freakishly*to the liking* of the bureaucratic claque that oversaw the ideological constancy of the Kirov, and for the most part, Sergeyev was left alone.

Unfortunately, others such as Leonid Yakobson, whose new works were quite innovative—and therefore banned by Sergeyev—paid the price for Sergeyev's go-along-to-get-along minuet with the bureaucrats. Makarova, having been viewed as a romantic ballerina, was not called upon to dance the newer works, and therefore savored the opportunity to work with Yakobson in his piece, *The Bedbug*. It was a ballet based on a play of the same name by Mayakovsky. It is astounding that it made it past the self-censoring commissars of the Kirov, because its theme was the

irony of the craven "NEPmen." The NEPmen were a caste of small capitalists, elevated in status during the Soviet New Economic Program (NEP).
The NEP was regarded as a temporary but necessary evil. It was imagined
that this parasitic caste would fall away at a more advanced stage in the
economy. But Stalin courted the NEPmen, and they proliferated like cock-
roaches. In a bedroom scene, a NEPman and his mistress squirm like
insects under satin blankets; in another, grotesque guests fox trot amid
the detritus of empty bottles, cigarette butts mixed in with flowers, and
flesh out a sleazy wedding procession. Yakobson cast Makarova as Zoya,
a kind of Giselle knockoff, a rebellious 60s teenager, whose movements
mimic the rock and twist dances of the era. She commits suicide when
her intended betrays her by marrying into the bureaucracy. Yakobson's
belief that Makarova could break out of the romantic roles and give life
to more genuinely drawn characters made her feel newly confident and
capable. When she danced the Beautiful Maiden in Yakobson's *Country of
Wonder*, she was named best Soviet ballerina of the year.

In 1965, Makarova entered the Varna competition, and won the
Gold Medal. More satisfying than winning it was working at close range
with Ulanova, who coached her with great scrupulousness in her interpretation of Giselle.

In the gulag atmosphere of the Kirov, Makarova went out of her way
to avoid conflict. Her single act of rebellion was committed against the
director of a tasteless film version of *Swan Lake*, who had no experience
filming professional ballet, and instructed her to dance Odile, "as if you
wanted to seduce me."[6] Declaring that she hadn't the slightest wish to
do such a thing, she walked off the set and out of the picture. Dudinskaya
and Sergeyev attempted to convince her that she was crazy to have let
such an opportunity go, but let it go she did, and Elena Evteyeva danced
the roles of Odette/Odile instead. Soon after this incident, she and
Baryshnikov were invited by Igor Tchernishov to work on his version of
a long *Romeo and Juliet* pas de deux to music by Berlioz, where Baryshnikov would dance Mercutio, and Valery Panov Tybalt. It was not officially
sanctioned, and so the dancers rehearsed it on their own time, working
long hours. Marietta Frangiopolo, much admired because she archived
historical material on world ballet, pronounced Tchernishov's work an
"evil flower that must not be permitted to blossom."[7] To that opprobrium,
Sergeyev added "formalism," "eroticism," "Western, not Soviet arabesques," and summarily banned it. The cast was psychologically spent.
Then they happened upon Gulyayev and Kolpakova rehearsing it,
Kolpakova having used her party connections to resurrect it, just before
leaving for the Kirov's third tour of London.

It was not Natasha's first London engagement. She had danced the
same role, Giselle, several years earlier. She felt more confident this time,
reprising the role without the burden of the toothache she had suffered
during her first London appearance. While having felt vulnerable to the

many attractions and luxuries that London had to offer, she denies that
she left the Soviet Union with the intention of abandoning her homeland.
Nonetheless, because of the *Romeo and Juliet* fiasco, she was feeling
alienated from the Kirov, and took comfort in the hours she passed with
her English friends, the Rodziankos.

Makarova reports that an unconscious will to separate herself from
her circumstances had begun to assert itself. When she joined fellow company members at a party, she was warned by several dancers that she was
being watched, and Irina Kolpakova instructed her to return to the hotel
in the company bus instead of accepting a ride with the Rodziankos.
She resentfully complied.

On September 3, 1970, Natasha was taking an elevator downstairs en
route to dinner with the Rodziankos, when she encountered two KGB
agents accompanied by Dudinskaya, who showed her a series of photo
proofs. For a reason Makarova is at a loss to explain, she circled the hotel
twice before entering the Rodzianko's car. The dinner conversation was
disjointed, and then suddenly, Irina Rodzianko began urging Makarova
to remain in London. Makarova says that she laughed, and tried to
change the subject to music, that defecting had never occurred to her,
but as the conversation continued, she silently began to consider what
she would leave behind if she did indeed decide to stay: her beloved
mother, the Kirov stage, the city of Leningrad, and her friends. It seemed
like folly. Then, after having weighed the liabilities, a flood of emotions
took over, which she says originated in her unconscious, registering her
fatalism, and she sobbed for 15 minutes as she realized that she did want
to stay. She asked her hosts to call the police.

Sergeyev, fearful of losing his position because of Makarova's defection (and soon thereafter, he did), wrote her imploring letters and
remained in London after the company had moved on to its next tour
stop, hoping to convince Makarova to change her mind, or at least make
the record for trying. Her decision was firm. Once it was made, everything that followed seemed anticlimactic. She had no job offers, yet her
photograph was in the daily newspapers, and reporters pursued her,
though she had little to say. Her defection had nothing to do with politics
in the broad sense; only despair at the limitations of the Kirov, and only in
the narrowest sense.

The company she had hoped to be invited to join—The Royal Ballet—
extended no such invitation. She performed the Odile pas de deux with
Nureyev on British TV, and was not happy with the result. At a party,
she proposed to Frederick Ashton that he set a piece on her, which drew
a reproachful look from the ballerina Svetlana Beriosova, and no enthusiasm from Ashton. It would be a year before the Royal Ballet invited
Natasha to dance at a gala for Queen Elizabeth.

She accepted an invitation to join American Ballet Theatre, and
moved to New York in the fall of 1970. The sudden move to a country

with few social supports forced Natasha to come to terms with her dreamy, impractical tendencies, and inattention to matters such as finance. As the questions from reporters narrowed down to a single theme—the scarcely disguised expectation that the dancer would use her "new freedom" to attack the Soviet Union—Makarova, who felt no such need, relied more and more on canned responses that expressed none of what she was feeling or thinking. She quickly came to the conclusion that she was completely alone in her new circumstances, and that her only real companion was her work. Natasha threw herself into the crazy-quilt repertoire of the ABT season, opening with *Giselle*, but also dancing in *Pillar of Fire, Lilac Garden, Romeo and Juliet, La Sylphide, Coppélia, La Fille Mal Gardée*, and Alvin Ailey's *The River* and *The Miraculous Mandarin*. When Erik Bruhn withdrew from partnering her in *Giselle*, Ivan Nagy replaced him. His patience, sturdiness, and gallantry during rehearsals made long and boring by translation, actually served to create a lasting bond between the two partners. Eventually, Makarova did dance with Bruhn, and speaks admiringly of him, lamenting that they met as his career began its decline. She valued his comments at rehearsals, "always in good taste and to the point."[8]

It was John Neumeier's *Epilogue* that permanently altered Makarova's attitude toward the expression of the emotional content in ballet. The ballet required the contradictory qualities of enormous energy and restraint of feeling. Having been accustomed to showing all her feeling, it was a new experience to tap into it intermittently. Makarova credits this work with having taught her how to better regulate her emotional energy in creating the role of Giselle.

In the pas de deux from *The River*, Makarova worked with jazz for the first time. She and Bruhn had some difficulty with the Duke Ellington score, and went to a discothèque, where Puerto Rican Latin Jazz was played, to see first-hand what would be expected of them. As she began to work with Alvin Ailey, her understanding of movement grew. She saw how jazz demands an immediate, spontaneous response, offering in return a greater range of freedom than classical ballet. Makarova's efforts paid off when a critic wrote that she danced jazz as if she had been doing it all her life.

Dancing Lise in *La Fille Mal Gardée* and Swanilda in *Coppélia* offered an opportunity to explore comic roles free to improvise. Dancing *La Sylphide*, staged by Bruhn, helped her to master the fleetness of Bournonville, with its lighthearted femininity. Even though she did not do her best work with the choreographer Anthony Tudor, whose sarcasm distanced him from most dancers he worked with, Makarova found that matching wits with him helped release much of the tension that had accumulated during her first two years in the United States.

She welcomed the opportunity to dance the Balanchine ballets and rehearsed ABT's *Theme and Variations* with Balanchine himself. She had

Natalia Makarova in *Other Dances*. Photo credit: Dina Makarova.

worked hard to master his counterintuitive technique of quick dense movements that spoke for themselves, free of interpretation by the dancer. His only criticism of her work was that she did not spot fast enough. (Spotting is the practice of whipping the head around in advance of the body during a turn, eyes trained on a "spot" towards which the turn, or series of turns, is advancing.) Not spotting fast enough causes the line of the body to falter and the turn to lose its attack. In the rapid deployment of Balanchine steps, the dancer must take care not to spend all his or her energy on the first in a series of repetitions, lest the later repetitions undergo an unintended diminuendo. One must dance truly, believing that he or she is not a human being, but a metronome. Makarova loved Balanchine's innovative, musical choreography, and regretted that she wasn't better at dancing it. She admits to having had problems working within the "no stars" entente that Balanchine stubbornly maintained. Natalia had to find a way to subordinate her presence without losing her artistry to the larger musical and stylistic concepts in Balanchine works. She was unable to embrace his abstraction of "pure beauty" that ignored, denied, and finally extinguished imperfection or, in the broadest sense, life as it actually is.

Natalia's own life, as it actually was, was far from perfect. She was exhausted, but learning! She rehearsed eight hours a day and then performed in the evenings. The athletic style of the ABT dancers seemed to contradict everything she had learned at the Kirov. They easily shifted from classical to contemporary works, relying on their individual body types to spirit them through a role or composition, instead of working more deeply with pliés, épaulement, or emotional responses, and arms and legs that were nearly equal in their expressiveness, as the Kirov had taught Makarova to do. It took Natasha a long time to interpolate the two worlds so that she could forge her own identity in the company. It required developing an understanding of her body, a process that can span an entire career. She gained insights that are best expressed by her:

> Maybe it is the knowledge of what must *not* be done in a romantic or a classical ballet. In both cases it is a particular system of restrictions concerning the positions of arms, hands, feet, chest, shoulders and head. If we stop observing these restrictions, all ballets will look alike, and the variety of aesthetic impressions will be lost. The spectators will lose more than anyone else, even those who are not experts in stylistic subtleties, for if they are only seeing dancers who approach ballet as a sport, they will never know the difference between the plastic beauty of *Giselle* and that of *Sleeping Beauty*, merely the difference between their stories.
>
> This sense of style I brought from the Kirov. Here are the roots of my oversensitivity to small details and my organic inability to "cheat" on the stage. When I dance *Swan Lake*, I try to make every finger "talk," and I know there are no limits to perfecting one's expressive means.[9]

The absence of the Kirov and its exacting teachers, and the burden of the now-classical, now-contemporary ABT repertoire, forced Makarova to become her own coach. At first, she worked away at delivering perfect Vaganova technique, never deviating from its orthodoxy. Then she realized that this practice was a potential obstacle, perhaps an unconscious mantle taken on as punishment for having abandoned her school of origin. Her penance prevented her body from "singing" when she danced. The irony is that Vaganova stood her in good stead when she danced contemporary works, but rendered her its prisoner in classical works such as *Swan Lake*.

> The political freedom I had found in the West...from petty oppression and humiliation, did not automatically warrant artistic freedom. By artistic freedom...I mean the freedom of synthesis, the freedom to assimilate the

best achievements of the world's ballet, the freedom of creation subordinated only to aesthetic criteria...I still had to fight to win my artistic freedom.[10]

After two years, Makarova decided to leave ABT. Two men entered her life: the impresario, Sol Hurok, and the man she married, Edward Karkar. Hurok often came to see her ABT performances, though careful not to develop a personal relationship so as to not jeopardize his connection with Soviet ballet contacts. During a covert dinner meeting in the Connecticut countryside, he urged Natasha not to tether her career to ABT, offering the opinion that she had the potential to cut a more international swath.

Having become disenchanted with dancing the classics without proper (read: Kirov) choreographic or musical support, Makarova began traveling internationally as a guest dancer. She performed *The Dying Swan* in Rio de Janeiro, *Swan Lake* and *Giselle* in South Africa, and *The Rite of Spring* at La Scala in Milan, where on the 1972 season's opening night performance of the opera *Un Ballo in Maschera*, Placido Domingo had been booed from the orchestra pit, apples having been lobbed at him. Having met with a much more favorable reception than Domingo, Natasha continued on to Stockholm, Munich, Zurich, Paris, and danced *Coppélia* in Berlin and then in the opera *I Vespri Siciliani* at the rebuilt Reggio Theater in Turin, then under the direction of Maria Callas.

The many performances helped Makarova better appreciate the stylistic differences between dancing the "tutu classics" and the "tutu romantics." One wonders whether what Makarova views as a conflict between her two worlds was in the end resolved by a third phenomenon —the artistic maturation that comes with experience and seasoning. Makarova became convinced that one could not settle for the precision that characterized the classics, where the dancer held her position to correspond perfectly with each musical rest. The dancer had to be free to move the story through the musical stops, and in her experience at ABT, that fluidity of style was neither valued nor encouraged.

In 1974, Makarova joined the Royal Ballet as a permanent guest artist. The atmosphere there seemed more gracious, free of the long and frantic rehearsal schedule that had been the norm at ABT. In the company's poise and style—which Makarova associates with the European way of life— she found refinement, where at ABT there had been chaos. After an injury during an otherwise successful *Swan Lake*, in which she was partnered by Donald MacLeary, Makarova was dissatisfied with her work in the season's remaining repertoire. She found that Anthony Dowell's somewhat restrained and distant partnering put her off. She abandoned an earlier, more subtle interpretation of Giselle for a more dramatic one that she had developed at ABT, and audiences found it overdone. To top it all off, her *Sleeping Beauty* "Rose Adagio" attitudes were said by British audiences to have been held too long. They had grown accustomed to Margot

Fonteyn's accented ones, frozen right on the note. At the Royal, however, Makarova was able to dance what would become her favorite role—*Manon*. Of this role, Makarova writes:

> She sees her own life apart from the mass of humanity, apart from society's moral prohibitions, and she lives without a backward glance. She lives according to the feminine dictates of her instinct, her will, her caprice; all the facets of the feminine character are vividly reflected in her...The Shakespearean "Tis better to be vile than vile esteem'd" is applicable to her. And she is ready to pay for her passions, for the pleasure of living fully, for not being satisfied with pale compromises or imitations....[11]

The role so fit Makarova that at the dress rehearsal, which happened to be on her birthday, she was so engrossed in the character's exile that she didn't notice the change in the music and when she did, attributed her lapse to being unfamiliar with the score, until she realized that the orchestra was playing "Happy Birthday." With *Manon*, she and Dowell finally developed a close artistic relationship when she understood that his reserve masked an insistence on authenticity, and as a result of their work together on *Manon*, they performed a much better *Giselle* than in their first effort.

In the summer of 1974, Baryshnikov phoned Natalia Makarova from Canada to say that he had decided to remain in the West, and was seeking asylum in Canada. En route to New York for an ABT engagement, she promised help find him a place with ABT. Makarova arranged with Lucia Chase for Misha to accept Ivan Nagy's invitation to substitute for Nagy in several of the works Makarova would dance over the summer. She found that Misha had matured as an artist and partner over the four years since they had seen one another. Their July 27th *Giselle* was tremendously successful, and Makarova considers him the only partner with whom she felt "as if there were an electrically charged field" around her, where a friendly rivalry supported their work. When Ivan Nagy was injured a year later, and Misha was put in for him in a January 1977 performance, he and Natasha danced without having rehearsed. Misha's decision to go to New York City Ballet meant that he and Makarova would stop dancing together. Even if they shared a common dance education and similar values, their tastes diverged, with Baryshnikov trending in a more experimental direction.

Of their collaborations, she believes that Jerome Robbins' *Other Dances* was the standout, which she attributes to their work with Robbins as he set it on them. She notes that while Robbins' choreography is much like Balanchine's, he never forced a dancer into a preconceived schema. There was always a margin of freedom as Robbins tried as many ideas as he needed until he found what fit both the dancer and the music. His images were exact for Makarova. She cites Glen Tetley's *Voluntaries* as another piece that was a perfect fit. To dance it, she knew she had to bring her mind to a state of near-despair, and challenge every sinew of her body to overcome it.

Makarova took a rest from performing in August 1977, settling into her life in San Francisco, enjoying her view of the Marin headlands, and giving expression to her vivid observations by painting. On February 1, 1978, Makarova gave birth to her son, André-Michel. She saw nothing new of interest emerging from young choreographers, and hoped that future performances of the classics would reveal new capacities of her own.

She asked herself whether she could live without ballet. The answer was that she could not imagine a life outside the art form. Three and a half months after giving birth, she danced *Other Dances* with Misha at the Metropolitan Opera House, undertaking perhaps the most intense preparation in her life as she struggled to get her body back. In a prologue to *A Dance Autobiography*, Gennady Smakov quotes the Chinese proverb, "Who rides the tiger can never get off,"[12] and it was in that spirit that Makarova tamed her truculently maternal body. She began private work with Janet Sassoon in her Market Street studio. She pulled everything apart, beginning with athletic tricks and then moving into more legato movements. Fouettés came back stronger than before. She traveled to New York, seeking Elena Tchernishova's coaching help. Tchernishova's diagnosis was that the body was in fine shape, but Natasha had lost her mental focus, and only by returning to the work could she regain it. In her opinion, Makarova was the kind of artist who danced better when something in her environment had gone awry and needed balancing. Childbirth had lent Natasha a womanly confidence and vibrancy. These were the qualities she was able to bring to her New York rendering of Kitri in *Don Quixote*. She then danced an inspired *Giselle* in Philadelphia.

On February 1, 1989, after 19 years' absence, Makarova was the first artistic exile to be invited to perform in the Soviet Union at the Maryinsky in Leningrad, on the stage where her career began, dancing two pas de deux from John Cranko's *Onegin* with Alexander Sombart. Prior to the trip, Makarova made a decision that this would be a good way to end her classical ballet performing career, completing the circle. Afterwards, her commitments took her in a different direction: She began staging ballets from the repertoire she had danced. Of this she says, "For a ballerina to give her experience to others and share all the nuances she learned through her professional life is precious. I like to pass on my knowledge of the art of classical ballet to a new generation of dancers."[13] A documentary of Makarova's historic visit, "Makarova Returns," was aired on BBC television, and that same year, she made a documentary for BBC called "Leningrad Legend" about the Kirov Ballet and Vaganova Institute. Among the productions Makarova staged were: *La Bayadère* for the Royal Ballet and Royal Swedish Ballet in 1989, for La Scala in 1991, Teatro Colon in Buenos Aires in 1992, Ballet de Santiago in 1997, Australian Ballet in

1998, Rio De Janiero in 2001, Hamburg Ballet in 2002, and Theatr Wielki-Opera Narodowa of Warsaw in 2004. She staged "Kingdom of the Shades" for San Francisco Ballet, *Giselle* for Royal Swedish Ballet in 2000, *Sleeping Beauty* for the Royal Ballet in 2003, *Swan Lake* for Teatro Municipal in Rio de Janeiro in 2001 and for Perm Ballet in 2005, and *Paquita* for the National Ballet of Canada for its 1990–91 season, for Universal Ballet in 1999–2000, and San Francisco Ballet in 2002. Makarova danced the role of Giulietta Masina at the 1995 Fellini Festival in Rome, where Jean Babilée danced the role of Fellini.

In 1994, Makarova wrote and hosted the BBC documentary "St. Petersburg to Tashkent" for the Great Railway Journey series, and appeared in the BBC Documentary on Tchaikovsky in 1997. She made her debut as a dramatic actress in the Chichester Festival production of "Tovarich," which moved to the West End Theatre in 1991. She played Elvira in Noel Coward's "Blithe Spirit" in the year 2000 at the Palace Theatre in Watford. She appeared in the play "Wooing in Absence" at the 1999 Charleston Festival, in 2000 at London's Tate Gallery, and in 2001 at New York's Lincoln Center. In 1991, she recorded narrations of *The Snow Queen, Prince Ivan and the Frog Princess*, and *The Firebird*, which received the American Library Association Award.

Of her decision to defect, she says that she has never regretted it. She says that having left a Soviet Union disfigured by Stalin's reign of totalitarianism enabled her to satisfy an artistic hunger which the Kirov repertoire was incapable of nourishing, and to dance what she wanted when she wanted without government approval or interference. As an artist, Makarova has never felt constrained, defined, or excluded by geographical boundaries. For her, "The art of ballet is universal; it speaks no single language, nor does it acknowledge any single nationality. It is beyond and above politics. My life as a ballerina crossed all frontiers, and my dance floor was the world itself."[14]

11

Maya Plisetskaya

Her arms have a special flexibility. They can twist like snakes, flutter and beat like ribbons in the wind, enthrall one with their slow, wavelike movements. In nearly all Plisetskaya roles there is a special, distincitve pattern of the arms and hands. Her famous exit in act 2 of *Swan Lake* relies for its effect on the remarkable accelerating, wavy movements of the arms on a straight, motionless body. It creates the image of a gliding swan, a proud bird sailing through smooth water.

—Critic Boris Lvov-Anokhin (1976, p. 107)[1]

Perhaps certain children are driven to rebel right from the beginning when they realize that their lives are little more than repositories or icons for adult narcissism or despair: discovering that they've been deceived for having invested heavily in the fable of their elders' lives sets them on a path of determined resistance. Maya Plisetskaya rebelled simply to live her life free of the import others assigned to that of her father, at the same time holding his legacy in high esteem. Refusal to be the icon left open the only remaining role: that of the icono*clast*.

She was born on November 20, 1925, in Moscow, into a family of notable performing artists. Her maternal grandfather, Mikhail Borisovich Messerer, was a Lithuanian dentist who, with his wife, moved his six children from Vilna to Moscow, where an additional six were born.

Maya's mother, Rakhil Messerer, was a silent film actress. Her aunt and uncle, Asaf and Sulamit (Mita), danced with the Bolshoi Ballet and the People's Artists. Her father, a government functionary in the coal industry, and a genuine communist (with a small "c," distinguishing him from the bureaucratized leadership of the Communist Party of the Soviet Union), was persecuted as an enemy of the state, sent to prison,

Maya Plisetskaya in *Swan Lake*. **Photo credit: Izogiz. Courtesy Dance Collection, New York Public Library.**

and executed in 1935 by Stalin's Cheka. During Plisetskaya's childhood, her mother, who declined to sign papers denouncing her husband, was sentenced to eight years in a prison for "wives [or widows] of enemies of the state." During this period, Maya was kept by her Aunt Mita. In a nation where inheriting private property was illegal, Plisetskaya could claim two rich legacies: one cultural and the other political. For most of her dance career, the Stalin-led regime counterposed them. When it served their aims, *apparatchiks* touted her talent as an achievement of the revolution, but in instances where she might be in a position to expose their pernicious nature, they sidelined Plisetskaya by banning performances of her choreographic works, denying her permission to travel outside the Soviet Union, and insisting that she write "Jew" on her applications to travel. While top government officials lauded Maya publicly, privately, lower-level officials kept their jobs as ballet commissars by re-seeding the cloud of suspicion always hovering over her. Though she came from a family of professionals and remained rooted in that petty bourgeois milieu, her belief that justice could be won by perseverance pushed any thoughts of defection out of her mind. Bureaucrats with access to ways and means to bail out of the nightmarish labyrinth of their own making were oftentimes in the best position to defect. Plisetskaya believes that such individuals projected their own worst tendencies onto her, utilizing their fiefdoms to ban her work and deny audiences the pleasure of seeing her dance.

Embittered and deprived of a political compass, Plisetskaya rejected Marxism and Leninism, viewing Stalinism as their inevitable endgame, rather than what it was: the bureaucratic degeneration of the revolution of 1917. Still, as an artist, she never stopped rebelling, using every opportunity to revolutionize ballet.

Plisetskaya offers high praise for her dancer uncle Asaf, who broke new ground in the display of tricks and men's solo virtuosity. She studied with him nearly every day of her ballet career. Among his other students were Galina Ulanova, Vladimir Vasiliev, and Ekaterina Maximova, whose outstanding work was on a par with, or more impressive than, Plisetskaya's.

Maya remembers 1929 as the year of her maternal grandmother's death *and* when people gathered to watch her impromptu dance performance to music in a local town square. Plisetskaya jokes that this story so lends itself to a cinematic retelling that she hopes nobody ever writes a scene depicting it in a film about her life.[2] She recounts seeing her first play, "Don't Joke with Love," at age five. She was so taken with the play that she acted out the part of "The Woman in Black" until she exhausted her family's patience, provoking her father to smack her on the rear. The next morning at breakfast, still smarting, she refused to speak. Her father asked, "Mayechka, you're not mad are you? Forgive me, it was just a joke. I love you."

"Don't joke with love," Maya shot back, as she struck the pose of The Woman in Black.[3]

In 1932, Maya's father, an engineer, was appointed General Consul to Spitzbergen, a Norwegian island above the Arctic Circle, and chief of the coal mines there. A Soviet icebreaker took Maya and her parents and eight-month-old brother Alexander from Oslo to their destination. In their two-room cottage, an electric light offered the only respite from the long winter darkness until the arrival of the long summer days. Maya spent all her time skiing. Amateur performances for miners' families in which Plisetskaya played small roles afforded an escape from the boredom. When Norwegian authorities sent her father a crate of oranges for Christmas, he insisted that it go to the miners' cafeteria. "They're not mine. They're state property." Plisetskaya offers this story as evidence that her father consciously and conscientiously took his distance from the trough into which most bureaucrats plunged their snouts. Most of them took or hoarded everything that wasn't nailed down—any scrap that might give off the faintest whiff of privilege—and many that would not. Perhaps his fate was sealed in December 1934, when he invited his lifelong friend, Pikel, to speak at a rally commemorating the death of Kirov. Pikel delivered an impassioned speech. In her autobiography, *I, Maya Plissetskaya*, the dancer writes,

> Only now, toward the end of my life, have I begun to see a terrible pattern. Pikel had been a secretary of Trotsky's. Everything, however peripherally or directly involved with the name Trotsky, was destroyed by Stalin with bloody fire. Father had been friends with Pikel all his life. Mother often told me how loyal a friend Father had been. When Pikel ended up without work and in political disfavor, Father took his old friend to Spitzbergen as his deputy. Before Spitzbergen, Pikel was director of the Tairov Chamber Theater. The destruction of the talented theater was, I fear, also tied to Pikel's political legacy. Meyerhold's death suggests the same to me: Trotsky. Meyerhold had dedicated one of his plays to Trotsky and that rankled with the ruthless, vengeful, treacherous Stalin.[4]

In the summer of 1934, Plisetskaya's Aunt Mita accompanied her to the entrance exam for the Moscow Choreographic School. The simple curtsy she did before the board at the end of the exam stirred Victor Alexandrovich Semenov, who immediately reciprocated with the words, "This girl we'll take." While there were only 30 applicants (today, the number of applicants can reach 1,000), she found herself mostly in the company of children of party functionaries who would drop off their fur coats at the director's office for safekeeping before class.

Plisetkaya's first teacher was Yevgenia Ivanovna Dolinskaya. She did everything a first ballet teacher should do and did it well: took a seat at the piano to emphasize phrasing, taught proper placement for the basic ballet positions, staged small performances, and had the patience required to teach squirrelly children ballet. At the choreographic school, Maya began working with Leonid Veniaminovich Yakobson. Their relationship lasted a lifetime. The school curriculum included Russian, arithmetic, geography, history, music, and French. Maya had to leave at the end of the first year because her family was returning to Spitzbergen. By spring, it was apparent that she missed her dance classes, and was sent home on the first available icebreaker, chaperoned by a bookkeeper who counted things constantly. Her second-year teacher was Elizaveta Pavlovna, whose father had been a soloist under the Czar, his mother a Maryinksy ballerina. While she had a "good eye," she could not give corrections in a helpful way, or as the Russians say, "couldn't write the prescription." Giving the ballet student even the simplest image is often the key to learning proper placement. Plisetskaya says that Agrippa Vaganova, for example, would instruct students to "Squeeze your rear end around an imaginary fifteen-kopeck piece through the whole class, so that it doesn't fall," and the result would be a dancer whose rear never looked unsupported, and whose pelvis and spine were always correctly aligned.[5]

Plisetskaya compensated for not having received a dance education she considered complete by learning from others. Her female classmates joined the corps de ballet of the Bolshoi; many of the boys died on the German front in World War II.

Shortly before December 1936, Nikolai Bukharin, Stalin's right-hand man, presented the new Stalin Constitution, and a few days later Maya's father returned from a new job in Moscow that came with a chauffeur-driven Emka to say that he had been expelled from the party. Maya didn't fully understand what "the party" was, or its role in her father's life. He soon lost his job, and became depressed and despondent. A few days prior to May 1, he was called somewhere and returned home all smiles, bearing two coveted tickets to the May Day Rally in Red Square. Maya's mother, pregnant, made her a new dress for the occasion. On April 30, the day before the rally, Maya's father was arrested at dawn. His last words, intended to reassure his daughter were, "Everything will be fine...Thank God, they'll settle this at last."

Her father's absence did not make Maya feel unique or strange at the choreographic school. Several classmates' parents were also under arrest, while still others' were instrumental in facilitating those arrests taking place. Maya was designated "daughter of an enemy of the people," and while this imposed strictures on her career in years to come, she was able to continue her dance education without bias or interruption. In her third year, Maya began to learn historical and character dance, which included Spanish, Roma, Russian, Hungarian, and Polish traditional dances. She enjoyed attending Bolshoi dress rehearsals. Children gained their first professional experiences by performing in the company's repertory. Maya danced the Breadcrumb Fairy in *Sleeping Beauty*, Flowers in *Snegurochka*, and The Cat in *The Little Stork*.

While Maya was at the dance academy, her mother was making inquiries and petitioning on behalf of her husband. She was seven months' pregnant when he was arrested. There was no money, and she began selling off what valuables she had to meet the family's expenses. On the occasion of Aunt Mita's *Sleeping Beauty* performance, they made a special effort to find Crimean mimosas to present to her, and though Maya recalls going to the theater with her mother, as the performance came to an end, her mother was no longer there, and she cannot remember at what point Rakhil went missing. Maya took the big bouquet to her aunt's house, and was invited to spend the night. Her aunt told her that her mother was summoned to see her father and had to take a night train before the several-hour ballet had concluded. At 12, Maya did not realize that her mother, arrested in the middle of *Swan Lake*, had been sent to prison. She took up residence with Mita, never realizing that the telegrams that in time came from her mother were actually sent by Mita. Had Mita declined to take Maya in, Maya would have been sent to an orphanage. Everything the family owned in their apartment on Gagarinsky Street was "redistributed," most likely to those responsible for jailing Maya's parents.

Maya's mother was taken to Moscow's Butyrki Prison with her new-born infant. It wasn't until 1989 that Maya and her family learned the date of her father's execution by firing squad—January 7, 1938. It took more than 50 years for him to be posthumously rehabilitated during Perestroika. When they interrogated Maya's mother, the Cheka pretended that her husband was still alive. She admitted, signed, and confessed nothing, and was sentenced to eight years in Camp Akmolinks Oblast in Khazakhistan in Siberia. Of the "wives of enemies of the people," all with infants, who accompanied her on the long train ride in a cattle car, many seemed to be widows, but Rakhil would not allow herself to believe that all of them were. With a matchstick, she quickly scratched Mita's address plus the four words "Taken to Camp Akmolinks Oblast" on a scrap of newsprint. She noticed a uniformed railroad crossing guard. She flicked the scrap of paper through the train's window so that it fell at the feet of the young female guard, who did not react. How the information traveled through many hands and over many miles back to Mita will never be known, but it proves one thing: that there was a network, however informal, of those who resisted in whatever minute ways they could the usurpation of the revolution by Stalin and his henchmen.

Asaf was decorated that year with the "Order of Labor of the Red Banner," and Mita with the "Mark of Honor." In their hands, these laurels became weapons with which to fight for their imprisoned sister. After writing many petitions and making her case known widely, Asaf and Mita secured Rakhil's release to "live free" near the camp where she had been imprisoned, and where six thousand "wives of enemies of the people" were detained. Mita went there and moved her sister to the small town of Chimkent. Maya's aunt and uncle, trading on their celebrity, obtained a rail ticket to Chimkent for Maya. Maya joined the horde of travelers hoping to escape arrest by deploying themselves as moving targets. She found her mother living in what amounted to the chicken coop of a one-room house occupied by a Bukhara Jew. Rakhil was giving dance lessons at a local club. After a 20-day stay Maya returned to Moscow. She prepared to dance the role of Paquita for a school concert. The audience was the NKVD. As she took her bows, Maya wondered whether, seated among them, were the individual agents who had taken her parents away.

The family's efforts paid off in Rakhil's early release. She and Maya's little brother returned to Moscow in April 1941. At her school's concert in June of 1941, Maya danced the Tchaikovsky *Impromptu* pas de trois staged by Yakobson. Many years later, a lifelong admirer told Maya that she never danced better than in that pas de trois. Cheers from the audience prompted Maya to take an exaggerated *réverence* during the curtain call, for which she was gently admonished by her Uncle Asaf. The Soviet Union joined the war the following day, and Moscow prepared itself for the onslaught of Germany's bombing. Mita learned that the theater would move to Sverlovsk and provided four train tickets to that destination. Maya, her mother and two brothers lived in a crowded apartment there, and Rakhil found work as a clinic registrar. But Mita's information was wrong. The Bolshoi actually went to Kuibyshev and the school to Vasilsursk. A remnant of the school remained in Moscow, moving to a new address. Maya went without class for a year and a half. Train tickets were difficult to get, but again, with help from a friend, she made the five-day trip to Moscow, but without the necessary rail pass. Her teacher, Maria Mikhailovna Leontyeva, helped her get back in shape. She danced the Queen of the Dryads lead for the school's panel at the end of the year, and graduated with an "A." She would at last begin her career in earnest.

Plisetskaya joined the Bolshoi upon its return to Moscow. She had become accustomed to dancing solo roles when the majority of the company was in exile and she was in the second company. When her career officially began with the Bolshoi, it came as a shock to Maya that she did not continue as a soloist, but was hired into the corps de ballet. This caused family conflict because her Uncle Asaf, as director, was in a position to promote her, but did not. As a means of adding to her income and getting exposure, partnered by Golubin and Kodratov, Plisetskaya made the rounds of the smaller Moscow concert theaters and clubs. During the government campaign celebrating the 25th anniversary of Komsomol (the Communist Youth), Plisetskaya was promoted, and danced the *Chopiniana* mazurka, crossing the entire stage in three jetés. Agrippina Vaganova was in the audience, after having worked with Maya on certain details of the mazurka that transformed it. She told her, "Come visit me and we'll do a *Lake* to make the devils turn green." Plisetskaya waited until it was too late for all but self-reproach.

Plisetskaya first saw Galina Ulanova in 1939, at the time of the signing of the monstrous Stalin-Hitler Non-Aggression Pact. In her autobiography, Plisetskaya recalls her first impressions of the famed Russian dancer:

> Her lines amazed me. She had no equal in this regard. It was as if her arabesques were sketched in with a finely-sharpened pencil. She had remarkably

well-trained feet...She seemed to speak softly with them. Her arms fit well into ideally drawn poses. The sense that she constantly observed herself from the side never left me. Everything had been carefully thought out and had a completeness about it. The difference between the Leningrad and Moscow schools was strikingly apparent. She didn't "fudge" anything, even once, during the entire performance [of *Giselle*]. Moscow dancers permitted themselves such liberties constantly—it was, frankly speaking, par for the course.[6]

Ulanova's Odette from *Swan Lake* and Juliet from *Romeo and Juliet* impressed the young Plisetskaya as well. In Ulanova's Juliet, she saw not so much a series of steps as the story, unfurled in movement very much as Shakespeare shaped it in his play. When it was Plisetskaya's turn to dance the role, she had the benefit of Vaganova's coaching. She coached her to do a very well-coordinated renversé, which won the hearts of the audience. Vaganova, who had a habit of giving her students nicknames, chose "red crow" for Maya, because the redheaded student was not always attentive to combinations and they had to be repeated for her, regarded by Vaganova as a waste of precious time. Maya danced Myrtha, the Queen of the Wilis, to Ulanova's Giselle. Her interpretation brought out the character's froideur and marble stillness in contrast to Ulanova's fleet-footed work. Plisetskaya never danced Giselle, always cast as Myrtha to Ulanova's, but Plisetskaya's *Raymonda* caught the eye of the critics and the public. Enjoyment of her new celebrity was tempered by transparent interrogations by the woman who washed the dressing room floor, or a former schoolmate who suddenly appeared to chat about old times, and then asked Maya whether she resented the execution of her father and jailing of her mother.

From 1947 to 1977, Plisetskaya danced *Swan Lake* more than 800 times on every continent except Africa. She danced three versions—those of Burgmeister, Berezov, and Chabukiani—of the Petipa choreography. Plisetskaya considers the ballet a divining rod because it is an all-consuming, demanding work, which totally exposes the dancer technically and artistically, leaving no room for imperfections. Perhaps one of the finest compliments Plisetskaya received during her career came from the famous filmmaker, Sergei Eisenstein. Upon seeing her Black Swan, he asked another dancer to "Tell Maya that she is a brilliant girl."

While the Stalinist regime prevented her from traveling abroad with the company until the early 60s, she was repeatedly asked to dance *Swan Lake* for such visiting dignitaries as Marshal Tito, Jawaharlal Nehru, Indira Gandhi, Shah Pahlavi, General George Marshall, Gamal Nasser, Muhammad Daoud, Haile Selassie, Prince Sihanouk, and Mao Zedong. Mao sent her a basket of white carnations after a performance.

One of her partners, Slava Golubin, was also her first romantic partner. Their careers were both going well at the beginning, but Golubin began to drink, destroying his career, and at the age of 34, took his own life. Her favorite partners in the early years of her career were

Maya Plisetskaya in _Don Quixote_. Courtesy Dance Collection, New York Public Library.

Yuri Kondratov, Nikolai Fadeyechev, Alexander Gudunov, and Alexander Bogatyrev. During a performance of _Chopiniana_ in which Maya danced, there was a coda in which the soloists danced sissonnes in series. Semyonova, who was dancing the leading role, bumped into Maya while turning and knocked her over. The resulting sprained ankle recalled a knee problem that Plisetskaya attributes to pronation of her feet. She consulted a recognized Moscow orthopedist who advised her to give up dancing because it was impossible to straighten her knee. Eventually, she learned of the work of a masseur by the name of Nikita Grigoryevich Shum, whom she credits with saving both her knee and career, using a combination of treatments including massage, paraffin, and herbs for four hours each day for two weeks. Other injuries included a dislocated ankle, broken toes, a torn calf, and a pinched spinal nerve. She relied heavily, as did many dancers, on the care she received from Shum. When he died in 1954, grateful dancers attended his funeral, and Ulanova placed a huge wreath on his coffin.

In 1948, Alexander Solodovnikov took over as artistic director at the Bolshoi. In her autobiography, Plisetskaya presents Solodovnikov as a commissar first and foremost, and an artistic director only by happenstance. In spite of her successes at Soviet-organized youth festivals in Eastern Europe, including receiving a gold medal, Solodovnikov did not acknowledge or utilize her talent, and snubbed her socially. It was not only the spectre of Stalin that haunted Plisetskaya's career. There was what she describes as her own "naïve disobedience,"[7] which cropped up again and again, even in instances where there were opportunities to work with artists she admired. She was cast in a piece staged by the legendary Kasyan Goleisovsky, who required that she trust his direction completely and unquestioningly, but she could not. She was given another chance in a Spanish dance to music by Rodion Shchedrin (whom she would eventually marry), and this was not a success either. A "hard case," Plisetskaya points out how easily and successfully this same choreographer worked with Vasiliev on the piece *Narcissus*.

Having understudied the role of the street dancer Mercedes in a performance of *Don Quixote* attended by Stalin, Plisetskaya was selected to dance at the cult-frenzied festivities marking his 70th birthday in December of 1949. NKVD agents were stationed at every portal checking identification, as performers were auditioned and re-auditioned. At the performance, Mao sat next to Stalin, and Plisetskaya, whose mantra had become "Let's see who gets whom!" was determined to turn this schizoid high/low point of her career to her advantage. The sanguine reviews mentioned her name! The watchdogs who had all along prevented her from taking her talents to venues outside the Soviet Union would be hard-pressed to continue their vendetta, and in fact they became friendlier, even Solodovnikov. Maya learned Kitri in *Don Quixote*, and made up her mind to trade on her new cachet to ask for a raise, as she was dancing principal roles, but receiving the pay of a third-level soloist. This deplorable practice is common in the United States today, but one expects better from a workers' state. Promises were made to "look into it," but nothing came of them. She danced Kitri splendidly if not perfectly, and backstage, Ulanova presented her with a book about Maria Taglioni. It bore the inscription, "I wish Maya Plisetskaya a great life in art."

Plisetskaya's accounts of touring the Soviet Union are replete with unfavorable comparisons of accommodations, flights, and surveillance practices with those of the West. She complains of unclean airplanes subject to delays, littered with the remains of the food passengers brought because none was available on board, and of intrusive surveillance by hotel maids, who counted linens before and after the guest left. Today, such comparisons would be more difficult to make, as Western travel is characterized by dirty, delayed planes, with no food provided on board, and capitalist surveillance is as American as apple pie, finessed via a cell phone or an RFID chip in a library record.

After Stalin's death in 1953 and a minor regime change in the Ministry of Culture, a deputy minister quizzed Plisetskaya to determine whether she could be trusted to travel to India with the Bolshoi. Her *Dying Swan* was the most popular of all the works performed, and once in India, she was sought out by Jawaharlal Nehru for conversation. Maya was unsparing in her rancor in response to being shadowed, as was everyone else in the company, by the NKVD. A former student of Vaganova made her way backstage after a performance to greet Plisetskaya. Her visit was

debited against Maya as an act of insubordination, and she was labeled
nevyezdnaya (unexportable) for future trips abroad.

Stalin's death did not end Stalinism, and the cliques that fought to
take charge did so via battles launched from competing bailiwicks. It
was easy to get caught in the crossfire. During Stalin's era, it was *de rigeur*
for artists invited to foreign embassy parties to turn the invitations down.
The regime punished anyone who attended, as these were viewed as
platforms for the auditioning of anti-Soviet spies. Under Khrushchev,
however, different ministries assumed contradictory stances toward such
invitations. The Ministry of Culture discouraged accepting them, whereas
the Ministry of Foreign Affairs insisted that artists accept. Who says this
nation was a monolith? And what was the invited artist to do? In any
case, the Ministry of Foreign Affairs apparently trumped the Ministry of
Culture, and Maya began attending these insipid events, where the KGB
(successor to the NKVD) gathered fittingly insipid and useless information, adduced primarily to document the gathere's attentiveness to his
duties. Plisetskaya's attending such affairs scored her the needed points,
resulting in opportunities to perform.

Plisetskaya was cast as the girl-bird Syuimbike in Yakobson's inventive piece *Shurale*, but was still not chosen to travel with the company to
Holland, Greece, China, or Sweden. At embassy parties, admirers would
demand to know why she hadn't visited their country, danced in their
exquisite theater, etc. Her exclusion from travel took place side by side
with national newsreels featuring her dancing. She was not excluded
from parties with the top rank officials of the *nomenklatura*, and their
friendliness made her question whether they were aware of her difficulties with the mid-level bureaucrats. As she eventually learned, "nice" is
not always synonymous with "good." Mita's husband, Grisha Levitin,
told her, "A man from the services whispered in my ear yesterday, 'Your
famous relative, the ballerina, will never travel anywhere. That's certain.
There's a ban on her.'"[8] When the full company was slated to take *Romeo
and Juliet, Swan Lake, Giselle,* and *Fountain of Kakhchisarai* to London, the
tour notice listed all the company soloists *except* Plisetskaya, renowned
for her interpretation of at least two of the works on the program. For
having come to her aid in asking to be permitted to travel there, a theater
acquaintance, Victor Gontar, Khrushchev's son-in-law, was not welcomed
into his father-in-law's house for a year, and a secretary who allowed
Maya to telephone the KGB official reputed to have ordered the travel
ban was fired.

Understanding that "success is the best revenge" in the game of
"Who gets Whom," Plisetskaya requested to dance *Swan Lake* at home
while the first cast was on tour. Her request was granted, and the performance drew an audience of supporters, with the Moscow appearance
shining a light on the government's decision to scratch her name from
the London cast. Plisetskaya gave her best performance ever to a packed

house. Servov, the KGB minister whose office she had called via his secretary's telephone line, attended the show with his wife. Those who clapped too loudly or shouted their approval were hauled out to the lobby by KGB thugs. As fans fought their attackers in the lobby, the event continued as something of a protest. The loudest clappers were interrogated, and Plisetskaya was brought in and "warned" that equal or more vociferous enthusiasm should be pre-emptorily curbed for the second performance, which was attended by Khrushchev himself, accompanied by Prime Minister Itsiro Hatoyama of Japan. He also attended the third performance, this time in the company of Muhammed Daoud, King of Afghanistan. It was October 1956, the year of the much-vaunted Khrushchev revelations. Khrushchev convened a meeting to hear General Serov's surveillance report on Maya Plisetskaya, served up to justify the travel ban that kept her from dancing abroad.

Maya met the composer Rodion Shchedrin in 1955. There was an instant mutual attraction, and as he drove her home from dinner with friends, Maya requested that he transcribe the theme from the Charlie Chaplin film "Limelight," so that she might set choreography to it. He agreed and sent it to her, but she was never permitted to use it. In March 1958, Shchedrin saw her perform in *Spartacus*, and called her the following morning to offer praise for her work. In order to prepare music to accompany the production of *Little Humpbacked Horse*, Shchedrin observed company class at the Bolshoi. He invited Maya to go for a drive with him that evening, and with that first date there began a lifelong relationship between the two artists. Shchedrin would share Maya's deep disappointment and sadness at being left behind during the company's very successful tour of France and Belgium. Those who were excluded from travel to Western Europe were sent to perform in Prague. After the Czech tour, Rodion and Maya took a brief vacation. Because they were unmarried, they could not stay together in hotels, and so slept in their car. They suspected that they were being tailed by the KGB when food they had set under the car overnight went missing. Rodion set a "trap," attaching a bell to the pot containing the food they left out the following night. In the event of another theft, the couple would be awakened by the bell and catch the pilferer. In the morning, they awoke to discover the food gone, and a rock in its place weighting down a note that said, "Thanks!" They decided to marry so that they could sleep in hotels while on vacation.

Among Shchedrin and Plisetskaya's friends was Lilya Brik, at whose salon of artists and intellectuals Maya met many of her fans. A campaign began among these supporters to overturn the travel ban against her. At long last, after many phone calls and letters and even a letter of self-criticism that she herself wrote to Khrushchev, Maya was summoned to the office of Alexander Nikolayevich Shelepin, Chairman of the KGB. He extended permission to travel abroad with the proviso that Maya "control her speech and behavior." He said that he was convinced that she would not defect, but mentioned in a jocular tone that they would cut off the hands of that talented pianist husband of hers if she did.

In April 1959, Plisetskaya toured the United States. She danced in *Swan Lake*, the *Stone Flower*, and *Walpurgisnacht*, and Ulanova danced in *Romeo and Juliet* and *Giselle*. Of her performance in New York, the *Herald Tribune's* Walter Terry said, "Plisetskaya is the Callas of ballet."

Like most touring companies, even those that are not shadowed and shepherded around by the KGB, dancers get only the vaguest suggestion of what the country they are visiting is actually like. Schedules, rehearsals, performances, and travel exhaustion are an obstacle to seeing much more than the inside of a hotel room, theater, rehearsal studio, and the main arteries to and from the airport. Still, Plisetskaya found the United States very different from what she had been led to expect. "But one thing was clear to me—immediately!—that America was a working land. Not a land of parasites, as we had been persistently taught since childhood." Those in the Soviet Union who promulgated "socialism in one country" wished to discourage hope for a socialist America, the better to pursue "peaceful coexistence" with what they depicted as a hopelessly and eternally capitalist power. Entire careers rested on that counterrevolutionary misappraisal.

In Paris, *Swan Lake* received 27 curtain calls. When Plisetskaya asked how French audiences liked her, the renowned French dancers Yvette Chauviré and Jean Babilée offered the opinion that the dancer had forced the audience to transfer its attention from abstract technique to soul and plasticity,[9] and overlooked what Maya saw as her imperfect bourrées because they were so intent on the angle of her swan's neck or the line of the arms. Among those who admired Maya's arms in Paris, was the actress Ingrid Bergman, who flew to the city especially to see Maya dance. They met at Maxim's, where Bergman said to her "You told me about love without a single word."[10]

Plisetskaya met the artist Salvador Dali, and was introduced to the couturière Coco Chanel by the *eminence grise* of the European dance world, Serge Lifar.

On the condition that Plisetskaya dance the role of Phrygia, Sol Hurok proposed that the Bolshoi bring a version of *Spartacus* by Leonid Yakobson to the United States in the fall of 1962. Yakobson's work was inventive, inspired, and remarkable for, among other things, marrying a step to each musical note. Maya had the privilege of working with Yakobson off and on for four decades. His creativity, artistry, stamina, and willingness to defend and fight for his visionary work fortified and inspired her.

The obvious question that comes to mind is "Why didn't Plisetskaya defect when she had the opportunity?" She wasn't a communist or a Stalinist, and the capitalist countries had every intention of courting her precisely because the Soviet Union had banned or restricted her work. In a partial answer to that question, Plisetskaya writes:

> In Pushkin's day, a nobleman's word of honor was more reliable than a Swiss bank account. I've read a lot about the honesty of the Decembrists, how faithful they were to their word, how they did not lie to Tsar Nicholas, did not try to twist the truth in order to lighten their prison sentences.[11]

And then there was the Bolshoi Theater. Its stage was like a womb, the only warm hearth to which Maya could always return no matter what. Of the Bolshoi, she writes, "...there was no stage so comfortable, the most comfortable in the entire solar system, in the entire universe, as the Bolshoi!"

In 1985, Plisetskaya was the recipient of the Soviet Union's most prestigious award, the Hero of Socialist Labor.[12]

She further writes:

> Maybe future generations will live freely and simply like cranes and swans, without visas, applications, travel commissions, idiotic limits on days, ridiculous forms...And then, maybe those who left won't play the national hero, proudly sashaying from state-supplied limousines to television cameras, and murmur to the bootlicking, shamelessly bootlicking—reporters about their exploit: leaving in time, running off, being sensible, and now returning with foreign passports and bursting with the greatness of their own heroism.[13]

12

Carlos Acosta

It seems extraordinary to think that Carlos Acosta, the very embodiment of balletic machismo, had never danced the lead in Kenneth MacMillan's *Romeo and Juliet* before this season; the role of the passionate young street fighter seems to be made for him. On Saturday evening (11th March 2006)—beg, borrow or steal a ticket—he gives the second only of two scheduled performances. He's dancing with Tamara Rojo, and the encounter promises to melt the gilt from the proscenium arch. Currently in terrific form, Acosta is the most recklessly ardent of lovers, dashing off bravura leaps and turns with stylish insouciance. Rojo, meanwhile, is a luminous and heartbreaking Juliet, and around them the Royal Ballet soloists spark and blaze...MacMillan's Verona is the perfect antidote to the British winter. There are blizzards forecast. Feel the heat.

—Luke Jennings, *London Observer*, March 5, 2006.[1]

Affectionately called "The Harrier Jet," "Air Acosta," "The Parachute," and "Lethal Weapon," Carlos Acosta was born on June 2, 1973, in Los Pinos, a tiny neighborhood on the outskirts of Havana, Cuba. His father, Pedro Acosta Acosta, was a truck driver; his mother, Dulce Maria Quesada Igualada, worked outside the home. He had two sisters at home, and five brothers and three sisters who were his father's children. Carlos was closest with his eldest sister, Berta Acosta Quesada. Marilin Acosta Quesada was the next oldest. When he was eight, Carlos' mother was hospitalized and then bedridden after surgery for a brain tumor. His father was serving a two-year prison sentence for a truck accident caused by drunken motorcyclists who ran a red light, in which one was killed. At 16, Berta had to do all the cooking and laundry. Later, at 26, the very sensitive and intelligent young woman exhibited symptoms of

Carlos Acosta in *Prodigal Son*. Photo credit: Asya Verzhbinsky.

schizophrenia. A schizophrenic aunt had committed suicide. Doctors concluded that the pressures of a hardscrabble upbringing were compounded
by Berta's genetic inheritance. Today, she is able to control her symptoms
with medication. Acosta says that he was raised in a humble environment,
but his family has had everything it needed. They never starved, and he
emphasizes that the poverty where he grew up was in no way comparable
to the abysmal levels in Mexico City or Brazil. Even when they had
nothing for breakfast but sugared water, they considered that enough.
They were happy.

In the 1980s, Carlos and his friends were learning break dance moves. When he began to hang around with guys who skipped school and stole fruit, his father stepped in. Desperate, Pedro asked a neighbor, Candida, "What would keep Carlos out of trouble?" She suggested Alejo Carpentier, the ballet school that her sons attended. Carlos auditioned in bathing trunks, and was accepted. At 10, he began ballet class, protesting to his father—because he wanted to play soccer instead. His father said, "Cuba needs soccer players like Norway needs bullfighters."[2] The newest boy stood at the barre doing "that tiresome movement." Accustomed to break dance steps, he expressed his exasperation by doing his plié in two counts. He would not dignify the silly exercise with a scintilla of artistry.

Neighborhood boys taunted him, calling him "Alicia Alonso." After three years of spotty attendance and doing his own thing, the school reluctantly pronounced Carlos an unworthy student: he failed to show up for performances, leaving his partners stranded. At half hour to curtain, the school would send out a search party. Inquiries about his son's whereabouts would prompt Pedro to grab the nearest "persuader"—a belt, a machete, a cable—and beat his son. Of the hardheaded "sculptor of my career,"[3] Carlos says, "Man, I was really scared of him. Once I told him, 'I want to be a normal person.' He pointed to the people in the street and said, 'Like them, with no future?'"[4]

Waking at five A.M. for school, Carlos then took three buses, with long waits between each one, to the studio. "I'd fall asleep and wake up at the end of the line. So I'd go fishing or play soccer with my friends." His truancy would have gotten him thrown out of most U.S. schools. He admitted that had he been a girl, he would have been kicked out in Cuba too. As a talented boy, he was not thrown out—exactly. At 13, he passed the qualifying exam, and was transferred to an academy in Villa Clara, but on arrival found that nobody expected him. With no classes at his level, he was asked to leave. He and Pedro slept on the bus station floor for two nights waiting for the next bus home.

Another "presence" in the Acosta home was Pedro's faith in the obscurantist practice of Santería based on the animist beliefs of Nigerian Yoruba tribes, whose slave descendants brought it to Cuban plantations in the sixteenth and seventeenth centuries. To hide it from Christian slavers, each Yoruba *orisha* was paired with a saint. Followers are assigned an orisha who best matches his or her personality and character. Not perfect, as are saints, they have singular attributes and powers but are prone to human folly. Ogun, Pedro's orisha, a warrior who helps others realize their human capacities, is also the god of secrets. His weakness is the alternate side of his strength: a tendency toward violence.

I grew up afraid of him [Pedro]. That made me lonely...very confused...As a defense mechanism, you put it away. I refuse to think about it, even now... But there are many layers.[5]

A Babalua assigned Carlos Elegua, the man-child diety of mischief but also the god of destiny, invoked to open a path of opportunity. Should he complain of pain, his father will make a small offering to San Lázaro. "I don't ask him what he does. That is secret. Some [followers] promise they will grow their hair or sacrifice a chicken,"[6] Carlos said, rolling his eyes, then collapsing back onto the sofa with laughter, still in pain.

Pedro enrolled Carlos in La Escuela Vocacional del Arte boarding school in Pinar del Rio. Carlos slept on his brother's floor on the weekends. Placed on probation, and at 13 finally having to prove himself, Carlos changed his attitude toward ballet. Ballet Nacional de Cuba came through with *Flower Festival in Genzano* and *Don Quixote*, and Acosta says he "fell in love" with the "tricks." He saw that by working hard he could be one of those dancers. He watched videos of the Cuban dancer Alberto Terrero and Mikhail Baryshnikov, Peter Schaufuss, and Fernando Bujones.

> You'd see a double cabriole and think, "if Baryshnikov could do this, then I'll try!" Most difficult to accept was that princely roles were only danced by the blue-eyed, blond males and not dark-skinned ones—even in Cuba.[7]

Among Latin American nations, Cuba stands out as the most advanced for having successfully combated machismo. Thanks to five decades of massive mobilizations led by the Federation of Cuban Women, Cuba is now one of the few countries in the world where *all* women are considered equal with men. They have child care, birth control, and abortion options, free education through graduate school, and equal rights on the job. Though machismo is widely repudiated, attitudinal traces remain, and so Carlos guessed that the very last thing a Cuban father would wish for was that his son become a ballet dancer. Pedro was a truck driver, and Acosta emphasizes that while it is not necessarily true that a truck driver is uncultured, in Pedro's case, he was unfamiliar with the world of ballet. As a young man he had admired it, but during Pedro's youth in the pre-Revolutionary era, the art form was inaccessible to him because he was Black.

Carlos says:

> One of the things that Fidel Castro and the Revolution introduced was that talent, not money, was important. Everybody has the right to be educated. Cuba has only twelve million people, but its dancers, athletes, and musicians are extraordinary. At the 1992 Olympics, Cuba won the fifth greatest number of gold medals. This tiny island! It shows how letting talent develop can be wonderful. Cuba produces many good male dancers. Yes, the teaching is good, but there are other factors. Cuba is a big family, and it is the same in the ballet school...they are good at dishing out the discipline. In this profession, discipline is very important...Dance is in the air, people are relaxed.[8]

Carlos was completely shocked by his father's decision to send him to ballet school. Perhaps the decision was *calculated* to shock Carlos. It was the decade before "the special period," when the two crop economy inherited from the pre-revolutionary colonizers bound the country hand and foot to Soviet aid. A demoralized segment of the population coveted the "better" life in Miami. For youth, turning away from the revolutionary process often meant refusing to achieve, using illegal drugs, and building rafts on which they hoped to float to Miami. There, they expected to find more drugs, luxuries, and support for their plans, however grandiose or modest. Pedro was probably not so calculating as to try to shock his son. His aims were uncomplicated. He wanted Carlos in an environment where he could thrive.

It remains a shock to Carlos that he prepared himself for a career that has taken him to the stage of the Royal Ballet. His incredulity sends him back to his pre-dance childhood, as if it were a primal scene violated by his success. "Some of my friends became thieves, delinquents, took off on rafts," he says, squinting slightly, as if trying to picture himself among them. "That's why he was making such a great effort to play the father's role. He would have behaved in a similar way if it had been fencing or basketball, but the first thing he encountered was ballet because of the neighbor downstairs, and so it was ballet."[9]

In 2003, Acosta produced "Tocororo," a loosely autobiographical mix of mime, spoken word, Yoruba-inspired music, dance, and classical and contemporary ballet. It presents the salutary if dissonant role of ballet in his life. It was performed in Cuba, with Fidel Castro in the audience, and by an all-Cuban cast of 30 dancers and musicians at Sadler's Wells and the London Coliseum. Acosta hopes to take it to Broadway when Cuban performers can travel to New York without first having to disavow their homeland.

Acosta says that all of his teachers contributed something—nurturing his technique, inspiring courage, or educating him to believe in himself. First was Lupe Calzadilla, mother of two famous Cuban dancers now living and dancing in the United States: Lorena and Lorna Feijoo. Today, Calzadilla divides her time between Cuba and teaching at San Francisco's City Ballet School. His teacher in Pinar del Rio was Juan Carlos Gonzales, who helped Carlos develop technique. "I was only 13, but he started to pay attention to me and set choreography for me and we were a big group—14 boys—but he made me do things beyond my level, and encouraged me to grow, and that's why I started to love it." Carlos realized he had potential when he overheard Gonzales saying so. Gonzales pressed him: "If you can do it, do it one better, and then keep on going."[10]

Acosta credits his having lasted those three years to his natural affinity for ballet. Gonzales convinced him that ballet deserved his full attention, focus, and commitment. Because of him, Carlos was able to attend the National School at 14, and pass the test qualifying him for the next level. "When I was 16, Ramona de Saa took me to Turin through a cultural exchange with Teatro Nationale di Torino. I studied and did mostly corps work. I returned to Turin, but dancing soloist roles. I was there 10 months, returning to Havana in July 1990. They proposed that I compete in the Prix de Lausanne, and I won the Gold Medal." Acosta went on to win the Italian Vignale Dance Prize.

"I was still in the school when I returned. I did my first year there, my second in Italy and my last in Cuba, condensed so that I could go to Venezuela and the Grand Prix at the Fourth Biennial Concours International de Danse in September 1990." He won the Gold Medal at the Grand Prix and the Frederic Chopin Medal, a Polish prize for artistry, the Men's Prize in the Young Talent Competition in Positano, and the Italian Osimodanze Prize in 1991. He won Cuba's Union of Writers and Artists competition, and a dance fellowship from the Princess Grace Foundation in 1995, as well as the 2003 National Dance Award from the UK Critics Circle.

Carlos finished his training with Lázaro Carreño.

> I learned to be quick, technical, and Lázaro respected me very much. He would mark a combination. I would do it alone first and then with everyone else. He could have behaved very differently towards me because I had many awards. He could have tried to put me in my place; but instead he encouraged me. He'd correct me, help me, and had a positive outlook towards me. To this day, I feel indebted to him and his classes.[11]

He praises Fernando Alonso, who designed the curriculum of the Cuban school, famously inflecting the Ceccheti and Vaganova methods with a Latin sensibility. Alonso took a scientific, materialist approach to his work. "When he taught us turns, he taught us physics so we would understand the science," says Acosta. "He was brilliant!"[12]

Acosta auditioned for the 1991–92 season of the English National Ballet. "[Artistic Director] Ivan Nagy saw me and wanted me as a principal." At 18, Carlos became the company's then-youngest member *and* principal dancer. He partnered Eva Evdokimova and Ludmila Semenyaka, and danced the Prince in Ben Stevenson's *Nutcracker*. Working with dancers trained in a variety of styles and schools amplified his range. After an injury, he returned to Cuba in 1992, joining the BNC for its 1992–93 season. In 1993, the BNC went to Madrid, where he danced in *Giselle, Don Quixote*, and *Swan Lake*. Few dancers, even *danseurs nobles*, find themselves with principal contracts at so young an age. How did Acosta achieve so much when he missed precious studio time in Cuba that students anywhere else would have coveted? "I was lucky. I had guidance, and everything happened at the perfect time; I took every opportunity, won all the competitions. When things looked dark, and I was about to veer off the path, something or someone arrived to put me back on track."[13]

Among those who arrived was Ben Stevenson, then artistic director of Houston Ballet, who saw Acosta at English National Ballet. Stevenson said, "I've seen just about all the young dancers, and I think he's by far the most exciting...I thought he was remarkable. He had amazing technical skills. He also had charisma."[14] Stevenson invited Acosta to join Houston Ballet. While in Spain, Carlos applied for a U.S. visa. He returned to Cuba for a visit and then continued on to the United States on the Spanish-issued visa. He left cheered on by the Cuban government and Alicia Alonso. Cuba had decided to export dancers in the same spirit that it has shared teachers and medical and technical personnel—as a gesture and an example of goodwill. Generally, Cuba's goodwill ambassadors travel to countries in the semi-colonial world. This was the first instance of a dancer going to the United States, not as a defector but as a supporter of Cuba's 1959 revolution.

Acosta made his Houston debut dancing the Cavalier in Nutcracker. While with the company, he danced in *Swan Lake*, *La Bayadère*, *Don Quixote*, Stevenson's *Britten Pas de Deux*, Harald Lander's *Etudes*, Jiri Kylian's *Symphony in D*, and the role of the Chosen One in *Spring*. He created the role of Frederick in Ben Stevenson's *Dracula* in 1997, and Misgir in the premiere of Stevenson's *The Snow Maiden*, partnering Nina Ananiashvili in 1998.

Lauren Anderson, Houston Ballet's most famous female principal dancer, is a frequent radio sports show guest because she predicts football game wins with 80% or better accuracy. Sports fansare drawn to Houston Ballet by Anderson's dual reputation as a dancer *and* football prophetess. She retires this season, the only African-American female principal dancer in a majority-white U.S. classical ballet company. Acosta became Houston Ballet's second Black principal. What changed when Acosta arrived? "Well, for one thing," Anderson jokes, "everyone started rolling their 'r's, and we watched a star evolve. He would do things that would raise the hairs on the back of your neck."

"Ben made it clear to Carlos that it's not about a bunch of big jumps and turns. You have to become 'The Prince' and at the same time be able to dance Basilio [the male who is a barber lead in *Don Quixote*]." Andrew Edmonson, Houston Ballet's Director of Marketing and Public Relations, agrees, "Ben's genius helped him find that. Lauren got a sensational partner in the bargain, and we all got to watch a great partnership blossom. At first, it was 'Anything you can do, I can do better.'" Anderson adds, "Ben told us: 'Don't let it get to you; you have to control *it*, you can't let *it* control you! Don't kill us, *or* each other. Learn how to be the two people who dance *together*.'"[15]

"Of course, that didn't stop Lauren from doing triple fouettés on a dime!" Edmonson quips. Lauren says Ben cautioned her

"Carlos has all the great steps, so you have to be the coquette." I would do single/triple for my fouettés to keep up with him and then relax for 16. So I'm a little cocky, but he gets two codas...He walked out and took off at a hundred miles an hour. He could be a little poopster, too, and say he didn't want to dance with me. He danced with Janie Parker and Martha Butler. And it wasn't about me being Black either.[16]

Edmonson explains, "He found in Lauren a partner with whom he could do *anything*. That can be scary." Lauren continues, "He still had peach fuzz when he went to London," "He got to do great modern and contemporary work while he was here," says Edmonson, "Christopher Bruce's *Rooster*, and Glen Tetley's *Rite of Spring*, which was killer!" Anderson adds, "All turned in, exactly what we were *not* used to doing." "He leapt in from the wings," says Edmonson. "—an explosion of energy, by far my favorite along with Robert Tewsley, doing *Sacre de Printemps*." Anderson recalls, "Carlos was *never* 'I know everything.' He was good at taking direction, even if he didn't agree. He has to make it make sense in his head. He's very smart and very positive, and so how can you not like working with him?"

Stevenson worried that Carlos could be tempted to "guest" too much. Edmonson remembers him saying, "If you're an artist of his caliber, it can stunt your development to spend your life on a plane and be without choreographers who know you making dances on you." Stevenson set the ballet *Dracula* on Acosta, and would have probably liked to have kept on going. *Snow Maiden* was a Stevenson piece danced by Acosta and Nina Ananiashvili, as well as Anderson. Lauren was blunt with Acosta: "Don't wait for Nina. Use me. We are a lot alike." Carlos did. Anderson and Edmonson agree that while professional on every level, Acosta is accessible, down to earth, and as practical as he is high minded. Anderson laughs in agreement that "he's Carlos from the block!"

Andrew Edmonson adds, "We see a lot of talented dancers here, but not a lot who see the big picture. You would see Carlos take young dancers, and awaken them to their gifts." Edmonson was impressed that in a competitive environment, Acosta did not hesitate to help those who, given more ambition, could have become rivals. "Where did that quality come from?" Anderson said, "He has a love of life, people, and dance. Some people got a little extra attention, an extra onstage glance. Everyone got what they wanted or needed from Carlos. I didn't have to hold back the energy. I could let go. I got to be vulnerable. There was someone onstage who could be 'bigger' than I was. I really *do* miss him." While on the subject of Black dancers, Anderson said, "We had a Black contingent at one time. Eight of us! Giving me the role of Sugar Plum Fairy with a white partner was one of Ben's biggest risks. There were letters..." Edmonson adds that many people misjudged Ben. "He was white, older, an Englishman heading up a U.S. ballet company" in what is viewed as a conservative part of the country.

People mistakenly assumed that Ben was unwilling to take risks. One of Ben's "risks" was casting a Black Romeo with a white Juliet, but Houston is where Carlos could do a radio interview in Spanish and go on TV dancing Don Q with Lauren during Black History Month.[17]

How was it when Carlos left? Edmonson says, "There wasn't a sense of 'How dare you leave me?' It was more like 'We want this to be your home,' and contractually, while Ben was the Artistic Director of Houston Ballet, Acosta remained a member of the company while dancing with the Royal Ballet."

"At the Kennedy Center during Don Q," remembers Anderson,

Carlos turns to me, and whispers, "This is for us, *Mamí*: it's our last opening night. I love you." I whispered back, "I love you, too." Then he takes my hand and shoves me forward. Forward, and then back and I saw that he had a tear in his eyes. Then out we went. This was not easy; we were screaming and crying during the whole performance. We used to scream at each other! Many a dress rehearsal I sat in the dressing room crying. He'd come back and say something else and I'd be, "Don't talk to me!" We let each other know how we felt immediately, instead of waiting for a better time than a dress rehearsal or an opening night—and *that* can be dangerous.[18]

People assumed they were lovers. "We never complicated it with anything like that. We had too much at stake. We spent *hours* on flights, talking." Much of what they discussed touched on the history of Black people in Cuba and the United States. Anderson said, "I was sheltered from a lot of prejudices, but they managed to seep into my life." Edmonson explains, "There are not a lot of Black dancers at auditions. You can easily feel excluded before the game starts." Anderson counters,

If you look like Carlos, you don't feel excluded. To be good at anything, if you have a bit of talent, you work at making it look good. It's an illusion. Carlos had the body and talent, even if he didn't have the drive, will and want. But Daddy came at him with that machete and some other stuff, and he found his ambition![19]

Edmonson continues:

"I'm gay, and after his having said something to correct a misimpression that dance is only for gays [with respect to men], I explained how aspects of what he said could offend gay people. He was very touched and very open to that feedback. That openness is part of knowing how to build a career.[20]

Anderson relates travel stories. First stop, Miami: She and Acosta are en route to an engagement in Santiago de Chile. Journalists have amused themselves by presenting as irony Acosta's enthusiasm for what they insist is "capitalist" technology, as if the bankers and landlords had invented the gadgets themselves. "On our way to Chile, we're in

Carlos Acosta. Photo credit: Asya Verzhbinsky.

Miami at a Cuban restaurant. The waiter crumbs the table using a plastic device." Carlos has never seen one of these, and knowing he's in the city where certain Cubans claim to lead a "better" life, shakes his head and exclaims, "Technology!" his shorthand for the Cuban vs. Cuban-*American* "wannabe" phenomenon.

In the crucible of touring, Acosta and Anderson's relationship took on a new aspect. "They were dancing five or ten Don Qs" in a row, says Edmonson. Anderson says of Moscow,

> There was a screamer in the front row every night. Menudo was in the hotel. People were rushing us for autographs. We were dancing at the Bolshoi, and staying at the Metropole. We had interpreters and drivers. They wanted to pay Carlos $3000, and me, $1000. He insisted that they pay us the same, and they did.[21]

Once in the theater,

> we both freaked out because of the raked stage. The one-upsmanship went out the window. We just wanted to do a good show. The applause was phenomenal. Carlos said, "Lauren, this is for the first two Black classical dancers in Moscow!"[22]

Former Houston Ballet dancer Tiekka Prieve (formerly Schofield) became Acosta's girlfriend. Having joined the company in 1988, she was a principal by the time Acosta arrived. Prieve and Acosta danced together for the first time in *Merry Widow,* and Prieve said, "It was a wonderful, comic piece. He had requested to dance with me, and later told me that he had had a crush on me." What was most satisfying about dancing with Acosta?

> Carlos is very passionate, personally and professionally, invested in everyone around him doing their best. You always felt that, for all his talent and being in the spotlight, he was always right there as a cheerleader for everyone, wanting people to succeed by offering confidence, or helping the boys with their tricks or turns. He was always on my side. If I stepped too far up on a piqué, it was never "Oh, you did that" after the show. It was more like, onstage, "Oh," and "Here I am for you."[23]

What was most challenging about dancing with him?

> He really is the center of the vortex. Whether it's the pas de deux from *Diane and Actaeon* or *Le Corsaire,* you are going to pale by comparison. It elevates one's level to dance with someone like that, yet it can be hard on the head trying to match that greatness.[24]

What brought them together?

> He asked me to guest with him in San Antonio, and we're driving back and he's like, "Your boyfriend is so lucky." It was very touching. That's the thing about him—he's very poignant. He spoke—and danced—from his heart. Six months later, I broke up with my boyfriend, and Carlos was like, "Would you like to go out on a date?" He taught me to dance salsa and meringue at the clubs we went to. I learned Spanish. I went to Cuba to meet his family, and they were so warm and welcoming. Berta and Marilin adore Carlos. Marilin is a tease—very witty and uses her wit to keep him in check. Berta is intelligent and reserved, but enjoys a good laugh. Even if their living conditions are not the best, if someone has a tape or a radio, there is music and dancing, and instead of a depressing atmosphere, it's uplifting and I'm sure that's why Carlos maintains such a close connection with his family. I saw him at the Met the other day, and he's still the same guy, connected with his culture; it's like a divining rod for him.[25]
>
> Our relationship lasted about three and a half years. Houston Ballet had always been a stable company, but at that point a number of principals like Janie Parker and Li Cunxin were leaving. There were administration upheavals. I wanted opportunities to travel and see the world, and the number of tours was declining. Carlos asked me to come with him when he went to the Royal, at the same time that he encouraged me to do my own thing. He wanted me there with him in this new experience. You knew he would be successful because of his personality and the force of his talent, but transitions for someone as young as he was are difficult. You're the new one, paying your dues. I danced with other companies in London, and with Scottish Ballet. I had to return to Houston for knee surgery. It was hard to be apart. When we moved to London, it was hard on Carlos—not necessarily the Royal Ballet, but the atmosphere in London.

Holidays were very important to me, but not to Carlos. I wanted to be with my family then, and he wanted to be in Cuba. Many times, I went with him, and missed seeing my own family.[26]

Tiekka's mother developed breast cancer, and she wanted to be closer to her and "reinvest" in what she saw as key: having a family, children, and settling down.

Carlos wanted those things, but wasn't ready. He was rising to the top. He needed to be immersed in his culture when he wasn't at the ballet. I wasn't willing to forfeit those other things, and so I went back to California. I started my new chapter and he continued his. He's making a stellar contribution, and not just because of his talent, but also because of his generosity. He wants to share his culture and knowledge, and has a lot of heart and he gives it, and that speaks enormously of him.

Ben was never one to condone relationships. Taking time to make ours public was harder on me than Carlos. He was positioned, doing every opening night. Being his girlfriend changed how I was cast. It was more detrimental to me. At the same time, I can say that Ben was also very generous. He is so skilled in bringing out the essence of the part you were doing, showing you the physical nature of the music. He has such a beautiful imagination and is able to communicate it. He demands that dance not just be acrobatic or about steps, but about the person doing the steps and the spirit and essence of the steps with music, not a mathematical or acrobatic endeavor.[27]

Prieve is married and has a son named Wilson. When she looks back upon her career, a single performance stands out.

My partner for a performance of *Don Quixote* at the Kennedy Center in Washington, D.C. was Sean Kelly. He came down with strep. I had worked very hard to prepare, and my East Coast family was coming to see me in our one tour that year. Carlos had danced Basilio the night before but offered to step in, which was very generous of him—but that's who he is. Ben said "No," but I went to him and asked. There was no rehearsal. At "half hour" we found out that we were dancing. Perhaps because we were in love we had that sixth sense about each other, but it was one of the best performances of my career. It was the one time that I felt I had matched him in energy and intensity. It was filled with moments where you truly feel that you are floating. Because of his generosity, I could throw myself into it the way you just *throw* yourself into an assemblé. I feel it went so well partly because we didn't rehearse. Working with it from moment to moment made it delicious. There was a resonance with the music, no anticipation, but just living it in the moment, kind of a metaphor for life.[28]

In 1998, Acosta joined the Royal Ballet, making his first appearance with the company in Forsythe's *in the middle, somewhat elevated*, and danced in Nureyev's *Raymonda Act III*, Ashton's *La Fille Mal Gardée*, as well as *Swan Lake*, *Diane and Actaeon* pas de deux, McMillan's *My Brother, My Sisters*, *Giselle*, *Le Corsaire*, *Rhapsody*, *Coppélia*, *Don Quixote*, and Balanchine's *Apollo*, and has performed the works of Nacho Duato and Antony Tudor. He has partnered such Royal Ballet standouts as Darcie Bussell, Marienela Nuñez, Tamara Rojo, as well as Lorna Feijoo and world-renowned dancers such as Sylvie Guillem (in Paris Opera's *Prodigal Son*), Zenaida Yanowsky, and Lauren Cuthbertson (in *Agon*). He made it clear to the Royal, as he had to ENB, that he did not want to be cast exclusively in exotic roles because he is Black, aware that he is dancing prince roles that most Black men never perform. He believes that ballet's racial barriers do not issue from casting decisions so much as the inaccessibility of ballet to Black children because it is perceived as and is a white-dominated art form. Most working class Black families cannot afford ballet school tuition or pointe shoes; why chase a dream that seems to come true only for the elite? Carlos hopes that his example poses a social challenge: "I am a rare animal, indeed. But I believe I am sending out the right message."[29]

Does Carlos want to return to Cuba? Definitely! Then why doesn't he? His departure from Cuba was a first, the first artist released to go to the United States as a cultural ambassador. He was not running away from Cuba's problems: just the opposite—he is sharing the island's best gifts. While he misses his family, he takes very seriously his responsibility to be exactly where he is.

Carlos laughs when he reports that his sisters say he was not very generous—that when he brought home mangoes or guavas, he would keep the biggest for himself. He finds this both amusing and slightly disturbing. He has been very generous with me—with time taken between rehearsals of *La Fille Mal Gardée* and performances of *Swan Lake*, inviting me to a rehearsal of "Fille." He is partnering Marianela Nuñez, and the choreography includes three successive lifts, each higher than the one before. The last is a one-handed *pressage* lift. Acosta's back hurts. He's had four ankle surgeries. He negotiates with the repetiteur: "I'll do the first two, but not the third today." The repetiteur says he must do all three or the rehearsal is over. Carlos gathers his things, signals me that he is leaving, and heads out the door. I assume that after changing, he'll come to collect me. The repetiteur and accompanist wait with me. Finally, the repetiteur suggests that we look for him, and after what becomes an unscheduled back of the house tour, we find Acosta in the Royal's famous canteen, eating a Snowball from the vending machine. He is very hungry, in pain, but smiles when he sees me, and offers me a piece of his Snowball. He apologizes and explains that he left because his back hurt and "if you let them do it, they will *kill* you!"[30]

In his dressing room I ask, "How does it feel to at one moment be on the Royal Opera House stage and then at the next in Cuba?" Glancing toward the voice recorder he has programmed for me, he says,

You learn to pull out one plug and put in another. When you go away, you enjoy the other environment, adapt yourself to it, and become someone else. I have to make a different life here because it's a different environment, so two things have to coexist at the same time. If I spoke perfect English, I'd never find the same words I can find in Spanish. But that's what happens when you have an international career. I try to recapture my original self in Cuba, be with my family, laugh with them, see them happy. My style is to remember who I am or I will get lost in the ephemeral illusions of who I am. I hang out with people who remind me of who I am. Inevitably you will be reminded of the person you are.[31]

He returns to Cuba for refreshment, pleased more than anything to see his family happy. "They love me; I have become everyone's father, even my father's father."

For Carlos, celebrity comes with no small measure of inner conflict, and a responsibility that does not include trying the impossible: being who fans require him to be to meet their own ego needs.

You can't make everyone happy, and not everyone has to love you. Some are looking for the nasty man, and they will find him, because it comes in the same package as the man they admire. They don't know me; they find a way to pull you down, and make you more insecure than how people normally feel. Some try to shape what you are, but I know who I am, and so I keep trying to do what I do best. Since this is not my country, and I don't belong here, and the environment is highly competitive, my tendency is to build a hermit personality around my genuine personality. I just can't be who I am in Havana here. It's like putting on a mask. You have to be polite, play whatever the game is, and when I leave, I can become myself again.[32]

How does this affect relations with friends and lovers? "I haven't been able to find the person I want to settle down with. It's not a question of the environment. If you find the right person, it wouldn't matter where you were: it could be Alaska." About friends, he says,

You learn how to approach people in a different way. It's a good, not a bad thing. It takes two people to understand differences; no matter what culture. You know when you are confronted with someone whom you have to try to understand. I pull the plug and put in a different plug. A lot of people can't cope with the drastic social differences. If I had my own family, that would be one thing—a framework, a haven. But when you are alone, you are forced to become better at this kind of understanding, because it's all you have and it's your only companion.[33]

He is also forced to become better at his work, because it too is his constant companion. For him, the alternative to moving forward is to return to Cuba or court depression. "Because a dancer's life is difficult and competitive, one tends to diminish the stature of any competitor, convincing yourself that they are not good enough—a subjective reaction present in nearly everyone." He says it's especially difficult for women because it requires believing you can be your best, and society's sexism makes women feel less worthwhile from birth, so they have to reeducate themselves to appreciate their own value.

Carlos rises from his chair and I see him fussing a trifle coyly with what look like three rolled-up charts on the top shelf above his dressing table. I ask him what they are. He pulls one down and says, "This is a poster of a photograph of me in Cuba that the Royal had specially commissioned." I look at the photograph and gasp: In it, Acosta appears to have leapt off the strip of beach beneath him high into the air. Majestic clouds backlight his head. Carlos smiles, and says, "It's for you!" I am overwhelmed: "But you only have three." "Yes, I have three, and this one is yours," he says, explaining the fundamentals of subtraction. He accompanies me downstairs, taking me backstage. Technicians are working in a roped-off quadrant. They signal that it's okay to cross the stage. Carlos offers me his hand as I prepare to step over the rope. I accept it, lifting and inclining my head, casting my eye a foot above and a bit beyond my extended hand, as I learned to do from my first ballet teacher, Nina Anderson, a former Ziegfield Girl. I lift my knee and extend my leg and pointed foot into *pas de cheval* before stepping over the rope onto the stage floor. Carlos Acosta's face lights up with the Chaplin-like warmth that makes him irresistible. He nods approvingly. "So you take *class*!" he says, as generously and encouragingly as anyone could wish for.

13

Muriel Maffre

But it was the glorious Muriel Maffre who reigned supreme. Her performance in the second movement [of "Symphony in C"], danced with heart-stopping purity and pathos...was unforgettable.

—Rick Nelson, *Miami Star-Tribune*, October 25, 2000[1]

Best of all was magisterial Muriel Maffre, in demeanor and bearing, the very archetype of a ballerina, bringing unmatched elegance to the Snow Queen, with one of San Francisco Ballet's finest partners, the warm and unaffected, Benjamin Pierce, as her King.

—Rachel Howard, *San Francisco Chronicle*, December 13, 2001[2]

[In Stanton Welch's "Taiko,"] Maffre extends her long arms like baskets of hope.

—Marilyn Tucker, *Contra Costa Times*, May 1, 1999[3]

"Muriel is a beautiful plant, but she cannot dance." With that pronouncement, Christiane Vaussard, Muriel Maffre's teacher, was preparing her mother for her daughter's eventual expulsion from the Paris Opera's prestigious ballet academy, which came when she was 16, with no notice, written or otherwise, to her parents. If Muriel felt cheated and bereft, she had sufficient self-assurance to find another way to dance.

I failed the exam for the company. It was dramatic. It was hurtful, but deciding to become a dancer had happened naturally, and I felt it was unfair because I was growing so fast; I needed a little time. I never doubted that I had something. I had to find another way to learn more and work; so many people had confidence in me.[4]

Muriel Helene Marie Maffre was born on March 19, 1966, to Monique Berteaux Maffre and Bernard Maffre, a newspaper executive, in Enghein-les-Bains, a northern suburb of Paris. When she was two, the family, which

Muriel Maffre in *Continuum*. **Photo credit: Chris Hardy.**

included her older sister Isabelle and would later include Chan, a brother
adopted from Korea, moved to L'Etang-la-Ville, about a half hour west of
Paris on the Seine. The Maffres descended from Huguenots, Protestants
who suffered centuries of oppression owing to what the Catholic aristocracy chose to regard as their rebellious religious views. They farmed, had
small enterprises, and adhered to a code of conduct that valued modesty,
asceticism, and a simple lifestyle, believing that hard work brings rewards.
So it came as a surprise when Monique Maffre enrolled in ballet class
right after Isabelle was born. She participated in performances in which
her daughters also danced. Later, in San Francisco, she and Muriel
took class together at LINES, where according to her daughter, "People
marveled."

Muriel and Isabelle started ballet with Nelly Delanou when Muriel
was four.

> My earliest recollection had to do with moving, movement, not having to
> talk, being able to just move. I had no idea whatsoever of what ballet was,
> nor had I seen it before; it was the small scale activity of going to class in
> the village and performing at the end of the year. Right at the beginning, at
> age four, by the end of the year, I was performing. After the performance,
> I felt powerful.[5]

In a film where she dances on a playground stage at age 11, the viewer can clearly see the very determined, self-possessed girl she was.

How did growing up as a Huguenot affect Maffre's relationship to ballet?

> The values that inevitably come out of that are not necessarily compatible with the ballet art form. They are about asceticism, emotional restraint and work. Anything superficial is just brushed aside. Artifice and make believe don't fit in with that culture. Also, there is a big resistance to hierarchy.[6]

Those contradictions could have proved too daunting, and Maffre might have stopped dancing. However, as the motivation to move and dance ballet took up residence within her, she became accomplished at remaining connected to the values associated with hard work, at the same time that she transcended the noumenal world, by consciously establishing a relationship with her intimate self.

Muriel was not the first member of her family to have a successful career in the performing arts. Her uncle, Didier Sandre, is a very well known actor. At 18, her father, Bernard, helped begin a theatrical group at his church.[7] It was in that group that he met and came to know Monique.

One day when Muriel was nine, she and her mother were running errands in Paris and passed by the Place de l'Opera Metro station. Monique asked Muriel whether she wanted to see the Opera. Muriel didn't understand what her mother was talking about. It was Monique's understated way of introducing her daughter to the Paris Opera Ballet School. She submitted Muriel's application, and at 10 years old, Muriel entered the school.

Muriel joined a complement of 600 applicants who were checked for height, extension, flexibility, and bone structure. There was a three-month provisional term, after which the school chose who would stay. Muriel was qualified to skip the first level on the recommendation of Claude Bessy, who was the school's director. Besides Vaussard, her teachers would be Claire Motte and Jacqueline Moreau. On her own, she studied with Claudie Jacquelin, who trained her according to the Russian school. Maffre regrets that Jacquelin didn't push her more technically, but believes that, as a very natural dancer, Jacquelin's emphasis didn't run in that direction. Having skipped the first level caught up with Muriel later when she had to repeat the third. At 14, she underwent a sudden growth spurt, losing a great deal of strength and coordination, and at 16, having failed the company entrance exam, was dismissed from the school. "I had to find another way to learn more and work." The "other way" was found at the National Conservatory for Advanced Studies, which offered tracks in Music, Dance, and Drama in a two-year curriculum with three hours of ballet classes daily, and four hours of pas de deux classes weekly. At National Conservatory, Christiane Vaussard once again became Muriel's teacher, having supported her decision to go there, knowing that she was a hard worker who loved the work, and that loving it was the key to achieving her goals.

While at the Conservatory, Maffre studied with Alain Davesne, Raymond Franchetti, Jacqueline Rayet, Yvonne Meyer, and Jose Ferran. She also continued her classes with Claudie Jacquelin. She graduated with a First Prize with Honors, and was immediately hired by Hamburg Ballet in 1983, where she remained for a year, and values greatly what she learned from Truman Finney, the company's then-ballet master.

Maffre was invited to join Ballet de Monte Carlo, which Pierre Lacotte and his wife Ghislaine Thesmar were hoping to revive, but circumstances required that they postpone their plans, and so Muriel found herself with a year off. She returned to France in June 1984, making guest appearances with other companies, and then in October of that year, entered the Paris Opera Competition. Claudie Jacquelin became her coach. The training was intense. For three months, they worked on every detail of the "White Swan" solo, which was part of her repertory, along with excerpts from *Carnaval de Venice*, and "L'Ombre" from Serge Lifar's *Les Mirages* (the Yvette Chauviré version). Muriel would go to Paris, take one or two classes, and then meet Jacquelin at her dance school in St Germain-en-Laye. They would take a section at a time, work on technique and the artistic elements, then discuss the work and work some more. They fine-tuned character development, entrances, and bows. Jacquelin would give Muriel keys to the studio to review the previous week's work on her own.

Winning the competition's gold medal became a vindication of Muriel's choices and decisions. Muriel danced in Spain for two months as a guest soloist in Zaragoza with Christina Miñana's company, and then entered the Moscow Competition in June 1985 with Jacqueline Rayet as her coach. Because of Rayet's other obligations during the competition, Monique and Claudie remained with Muriel in Moscow for the first two weeks. During the third week, as a member of the competition's jury, Rayet was not very available. Muriel did very well during the first two weeks. "During the last week, my interpreter was with me all the time, driving me a little crazy, making an unnecessary fuss over me," Maffre explains. "I danced 'Black Swan' and *Raymonda* for the last round. It did not go well, and that was a huge disappointment." In the soloist category, men and women competed for the same prize. Maffre was the only woman soloist, and received a diploma, though there had been discussion about giving her a bronze.

I remember falling asleep on one of the benches in the Bolshoi while waiting for the results, which were announced at three a.m. Competitions are incredible; you develop quickly under the pressure, and meet lots of people. The good things are the experience, prep time, working to develop as a soloist and the exposure. The bad things are: How can you value someone's dancing, and assign a mark to it? There are lots of politics involved, depending on the location. In Russia, a Japanese dancer never wins. If they want to give a political favor to France, they award a prize to the French. But within that framework, it is fair. Yuri Possokhov and Alex Ratmansky remembered me from the competition. Also, a few years ago, when I traveled to the Ukraine with Yuri's group, I visited with Vadim Pissarev, who was one of the medalists at the competition. It's a huge challenge, and if you rise to it, you get stronger in your mind, it tests your endurance, stress management—a crash course in what you face in your career.[8]

The competition also helped Maffre locate the right star by which to navigate accumulating career pressures and steer her own development. How did her approach to her work change?

I'd choose a direction and go all the way with it, and then realize that maybe it was not the right choice. There was a huge disappointment [with] the reali-zation that something I believed in or thought would work for me—didn't, and the shock that I didn't realize sooner, or that people didn't guide me. I eventually saw that nobody's going to understand what I want to do, what my standards are for my dancing. For example, when a teacher or a choreographer approaches you and says, "Dance full out and I'll tell you when it's too much," and then they forget that they had that conversation with you, and you perform that way, and they say, "Uh oh, what is she doing there?" You have to trust your own eye, you have to be vigilant, and educate yourself.[9]

Many dancers find it difficult to watch their performances on video or DVD. Maffre says,

I do watch myself on tape. I've become more accepting, less obsessed about things. I enjoy it more after I let a little bit of time pass. When the feelings are too fresh in your mind and body, what you see on the tape oftentimes doesn't match what you feel as the performer. There was a time when I would never watch a taped performance in the middle of a run; now I have more maturity and want to make changes in a timely manner if necessary, working in detail and trying ideas.[10]

In June 1985, Maffre began dancing with Ballet de Monte Carlo. During three of the five years that she danced with the company, it was under the direction of Pierre Lacotte, who brought Maffre in as a soloist. "He trusted me, believed in me, and cast me," Maffre says. After two years, he promoted her to Principal.

Pierre was interested in reviving repertory from the Romantic Era, as well as from the Ballet Russes. He invited many young choreographers to create new works. After five years, I felt that I needed to expand my horizons. I had

heard about San Francisco Ballet through French dancers, Karine Averty and
Jean-Charles Gil, who had danced there. The company came to Paris in 1989.
I flew up to Paris, and took one or two classes with the company and met
with Helgi Tomasson, the company's Artistic Director. I invited him to see
me perform the next week. Unfortunately, the performance was cancelled.
Fortunately, I happened to run into him on the street in Monte Carlo, and
we ended up in my living room watching videos. A few months later, he
called me to offer a contract.[11]

It was not a difficult decision for Maffre to join San Francisco
Ballet.

I felt that I had been in that world of dance in France for too long; it was so
familiar to me; the background of the Paris Opera history was following
me. Helgi was going to give me a soloist contract, and then I insisted, and
he was able to find a principal contract, which was gutsy of him because he
had not seen me onstage, and gutsy of me because I didn't know whether
I would be at the same level as the company was. I arrived in February,
1990. The company was performing William Forsythe's *in the middle, somewhat elevated*. I had been dancing it in Monte Carlo, so within two weeks,
I was onstage with Christopher Boatwright. That helped me become
accepted. I felt comfortable right away. I was thrilled from the beginning.
It was an exciting environment where I could learn a lot: The lifestyle, new
people, and I knew enough English.[12]

Maffre says that when she arrived at San Francisco Ballet, she wanted
to dance like American dancers. She wanted their strength and power and
began to move in that direction. After seeing tapes of her performances,
she realized that the style did not fit her, but there was something there
that could be incorporated into her own dancing without turning her back
on her training and the dancer she was. "That was my journey," she says
of that discovery,

trying to find out what this was all about. What helped me was an encounter
with Alonzo King [Artistic Director of the LINES Contemporary Ballet Company, headquartered at the San Francisco Dance Center in San Francisco,
where he also teaches class]. I loved his teaching. I took class with him during
my free time. My relationship with Alonzo evolved to where he invited me to
perform with his company. After a few performances with LINES, I had to
pull back because of conflict of interest with SFB. In some ways, I felt that
I was betraying Alonzo. After that, it took me awhile to go back to his studio.
Personally, I did not see it as a conflict of interest because they are two very
different kinds of companies. People go to each because of that. Apparently,
there was a fundraising issue.[13]

In Europe, including France, the major companies are state-supported.
Did the problem arise from the fact that dance companies here are supported with private, rather than public funds?

Here it totally has to do with private support. Private funding affects conditions immensely in every aspect from the hiring of talent to the building of repertory.

When I came here I was very impressed with and inquisitive about the precision of the dancers, the legwork and balance, and how they presented themselves with virtuosity and energy. That was something I was lacking and it was very, very attractive to me, and I was on a mission, convinced it was something I could acquire and that it could work for me. And I tried, and just hit a wall. I was watching films of myself and just could not recognize myself. It didn't work for me. For me, Joanna (Berman) typified the clarity, Evelyn (Cisneros), the radiance and heroics, and I had to step back and think, because even though I was becoming stronger, something of who I was as a dancer was getting lost. So, I went back and tried to understand who I was as a dancer, what quality I wanted to bring out, and did a little triage of what I should keep of that American way of dancing, and what to keep of my own training, and what I was learning from other people like Alonzo. What was unique from childhood that made me want to stop playing, or abandon a game and take class? What feelings did I have onstage before and after a performance? What kept me going? I had gotten caught up in that whole system of multiple influences and politics and the feedback of a regime that produces that, and it created an amalgam of things, and I got lost in it.

No matter how much you do, the more you grow, the more you perform, the more lonely you are, because you learn that the only one you can trust to help you is you, because only you really have a sense of your needs and potential and how much of those you want to satisfy and realize.[14]

Maffre relies on coaching only up to a point because ultimately she has come to believe that as a dancer she is alone with her work, and that is "very hard" for her. Monique sheds light on possible reasons for her daughter's dogged self reliance. While at Paris Opera, she was seen as an outsider, in part because of her height and build, but also because of her anti-hierarchical values, where she had the temerity, on one occasion, to rinse her contact lenses in a high school faculty bathroom sink. In a comedy of errors involving a broken lock, the teacher who chastised her accidentally got locked in the bathroom. Maffre was made to write an essay as a show of remorse. She wrote, but with no remorse, merely disclosing the facts of how the teacher's gaffe had hoist her on her own pétard, and she was then more harshly disciplined for that than the original offense. Other incidents, such as being caned in the course of a correction, or removed from a list of students going to Japan because she was cutting up with a friend after a performance in front of school's director, were not as amusing.

Did any breakthroughs occur at SFB in the context of all the difficulty?

I had hit the wall with *Swan Lake*, and was not happy during that time. It was when the [San Francisco War Memorial] Opera House was being retrofitted, and we began dancing in other venues. The whole period was kind of a shift.

There were some changes in my life in 1994–95. I was 28. I underwent a complete change in my body and everything at that age. I was happy to have made that realization, and come to an understanding with myself, and I let go of the things that didn't work for me, technically or with my dancing. I was looking for a different approach.[15]

Were the roles that Maffre was cast in changing also?

It was a time that I wasn't getting used much. I danced in *Violin Concerto* and a couple of other roles. I tried to nourish my life with other things because it was not fulfilling. I enrolled in the degree program at St. Mary's. I made a decision that it was not what I was given or not given to dance that would make me a good dancer; it was *what I did in terms of my work*, my investment or commitment, day-to-day. I had to separate ambition from my other journey, develop my practice separate from my artistic goals. Then everything started to change. I began feeling more secure and developed a way of dancing that made it possible to free myself from many things. I separated from Jean Baptiste Bello-Portu,[16]

the man with whom Maffre had come to the United States.

Muriel met Randy Candler on a San Francisco MUNI bus. It was "a completely liberating feeling" that he was not connected to the world of ballet. She credits Candler with having given her enough self confidence to open up to the world outside of ballet. While she was acutely aware of that world, until she connected with Randy, she lacked the basic self confidence to tackle it.

I was alone for two years, and very adventurous, curious, going to lectures on childhood education, mountain biking on Mount Tam, but as a woman, I lacked self confidence. I had an instinctive behavior, a maturity and an emotional sense. Being with Randy advanced my social outreach. The relationship went as far as it could go, because with all that Randy gave me, I was becoming more comfortable with myself, completing my study program, involved intellectually, but something was missing artistically in my life. I could not compromise with that. It is still difficult to talk about, even though it's been a few years. I was feeling trapped, and not going in the direction I wanted to go.[17]

Deciding to separate from Randy didn't accelerate Maffre's ability to pinpoint her artistic focus, however.

I had lived with Jean Baptiste for eight years; I had been thrown off balance when it ended; with Randy, I invested myself in my dancing and channeled the emotional ups and downs into that, but with less intensity. I almost let it happen instead of suffering.[18]

One change was getting the roles that she wanted. Muriel had begun to get more and more, and describes her relationship with Helgi Tomasson as having been "very privileged."

Muriel Maffre and Christopher Boatwright in *New Sleep*. **Photo credit: Marty Sohl. Courtesy San Francisco Performing Arts Library & Museum.**

He has been very, very respectful of my process of work, and my work in general, and I think that's what has allowed me to take my time and make it work." Maffre believes that this is attributable in part to having joined the company as a principal dancer instead of coming up through the ranks, where the memory lingers that "you were once in the corps."[19]

At the very young age of 11, Maffre realized that because of her height, she would have to be a soloist, as it was unlikely that she was would be hired into the corps de ballet. Because of her height, also, the choice of dancers to partner her has been limited. Among those she cites as outstanding are her current life companion, Benjamin Pierce, Christopher Boatwright, who danced with San Francisco Ballet and LINES Contemporary Ballet and died of HIV/AIDS in 1997, and Yuri Zukov, who danced with San Francisco Ballet. Of Boatwright, Maffre says,

When I joined the company, I danced with Christopher Boatwright, which was incredible. With Christopher, there was an instinctive rapport. Benjamin has been the best partner, and I think that is because I have connected with his sensibility and intellectuality. We didn't always get along in the studio because of different work methods. He was trained at the National Ballet School in Canada, and then at SAB and ABT.[20]

Maffre's first impressions of Pierce were that he was young in age and experience.

> I felt he was very ambitious: all that energy, wonderful, verging on being a little arrogant. There was a time when my level of concentration was unshakable. He was reading that as being serious, even severe. That created some communication problems. It reached a climax, and after that there was no communication at all. It was during *Western Symphony,* and that period when we were dancing a lot together outside of the Opera House, and he was scaring me some. I was becoming more aware of who he was, his sensibility, intellect, and interest in art. Eventually we started to talk, little by little. There is something in Ben's behavior that is there to cover his hyper-sensibility. It's a kind of protection, very gregarious, always funny and clowning, so people would not attack him if at an odd moment he showed his vulnerability. During tours, we spent time together, going to art galleries and museums, and built up a friendship that led to a more serious involvement that began in 2002.[21]

When Muriel mentioned to former SFB dancer Jim Sohm (now administrator of the school there) that she had been taking college courses by correspondence, how could she have guessed that a conversation he would have with a pioneer of another kind, Claire Sheridan, would result in a highly successful college degree program for dancers, where Muriel would be one of its first and most famous graduates?

Sheridan had founded the dance program at St. Mary's College, and taught jazz dance in cities around the world. At 43, she found that her dance injuries had taken a toll, and she wanted to retire. While teaching in post-war Sarajevo, Bosnia, she contracted an infection that nearly took her life. She reports that at the time, she didn't care if she died, because without a dance career, it felt as if she had no identity or purpose. After her recovery, she taught dance history at San Francisco Ballet's summer school. She was watching the company rehearse one day, and realized that the dancers she was watching could easily harbor similar feelings about having no identity once their dance careers ended. In a conversation with Sohm, he mentioned that Maffre was sometimes asked when she was going to get a "real" job. Sheridan's reaction was, "How insulting!" She reasoned that most people have no idea what is required of dancers, and how dancers in major ballet companies can "dance rings around" graduates of college dance programs, which require very little of their students. Dancers needed a way to earn a college degree easily, without having to work at a dead-end job while they slowly slogged through years of evening courses. What could she do to help these artists transition from the stage to a new life? The St. Mary's College administration in Moraga, California, agreed to host a program where Bay Area dancers could attend Sunday night and Monday classes at a downtown San Francisco hotel, add "life credits" from their careers to their classroom credits, and pay only

$13,000 tuition for a Bachelors of Arts degree in the Performing Arts. Muriel was among the first group of 18 to enroll, and at this writing, LEAP (Liberal Education for Arts Professionals) has graduated its third group, having expanded to Los Angeles and New York, and is hoping to add Las Vegas. A mission of St. Mary's, where the curriculum resembles the St. John's College "Great Books" program, is to serve the underserved. It was easy to argue that higher education "underserves" dancers—so many graduate from high school with degrees that fall far short of an academic diploma.

Of Maffre, Sheridan says,

> I will always be grateful to Muriel for being in the first group, because she led the way. She's a star. Why does she care about this? She has such a hunger that she would have done it on her own! A lot of people followed her: Yuan Yuan [Tan], Damian [Smith], Gennadi [Nedvigin]. Also ethnic and modern dancers, though they don't need it as much...because their professional life doesn't begin at 16 or 17, as with ballet dancers.[22]

LEAP graduates have gone on to get Master's degrees at Duke, Columbia, and Boston University. The New York students will range in age from 20 to 65, and include Clover Mathis, a founding member of Dance Theatre of Harlem, who, at 60 years old, currently works as a nursing attendant.

What did Muriel show Sheridan in the course of her studies?

> Much of what is fascinating about Muriel comes through in her writing. In America, we separate intellect, soul, intuition, body. For her, they're equal, blended. Dancers, like Europeans, are viewed here as "arty," athletes as "dumb." Muriel once wrote, "I think through my body and dance through my mind." She can't separate them: She's not doing technical tricks; she's completely absorbed by the character, not like a dancer acting the part. She *is* the part, has thought about it so carefully and intellectually. Though she gives off an unapproachable, elitist vibe, she is actually quite open and has done these things to be accessible, willing to help others, talking other dancers into joining the program. Several times, she'd call me in tears while reading Plato, not understanding, freaking. She was struggling and a pioneer. She created a website called "Dancerhood" for dancers. She worked so hard to get the logo right. Why a website? To give her fellow dancers a way to express themselves, show that they're well-rounded, and like Diaghilev, encouraged them to visit museums, read a certain book, reaching out to dancers to become better by reaching out to other art forms. In 2000, she began her own little LEAP program at San Francisco Ballet for the advanced summer school students to meet on Saturdays to talk about the art of partnering, facing adversity, to get them talking. She made t-shirts and transformed the SFB library into a cafe, brought in [cafe-style] umbrellas and refreshments. She had them write essays and papers about what they got out of it. Kristine Elliott (former ABT principal dancer) spoke about her trip to the South African townships, and how she raised money

to bring young dancers from South Africa back to San Francisco to study with Richard Gibson. The ground rules were spelled out in a menu: There was no right or wrong, smart or stupid: students were urged to "resist the beauty contest."[23]

Sheridan spoke of Maffre's post-LEAP efforts.

A few weeks ago, I attended a choreographic workshop Muriel asked Helgi to let her organize. There were two rules. Anybody in the company could set choreography within the allotted two week period, but they had to set it on least four members of the corps. It was highly successful: Finally, members of the corps had a chance to shine and be seen in a different light. Think about what she does to bring those below her *up*. She's not threatened by them. She helps us fund raise. She sat next to someone at a luncheon and then LEAP received a check for $25,000. She did *Ballet Mori*.[24]

Ballet Mori, a collaboration between Maffre, choreographer Yuri Possokhov, Ken Goldberg, a University of California, Berkeley, Professor of Robotics, Randall Packer, a composer, and Benjamin Pierce, who designed the set and costumes, was a one-night performance at the San Francisco War Memorial Opera House on April 4, 2006. Seismic waves from the Lawrence Livermore Seismological Laboratory at UC Berkeley were transmitted via computer hookup to the stage at the Opera House, and Maffre responded to the sound waves using movement set by Possokov. The eight-minute work, where the earth was the conductor, brought the audience to its feet in a standing ovation. Underpinning Maffre's stirring performance was the spiritual impact on the collective unconscious of a multi-generational, multi-national audience, most of which had never been brought so close in a sensory way to the earth's interior.

At LEAP, Maffre wrote an intellectual biography to examine "why I think the way I think. What part of my upbringing and other life experiences influenced the way I think?" Courses in sociology, psychology, cultural anthropology, and visual arts provided a foundation for a portfolio of essays. Maffre's topics were: The subculture of Ballet, Alternative Family Formation: Adoption in France, The Subculture of the Gijou Valley in Southern France, The Psychological Adaptation to Immigration, and Appreciation of Visual Art: The Nabis (a French school of art centered in L'Etang-la-Ville).

I had entered the program because I thought that doing all this work would make me aware of the potential I had, and evaluate where to go next, and I became aware that I love writing and scholarly research. As I did research on art, it created a connection with art and museums. With Ben, there is an incredible exchange about art all the time. His dad is a lithographer and his mom is a textile artist. She taught at the Smithsonian. He picked up a lot of it from his dad, took a few drawing classes. The rest came naturally. He stopped dancing because of a back injury and his interests began to shift. He became more passionate about what he was doing outside [of ballet]. He went to film school. He met people who had confidence in him, connected with [the public TV program about art in the Bay Area] "Spark," and now he's very passionate about developing his own films, his own work.[25]

When he was a student at San Francisco State, he made a film around [Maffre's] *The Dying Swan* with no budget.

It was a student project. We took over one of the studios at City Ballet and shot the dance part in five hours straight. The next day, Elizabeth from the LAB, let us use the Gallery space to shoot the other scenes. The response was so great that we want to re-shoot it to bring the production values up, so it can be presented at festivals. We developed the narrative and pushed the aesthetic. I wrote a treatment, a script and descriptive of all the different elements in the film.[26]

How was she able to simply sit down and write all those things with no prior experience? Maffre referred to the preparation she received from LEAP:

You're exposed to that level of thinking and methodology in school, and this can be applied to anything you do in your life. I bought books, and I just did it: script, location, time of day, what happens, very factual, placement, action. The treatment is really a short story, so you know what is happening with the image and its quality.[27]

Maffre's life is centered in the United States. What is it like to return to France?

You feel that you float in between. You're not quite French. When I returned one year, I was visiting my grandmother at her vacation home, with so many memories of the Loire Valley where she lived, and then, suddenly, there was no emotional attachment. After that, it was just me visiting. I still have my family, feel very comfortable with them, but it's a world where I was not able to develop myself as an adult, and *here* [the United States] is the place where I've become who I am and where people have given me opportunities.[28]

Did she utilize related feelings and insights around this in her portrayal of Medea in Yuri Possokhov's ballet *Damned*? "Yes, being a castaway, not fitting in, feeling inadequate."

Maffre will have retired at the close of the 2006-2007 San Francisco Ballet season. What's next for her?

I'm very interested in public intellect. If you understand those dynamics, you have a better sense of how the public can be drawn to one form of art and not another, and how you can communicate. The public as a group or a body— the intellect of that body—is different than the individual and affects any events that are public. Showing art in a museum is creating a dynamic. Mixed bills in a ballet company should be curated so that programming an evening doesn't consist of just an appetizer, main course and dessert, in a superficial way. There is a way to make it more powerful and meaningful. Organize it thematically, or in a way meant to affect people. Focus on the qualities in more subtle ways, so it doesn't remain a jewel box, or realize that it's a ballerina in a jewel box. For instance, looking at the theme "reflection," there are a few ballets that deal with mirrors like the duet in Bintley's *Dance House*. It's about creating connection on a different level and bringing different light to these works. One season we had "white ballets." Instead of trying to balance each program with one, put them all in one evening and see how white can look different or can be used for different purposes.[29]

Will Maffre's concerns lead her to form her own company, someday?

It leads to more than a company: a theater as a venue where I would organize programs. There could be video, photos to make it a whole, to make it relevant. I always feel sorry when people look at ballet just on the entertainment level, and it never, ever should be. I created the Dancerhood website, a virtual neighborhood for dancers to write, talk about their experiences, anything dance related. One page showed work dancers did outside of dance, such as writing and painting. "Pick" was a page of dancers making suggestions. I managed to put all the information in the first pilot, committed to make it work, then got too busy with my studies, and took it offline. I still like the idea very much. Peter Brandenhoff wrote about his experience in South Africa, teaching and dancing. Brook Broughton wrote about her experience as a corps member. I had written a piece on Homer Avila [a dancer who continued to dance after losing a leg to cancer], whom I met to take class at LINES. After class I introduced myself, and we talked for half an hour and I could not tear myself away and interviewed him for two hours on another occasion. He took me step by step through his experience with the surgery and then up to the present. I wrote the story, posted it, and then he called me just before he performed with AXIS—I could feel a change in his energy. He seemed kind of sad and insisted that we have a drink, but I had to go to France, and we never connected, and then I went up to LINES one day to take class and saw that there was a memorial for him.[30]

Where will Maffre go with this? Her next step is to acquire a Master's degree in a discipline that links the arts with people. How does her family feel about her goals? "They're always very supportive, bringing their own understanding to it, which is very different than mine." Are they looking for more definition? "I guess yes. They ask, 'Have you made a decision?' It's the Protestant work ethic. 'Put a name on what you're going to do.'" Monique reports that when she was a child, Isabelle (now an interior designer) hid a painting project from the family, interpreted as part of a jealous response to Muriel's success. Was Isabelle the symptom bearer of Muriel's career?

Muriel Maffre in *The Dying Swan*. **Photo credit: Chris Hardy.**

> We reconciled when she created a family. We had some issues when were kids, and it really began to accumulate as I became more successful. The struggles we both had brought us closer; understanding each other's struggles helped us see that neither of us had had it easy, even though it might have seemed so; I reached a point where I had to write her a letter about my own experience, my relationship with my mother. She has never talked about that letter, but I think it helped.[31]

Evidence that it did can be seen in Isabelle's opening up her home and heart so that interviews for this book could take place with Maffre's family. Is the relationship harder between siblings than parent and child?

> There are things my sister did that hurt me profoundly, but I think the heritage you get from your parents weighs more and is more difficult to resolve. What is amazing, and I find it everywhere, is the resilience of kids, and human beings in general. Homer Avila exemplified this.[32]

Maffre ended her application for admission to St. Mary's College with the following parable: The Hasidic Rabbi Zusya was asked on his death bed what he thought the kingdom of God would be like. "I don't know," he replied. "But one thing I do know: when I get there, I am not going to be asked, 'Why weren't you Moses?' 'Why weren't you David?' I am only going to be asked, 'Why weren't you Zusya? Why weren't you fully you?'"

14

Arthur Mitchell

Agon [danced by Arthur Mitchell], as Balanchine choreographed it, had an atomic-age urgency, it had thrills, danger, apocalyptic energy. And it was wall-to-wall dancing, without even the shadowy pretext of a competition before the gods.

—Arlene Croce, "The Spelling of Agon," July 12, 1993 *New Yorker* [1]

Arthur Mitchell grew up a few blocks from Sugar Hill in Harlem, and the imprint and influence of its striver constituents have remained with him all his life. The first child of Arthur Mitchell, Sr. and Willie Mae Hearns, Mitchell was born on March 27, 1934. His father was a janitor and tradesman. His mother was a homemaker who also looked after other people's children. Arthur had two sisters and three brothers. Mitchell has pleasant memories of Sunday mornings when his father rose early to prepare fried chicken or pork chops and cornmeal pancakes, but the elder Mitchell's penchant for hard work and pleasing the family were not enough to sustain him. Suffering enormous frustration and having struggled with alcoholism, he eventually deserted his wife and children. Asked why he was so successful, Mitchell consistently gives one answer: "I was the father of the family at age 12, never a child, really. I couldn't believe in Santa Claus, because I was the one earning the money to buy the presents."[2] If the saying "Go with what you know" ever applied to anyone, it is Mitchell, who has sought to reprise the patriarch role and recreate the hierarchy required to support it in his professional life, to go as far as he could with what he knows.

At three years old, seeing older children enter and leave the local elementary school, and feeling a sense of entitlement at least equal to theirs, he simply followed them into the classroom. He was thrown out

Arthur Mitchell in *Among the Moderns.* **Courtesy Dance Collection, New York Public Library.**

the first time, but because he persisted, he was finally admitted, in spite of being underage. He says he then demanded to sit in the first row. The insistent desire that his reach exceed his grasp drove who he would become as an adult.

Arthur took over what had been his father's janitorial duties, ran errands, sold newspapers and found work at a butcher shop so that he could bring meat home to his family. He attended Junior High School 43, and loved to read. He claims to have been a member of two neighborhood gangs, The Hilltop Lovers and The Rebels. On one occasion, he was jumped by a gang of white boys. One of them yelled, "Hey, there's a nigger!" and cut his cheek with a switchblade.[3]

Talent school representatives would go door to door in Arthur's neighborhood in search of gifted children, or more accurately, parents willing to enroll their gifted children in classes that offered 15 minutes of dancing, 15 minutes of singing, and 15 minutes of acting. CBS operated a school offering such classes at its Madison Avenue studios. Willie Mae Mitchell signed Arthur up. His junior high school guidance teacher noticed Mitchell dancing the lindy hop and jitterbug, and suggested that he audition for New York's High School of Performing Arts, still a pilot program in 1948. Coached by an old vaudevillian, Arthur danced a three-minute jazz routine to Frank Sinatra's "Steppin' Out with my Baby" in the manner of Fred Astaire, and dressed in a rented costume of black tails, a white tie, and a top hat. He reports having heard throughout his life, "Kid, you've got style," and believes that it was style, not technique that "sold it" to the Performing Arts jury. (At 15, he auditioned for the Paper Bag Players, and saw the audition notes, which read, "Very talented, but needs technique.") As so many of the school's male dancers start out believing, Mitchell was convinced that he was the least prepared of any of the students, and the school's Dance Department director warned him that he would have to work hard if he wanted to stay. Mitchell took advantage of all opportunities to catch up, and studied with LaTanya Newman, Gertrude Shurr, Robert Joffrey, and Merce Cunningham, and danced with a small company headed by Shirley Broughton,.

In their senior year, Performing Arts dance students were expected to audition for companies and college dance programs. During those auditions, Mitchell was confronted with institutionalized racism. He had believed that his talent would be sufficient to get him jobs anywhere until the day that choreographer Gower Champion told him that he couldn't hire him for a TV special because of his color. (Ironically, Champion ended up hiring him many years later for a different project after dancers such as Mitchell had broken the color bar.) Mitchell danced with Donald McKayle at the 92nd Street Y, and with Mary Hinkson, then of the Martha Graham Company, whom Mitchell regards as the best dancer he has ever seen. He met Karel Shook at the Kathryn Dunham School. Shook, who taught there, and would become a lifelong friend and collaborator, believed Mitchell's style and carriage were best suited for a career in ballet, and encouraged him in that direction.

In 1952, some of Mitchell's Performing Arts classmates decided to try out for the musical "Four Saints in Three Acts." Arthur went along for the ride, not intending to audition. The woman running the audition noticed him, and gushed, "Oh my dear, you'd make a perfect angel! Come inside."[4] Mitchell was given a leave of absence from Performing Arts, and the following day, Bill Bowers was setting choreography on him before Arthur had even seen the show's book.

Mitchell auditioned for Bennington College in Modern Dance, and was offered a scholarship to the then-all women's institution. P.A. dance students had to choreograph a senior project, and Arthur set his to music by Bartok. Arthur's work prompted Lincoln Kirstein, a member of the senior project's adjudicating panel, to offer him a scholarship to the School of American Ballet. Mitchell recalls having seen a performance where a ballet dancer "bourrée'd across the stage and seemed to float."[5] That image and his teacher Nanette Charisse having offered the encouraging words, "Arthur, you should do Ballet," helped him decide to accept Kirstein's offer.

Mitchell chose a ballet career at a time when the 1954 *Brown v.Board of Education* Supreme Court decision favoring school desegregation had become a rallying point for the U.S. Civil Rights Movement. Did Arthur want to be the Jackie Robinson of ballet? No, he simply wanted to dance in any style or discipline he chose, including and most determinedly ballet. *Did* he become the Jackie Robinson of ballet? Very much so, but he also became a dancer and choreographer who happened to be Black, an identity that diminished the self-styled noblesse oblige of the white and socially elite world of ballet theater. No matter how talented Mitchell was, history strongly suggests that he would have been less likely to have been as successful had there been no Jackie Robinson, *Brown v. Board of Education*, and massive mobilizations of Black people and their supporters for civil and human rights.

The first time that Mitchell came face to face with the awesome and imposing Lincoln Kirstein, Kirstein said to Mitchell, "You are a Negro," to which Mitchell replied, "Yes," and then Kirstein added, "George and I like you, but in order to get into the corps de ballet, you have to be equal to a principal." Mitchell said of himself, "I am maniacal about what I believe," and driven by that mania, he worked to prove his mettle.[6] He knew Kirstein as the individual who had raised $5,000 to bring Balanchine to New York to start the School of American Ballet, and learned that Balanchine admired the tradition of musicality in Black culture, having hoped, according to Mitchell, to start the school with eight Black students and eight white students, though the composition of the school has at no time approached that ratio.

Mitchell found that ballet was much more a function of hard work than glamour. While rehearsing the punishing choreography in the 1954 Broadway production of "House of Flowers," he was injured after Carmen de Lavallade fell on him as he was going into one of the piece's famous knee slides. He broke both knees, and had to be hospitalized. Mitchell cites words that Pearl Bailey once spoke to him: "See those people down there in the orchestra? They're very fickle. See those people in the balcony? Once you've got them, they're yours for life."[7] Thereafter, Mitchell always made sure that his cheekbones were lit instead of his forehead, forcing him to hold his head high with his hand extended a foot higher than his head in order to be seen by his balcony devotees.

After three years at the School of American Ballet, Mitchell made a guest appearance on the TV soap opera *Look up and Live* and met John Butler, whose dance company was on its way to Europe. Before he knew it, after having danced in "Goldilocks" on Broadway and made the film version of *House of Flowers*, partnering Mary Ann Niles and dancing with Glen Tetley, he was on his way to Europe with Butler's company.

In 1955, while in Europe, Mitchell received a telegram from Lincoln Kirstein inviting him to join New York City Ballet. His first thought was a practical one: he was still the head of his household, and NYCB paid $90 a week and medical benefits. He had proven the naysayers wrong: A Negro could dance ballet in the United States of America in the twentieth century. He agreed to sign the NYCB contract if there was no fanfare about his being Black and no special press announcements trumpeting "Negro Breaks Barrier." He hoped to slip into the company as discreetly as possible in his debut as Tanaquil Le Clercq's partner in the Fourth Movement of *Western Symphony*. Hardly a discreet role, it was still one in which he could be seen as a dancer who happened to be Black. And he was: As he came on stage with his partner, he heard a gasp from the audience, followed by the unmistakable words, "They've got a *nigger* in the company!"[8]

Mitchell recalls an atmosphere at NYCB where everyone worked together in a spirit of friendly competition. What did Mitchell bring to the company that the other male dancers did not? "I was not the strongest technician, but I was the strongest dancer to do all styles."[9] Erik Bruhn was Mitchell's role model, and he says that when Erik arrived in New York in early November, Mitchell invited him to Harlem to join his family for Thanksgiving dinner. He describes what it was like to stand behind Bruhn at barre, admiring and learning from him, but also thinking, "I have something, too." Later in life, he sought to imbue Dance Theatre of Harlem company members and students with that same "I have something, too" sense of self worth.

Describing Balanchine as "old school," Mitchell recalls that his mentor never raised his voice in anger. In Mitchell's opinion, Balanchine was first and foremost a musician who possessed the profound understanding that there has to be rhythm before you can set steps. The ballerina Maria Tallchief advised Mitchell to listen to every word Balanchine said. Mitchell took that advice a step further, and attached himself to costume designer Mme Barbara Karinska, and lighting designer Jean Rosenthal, to become expert at both crafts. Mitchell assesses his overall experience at NYCB as "a glass half full." His hard work made him a quick study. Company recognition of his efforts often took the form of a last minute phone call during a matinee intermission reporting that "Jacques sprained his ankle," and urging him to come "right to the theater" to learn a role that he would perform that evening while a dancer in the wings called out the steps to him.

Partnering spotlighted the race issue. Mitchell says he saw the conductor's head "shoot up" from the orchestra pit at the sight of him dancing with a white partner. As the curtain opened upon a single couple, him Black and her white, a murmur of shock and disapproval bristled through the audience, but as the piece continued, the audience was won over, and the pair received a standing ovation. Parents called to say, "We don't want our daughters dancing with that _____." Balanchine's response was, "Then the girls are out!"[10] The Board revolted against Mitchell opening *Stars and Stripes*, and threatened Balanchine that there would be reprisals, urging him to "pull it." He didn't. Balanchine cast Mitchell to partner the (white) Sugar Plum Fairy in *Nutcracker*, declaring, "I hope that [the pro-segregation] Governor [Orville] Faubus is watching!"

In "In Balanchine's Company," former NYCB soloist Barbara Milberg Fisher recalls a conversation overheard between Balanchine and Kirstein:

LINCOLN (concerned)   But what *will* you put him in?

BALANCHINE: (two sniffs)   *Swan Lake.*[11]

Noting that Mitchell possessed a noble bearing rarely found in American dancers, Fisher nonetheless reminds readers that ballet companies did not hire Black dancers, no matter how talented they might be. She says that Balanchine cited the story of Alexander the Great and how he tackled the Gordian Knot—"You don't waste time trying to untie it; you slash it in two"[12]—and cast Mitchell in the "white ballet," *Swan Lake*. He offered no apologia, and moved on to choreograph *Agon* on Mitchell in 1957. In the studio, he paired Mitchell with Virginia Rich, precisely to point up the beauty of their contrasting complexions. He worked with them on placement so that Mitchell's black hand would not upstage Rich's white arm. If Mitchell wished to subordinate his Black identity to his dancer self, it is apparent that Balanchine was coming at the question from the diametrically opposite perspective.

Diana Adams danced with Mitchell in *Agon*. *Agon* represented the third major collaborative Stravinksy-Balanchine effort inspired by the Greek antiquities. Dancing Agon along with Puck in *Midsummer's Night Dream* rendered Mitchell's style unforgettable to ballet audiences. In the 15 years that Mitchell danced with the company, he attained the rank of premier danseur, while continuing to excel in jazz and modern ballets such as Jerome Robbin's *Interplay*, John Taras' *Ebony Concerto*, and John Butler's *The Unicorn, the Gorgon and the Manticore*. Between seasons with NYCB, Mitchell danced as a guest artist with other companies, as well as in musicals and on television. In 1966, in a collaborative effort with Karel Shook, he organized the short-lived American Dance Company.[13] Accepting USIA funds, he helped establish the National Ballet of Brazil.

While he doesn't think that George Balanchine was grooming a "successor," it is Arthur Mitchell's opinion that Balanchine was preparing him for more than just a performing career. He believes that it was Balanchine's intention to plant seeds in the minds and consciousness of his dancers, hoping that they would bear fruit. He says NYCB dancer Gloria Govrin objected when Balanchine cast Mitchell in a corps spot in *Don Quixote*. "Mr. B., why are you putting Arthur in the corps?"[14] Govrin asked. "Because one day he'll be a great director, but in the meantime, I don't want him to forget everything," was Balanchine's reply. The more Mitchell began to think like an artistic director, the more of an effort he made to recruit non-white dancers to New York City Ballet. He approached Balanchine with the idea that the first violin in *Concerto Barocco* be white, the second black. He was hoping to convince Sarah Yarborough, then a student, to join the company, but she joined Harkness Ballet instead. He tried to bring Chita Rivera into NYCB, but instead she signed a contract to star in "Can Can."

In 1968, Mitchell had been en route to Brazil when he received news of the assassination of Dr. Martin Luther King, Jr. in Birmingham.

> I said to myself, "Arthur, why are you going to Brazil when a company should be started right here in America? Like most people, you're sitting back and seeing all the problems but doing nothing about them." When you pay homage, you do the thing you do best. I decided that training Black ballet dancers and forming an all-Black ballet company was the greatest tribute I could pay to Martin Luther King.[15]

In 1969, at the age of 32, Mitchell resigned from NYCB, and with Karel Shook (who had been ballet master at Dutch National Ballet Company) began what would soon become Dance Theatre of Harlem. In 1968, they had started with 30 students as a dance program in Dorothy Maynor's Harlem School of the Arts, having initially held class in a garage. In 1969, the school moved to a church basement, its enrollment having grown to 250, and with a Ford Foundation matching grant of $150,000 opened its doors in 1971 as Dance Theatre of Harlem.

> I quickly realized that I couldn't have just a school because my dancers wouldn't have had anywhere to perform. That's why I established the company. You may begin something for social reasons, but after a certain point, what you're striving for as an artist will outweigh anything else.[16]

Today DTH is located on 152nd Street and Amsterdam Avenue in Harlem. Each year the school enrolls 1,000 students between the ages of three and seventeen, and offers adult classes. Its Dancing Through Barriers outreach program has exposed thousands of youth to dance theater, including to the "back of house" components: lights, costumes, and sets—all introduced by company members. At the end of each year students perform live in a local theater. DTH has hosted a community open house one Sunday a month where students and visiting musicians perform to an SRO audience. Conceived of as a training ground for Black

Arthur Mitchell as Puck in *Midsummer Night's Dream*. Courtesy Dance Collection, New York Public Library.

dancers, Mitchell views himself as a citizen of the world who is the continuator of the Balanchine tradition in Harlem. Balanchine, who had served on no other ballet company's board, agreed to serve on Dance Theatre of Harlem's, as did Lincoln Kirstein in its formative years. Arthur Mitchell has received 13 honorary doctoral degrees for his community outreach efforts, including from Harvard and Princeton universities and was inducted into the NAACP Image Awards of Fame. In 1993, he received a Lifetime Contribution to American Culture award from the John F. Kennedy Center for the Performing Arts, and in 1996, he was awarded the National Medal of Arts by President William Jefferson Clinton.[17]

In 2005, Dance Theatre of Harlem announced that it was suspending performances for an indefinite period owing to financial difficulties. The company repertoire had embraced all genres, with an emphasis on contemporary ballets. Mitchell had wanted to present a Giselle that made sense in the context of the African American experience, and based on research of Creole Society in Louisiana, developed a version of the ballet staged by Frederic Franklin in 1984 with sets by Carl Michel, where the lovers come from different sides of the tracks within the Black community. According to Mitchell's research, certain pre-Civil War Blacks were called *gens de couleur libres* (free people of color). By 1812, they owned sugar and cotton plantations worked by slave labor, and ran lucrative industrial and commercial businesses that enabled them to send their children to private schools in the North or in France. They adhered to a caste system similar to that of European society. There were local legends of bayou spirits similar to those of the German wilis.[18] While purists in the United States found fault with *Creole Giselle*, the reviews of the British tour were laudatory, and according to Mitchell, Margot Fonteyn pronounced it "marvelous." The company not only toured the U.K., but went to the Soviet Union in 1988 as part of a U.S.-Soviet cultural exchange, toured Cairo and other cities in Egypt in 1990, and in 1992, Mitchell took the company on a highly successful tour of post-Apartheid South Africa. In the mid-90s, the company performed in Monte Carlo and at the Festival of Two Worlds in Spoleto. In February 1999, DTH toured historic Black colleges while students from the school performed in Hong Kong at Lunar New Year celebrations.

When Helgi Tomasson assumed artistic directorship of San Francisco Ballet, its former director Michael Smuin's piece *Song for a Dead Warrior* was taken out of the company's repertoire, and the costumes and sets were stored in a warehouse. "Helgi wanted to burn it, but I considered it one of the most phenomenal ballets I had ever seen, and I got it for $2000—an endangered species of a ballet that NYCB told me would have cost $2 million to reproduce."[19] DTH danced the Smuin work at the New York State Theater at Lincoln Center in March 1993. Among the triumphs of the company's repertoire was Agnes De Mille's "Fall River Legend," which catapulted the dancer Karen Brown to national prominence. She later became the director of the now-defunct Oakland Ballet Company. Former DTH principal Virginia Johnson became Editor-in-Chief of *Pointe* magazine, the only U.S.-based magazine devoted exclusively to ballet. In an October 1999 *Dance Magazine* piece on the company's 30th anniversary, Johnson is quoted as saying,

> We went to small towns where they'd never seen blacks before...We had an enormous impact on many narrow-minded people. And not just whites. Some of our people felt, why do ballet? It's only the white man's art. Our repertory showed that many classics were applicable to blacks. That's why Mr. Mitchell commissioned a Creole *Giselle* and an African *Firebird* for us to dance. He gave us a personal and social connection with them.[20]

Arthur Mitchell has adopted wholesale the "Ballet is woman" view famously attributed to George Balanchine. Paraphrasing his mentor, he says,

> If you want something done, get a woman. Women have a tenacity that men don't have. So all the things I heard, I now understand. Man is egotistical. Woman has endurance because she carries a baby for nine months. If you ask a group of little girls to get in line, they automatically do that. The man takes offense, takes it personally. Getting men to take corrections is very hard because the male ego gets involved. When you give a man a correction, he'll protest: "Well, I. . ."[21]

In Mitchell's view, Balanchine didn't have strong male technicians at first, but because he "understood" the female body, and because he had a very short time in which to turn out dancers, he created the circumstances where there was "nothing they couldn't do." Mitchell applauds Balanchine's biological determinism while choosing to ignore the likely possibility that girls line up without comment because they have been drilled from early on to do as they're told, and not because their egos are weaker than men's or that Balanchine built his oeuvre around women not so much to elevate them as to subordinate male rivals. Is there any more unimpeachable license than an artistic vision that places women on a pedestal? Mitchell's orthodoxy, which requires strict adherence to determinist views, is both embraced and criticized by those who have worked for him.

In an article by Valerie Gladstone in the October 1999 issue of *Dance Magazine*, Eddie J. Shellman, who danced with DTH for 23 years, is quoted as saying:

> I learned all about theater, opera, music, Kabuki and administration. And what an impact we have had on the world. Mr. Mitchell is strict. But someone has to be strict or you get lax. He tries to find in you what you can't see. It makes you a better artist and it makes you a better person. Largely because of his effect on me, I was able to establish my school, the Shellman Dance Academy in New Jersey.[22]

Robert Garland, who was choreographer in residence with the company, says,

> It's given me an opportunity to explore my own culture and develop a new audience for ballet. Mr. Mitchell is a father figure for many of us. Working with him, you realize that the world is much bigger than you are, that you need to get out of your own comfort zone and do something useful. Our tour to South Africa in 1992 changed our lives. When we went to the townships, we saw how badly the kids wanted the arts and how transforming they can be.[23]

In the same article, then-President of South Africa Nelson Mandela is quoted as having commented upon a DTH performance, "This is one of the most delightful evenings I have enjoyed. I have forgotten all the troubles I have had in my life."[24]

Mitchell echoes the sentiment that he is "just like a father" to the company. Some hold a negative view of his authoritarian approach, suggesting that he is something of a latter-day Bonaparte. "My brother once told me that I am the most self-centered, egotistical person he has ever met," Mitchell says, laughing. The twinkle in his eye suggests that there is more to the story. "I told him, 'Yes, and that's why I have been so successful in my life.'"[25] At times, the *l'état, c'est moi* hubris can wax more patronizing than sheltering. In 1997, dancers' frustration with Mitchell took the form of a bitter strike against the company. "To this day, they [the dancers] cannot tell you why they went on strike. *To this day*!" Mitchell says.

> You see, if they cannot get to me, they get to the dancers or the staff. I said, "Why are you striking?" The union told me "You're giving more benefits than the union does." It's acceptability—because all their friends were in the union. But this is DTH, we only have a budget of this much money. You've got *everything*! I sent you to school...See, they're my kids. At a certain age, kids want to rebel against the father.[26]

Articles in the May and July, 1997 issues of *Dance Magazine* cite at least two motives for the only strike by unionized dancers in U.S. history:

> Dancers went on strike January 22, picketing DTH and forcing Mitchell to cancel auditions for new dancers on February 7...The twenty-nine-year-old company ran into trouble in October when management offered a contract that removed long-standing benefits such as extra pay for certain overtime and designated rest periods between performances. The company had also started enlisting what it called "floaters," non-contract dancers who filled in roles. Angered by the apparent disloyalty and indifference to their health, the dancers struck. The union cited management's attempt to eliminate penalty pay and free-day pay from the contract.[27]

A tentative settlement was reached by February 9 with a five percent wage increase. However, the dancers lost penalty pay and free day pay, the provisions they had struck to keep. Lenore Pavlakos, representing the striking dancers, explained that they had agreed to go back to work because they would be compensated in overtime pay. Another dancer, Cassandra Phifer, who had danced with DTH for 22 years, said, "Dancers are notorious for not standing up for themselves. Never before has the company stood up with this kind of vehemence."[28]

Ikolo Griffin, now dancing with Smuin Ballet, joined DTH a month prior to the September 11, 2001, attack on New York's former World Trade Center. As San Francisco Ballet School's first outreach program student, he joined that company's corps de ballet. Commenting on a Dance

Theatre of Harlem outreach event at Stanford University that he observed
while still at SFB, he said,

> It was the best lecture demonstration I had ever seen, so well-rehearsed! The
> dancers did everything you could do at the barre. The narrator said, "This is
> a *passé*! *What did I say?*" and the audience would respond, "*passé*!" They
> brought the kids on to do their own moves and the narrator said, "We're
> going to show you how your moves are related to ballet." Then to that one
> fantastic kid who always shows up, they'd say, "See, what you just did—
> that's called a *plié*."[29]

Griffin decided to audition for DTH. He was offered a soloist
contract, and when Helgi Tomasson wished him good luck but did not
fight to keep him at SFB, he accepted the DTH offer. He danced the title
role in *Prodigal Son*, understudied the title role in *Apollo* staged by Jacques
D'Amboise, and danced Artie in Michael Smuin's *St. Louis Woman*, the
very best roles in the company. He had a good professional relationship
with Mitchell, but says that Mitchell's method was to break a dancer
down in order to then build him up. According to Griffin, Mitchell
was adept at the breaking down part, but over the years, faced with hip
problems, fatigue, and the financial losses sustained in the wake of 9/11,
Mitchell had lost the optimism that would have otherwise spirited the
building up part. Griffin said,

> My ego completely protected me, and you need that with him or he'll walk
> all over you. Still, he had great things to say. He definitely drew out the artist
> in me, gave me the opportunities to do the roles that brought that out. It was
> exactly what I needed—to do the body of work to gain the experience. He
> absolutely had a vision of a Black ballet dancer and knew how to sell that
> product.[30]

Griffin had been excited to work with an iconic father figure for Black
people, "someone whose name was in the history books."
Griffin believes that before he was beset with these problems, Mitchell
had had a more inspired view, "The company was fantastic in its heyday,
when there were 80 dancers—huge—a different period. It was the Golden
Age of Ballet and the Civil Rights Movement had won important victo-
ries." He emphasizes that Black arts organizations were hit hardest by
the collapse of private funding after 9/11, and DTH went down too.
Griffin was inspired by DTH principal dancer Donald Williams.

> Up to then, the Black dancer who had the biggest influence on me was Chris-
> topher Boatwright. I'd seen Christopher as I grew up in the school and com-
> pany at SFB, but never got to know him well. He had a lot of energy, and
> presence, but was frustrated that while he was cast in the role of Siegfried
> in Germany, Helgi would not let him dance it in his native United States of
> America. He was very helpful to me. I remember visiting him in the hospital
> when he was dying, and the outpouring of love for him at his memorial

meeting. Outside of him, I didn't have a role model until I met Donald
Williams at DTH. He became my ideal of how to shape my style, technique,
and presence—his amazing partnering, and masculinity! Donald Williams
was such a beautiful dancer. When I do a pas de deux, I channel him.[31]

In Griffin's view, Arthur Mitchell was a visionary in the way in which
he conceived of the company and made it a destination for Black dancers
and audiences, and broadened its outreach and appeal by touring it
throughout the world. On the other hand, he criticized Mitchell's short-
sightedness in his dealings with the union and approach to winning
financial support after 9/11:

He eventually brought the company down [under the crushing impact of
9/11] because of the stubborn and unorthodox way that he dealt with the
union and the dancers. It was inevitable that it couldn't return to what it
was. At the same time, it was amazing for all these Black dancers; he
had given them jobs and opportunities that ceased to exist on the same scale
afterwards.

The union didn't really exist up there in Harlem. It was crazy. We had to
sign waivers giving up overtime pay. We received late paychecks—an outra-
geous thing that you just don't do to people. We did a show at a casino and
were asked by Mr. Mitchell to sign a waiver to give up our per diem, our food
money, promised that we would get food vouchers—the same as cash—
except that you could only eat at one place, where the casino staff ate. We
had to sacrifice so that the company would be invited back. Well, the food
was terrible, and we were never invited back. We got sugar coated promises
that verged on the fantastical. Even as the company was about to close, he
said, "We have a show in September." There was no show. When we returned
from Europe to the Kennedy Center in 2004, we sensed something was
about to happen. In rehearsals, he was complaining that we weren't trying
anymore—and we're talking about ballets we'd performed one hundred
times, like *Firebird*—he was yelling at us over trivial stuff. I was invited by a
regional company to do a guest *Don Quixote* in 2005, so I asked to meet with
Mr. Mitchell. First, because I had been promoted to principal, I asked for the
pay I was entitled to. I was told, "I can't do that." Then I asked, "As a principal, what will I be dancing this season so that I can prepare and know what
to focus on?" He said, "Focus on everything." I asked for a six week leave to
do the guest Don Q. He said, "No, I can't let you go." That was three no's:
When Joffrey came to town, I auditioned and was offered a job. I asked
Mr. Mitchell again for my pay increase. He said "No." That's when I realized
that the company was closing. We just hadn't been told. He told the dancers
not to take other jobs and so they lost out. Maybe 20 out of 40 are dancing
now.[32]

In Griffin's opinion, were the company to be revived, Arthur Mitchell
should act in an advisory capacity. His vision and contribution have been
singular in the history of Black America and beyond its borders. Griffin
offers an anecdote to illustrate Mitchell's success in making the company
into an ambassador of Black culture.

After a DTH performance in Ireland, Griffin met an audience member who introduced himself with these words,

> You know, I'm a lawyer, and I work hard all day. My wife tells me we're going to the ballet tonight, and I'm thinking, "Oh, good, I'll get a chance to sleep." But then when the curtain goes up and I see those *bodies*, I say to myself—"Holy hot-cross buns!" I perked right up, and was riveted: I couldn't for one moment take my eyes off those dancers![33]

"That's what we did thanks to Mr. Mitchell's vision and help," Griffin says,

> and what incredible dancers we were: Rasta Thomas, Ikolo Griffin, Kellye Saunders, Alicia Graf, Duncan Cooper, probably the technically strongest in the whole history of the company! We could have done *anything* as well as any other company, if not better. The women in our company had a different line than those pre-pubescent white girls, but they were beautiful, sexy, luscious, and they knew their power! And for me *that power* was Dance Theatre of Harlem![34]

15

Carla Fracci

Carla Fracci is one of the best dancers in the world and possesses three vital ingredients with which to interpret the unforgettable Giselle: the ability to relive the ingenuousness of a peasant girl in love for the first time, the capacity to imagine herself as the spirit of the dead girl who dances on her grave, the energy to confront the enormous physical challenge required by the role. Her miming is by now famous; famous are the movement of her arms and agile feet. Besides this, she is young and charming: in sum, *she is absolutely something to see.*

—Paul Hertelendy, February 1970 *Oakland Tribune*[1]

Like the Giselle she has so stirringly interpreted, whose roots are in the earthbound surroundings of a humble cottage in the first act, but who appears to float immeasurable sacred inches above the forest floor in the second, Carla Fracci, from a working class Milanese family, rose to uncharted heights on wings she fashioned herself as the spirit muse of international ballet. The secret is in her heart. Her grace, nobility, and artistic freedom issue from the crucible of her modest, hardscrabble origins and not despite them. Her instincts relayed the message that becoming a ballet dancer would mean honest, disciplined work, where candor and intelligence would find their echo in art and beauty.

Carla Fracci was born in Milan on August 20, 1936. Her father was drafted into the Italian armed forces and stationed in Russia during most of World War II. When she was seven years old, Carla was sent to live with her grandmother in Crimona, the city renowned for its Stradavarius violin, near Bologna, where she enjoyed the freedom of country life. Her mother worked at a Milan auto plant making wheel bolts. Upon her father's return, the Fracci family, which included Carla's sister Marisa, moved back to Milan, where her father took a job as a tram conductor.

Carla Fracci with Erik Bruhn in *Romeo and Juliet.* © **Martha Swope.**

Her parents were very young, and enjoyed dancing the tango, rumba, and waltz. Carla shared their enthusiasm for "ballroom" and loved to dance with her uncles. An orchestra conductor and family friend recognized the child's talent and persuaded Carla's father to enroll her in La Scala's dance academy. For a humble family, a tuition-free dance education at La Scala offered a tremendous opportunity. Carla presented herself as one of 300 children who auditioned. She was small and fragile, with a fine-featured symmetrical face. The children were divided into three groups. The first group was sent home, rejected. Those in the second group were immediately accepted. Those in the third were summoned to return for a second audition. With her delicate ankles, Carla was placed in the third group. Seeing Carla again among the others, one of the jury members said, "She's very thin, small, pretty. Let's take her."[2]

Carla entered the school when she was nine. She knew nothing of ballet at the time, never having seen a performance. Her teachers at

La Scala were Estorina Mazzuchelli, Paolina Giussani, Edda Martinioni, Esme Bulnes, and Vera Volkova. During her first year, she didn't understand why if you were to dance, you had to remain at the barre for so long. She wished instead that she were back in Crimona dancing out of doors and running free in the country air. Then, with some other children, she was given the role of the page holding a mandolin in a performance of *Sleeping Beauty*. The children lined the stairs down which Aurora would walk. Margot Fonteyn as Aurora descended, as Fracci likes to put it, "straight into this young girl's heart!" She waited after the performance to see what would happen, and saw Frederick Ashton arrive to correct just *one finger* on Fonteyn's hand. When she saw that even someone as perfectly beautiful as Fonteyn could receive such a minute correction, it clicked. That was what ballet was—to see how to dance so precisely and carefully through the eyes of a teacher. Fracci says that it opened another world to her.

She shows me how delicate her legs are, especially her ankles. "Can you imagine as a child how *magra* [thin] I was—and my ankles!" she says, laughing. Fracci realized that because of the weakness in her ankles, she would have to "work like crazy," the first to arrive in class, standing at barre repeating her *coup de pied*, or taking advantage of the heat to stretch. "I wanted to be like Margot Fonteyn, to have that light in my eyes. I tried to form myself like her, working first with Edda Martinioni and then with Esme Bulnes."[3] Fracci graduated in 1954, and her *passo d'addio* [farewell dance], the qualifying student showcase event at the Opera House, took place in 1955, on the same evening as a new production of the opera "La Sonnambula" directed by Luchino Visconti and starring Maria Callas. Visconti's assistant Beppe Menegatti, then 24, found Fracci enchanting. He circulated among the audience during the opera's intermission, urging as many people as he could to stay to see the new promising young dancer. Beginning with that evening, Fracci was hailed as the ballet's rising star. Carla and Beppe would marry seven years later in 1962.

In 1956, the French ballerina Violette Verdy was to have danced the title role in Alfred Rodrigues' *Cinderella* at La Scala, but was called away at the last minute. The artistic directors debated whether to put Carla in as a substitute. Some feared that she was too inexperienced. She spoke up and said, "If you choose me, you will be able to decide!" She was put in and went to the theater on New Year's Eve morning to rehearse with the orchestra, and like the character she danced, her debut in a full-length ballet was a triumph. Later that year, Anton Dolin invited Fracci to dance the role of Fanny Cerrito in his *Pas de Quatre* at the 1957 Nervi Festival. The other three dancers were Yvette Chauviré, Alicia Markova, and Margrethe Schanne. Fracci describes herself as the "unknown" of the four, but in 1958 she was promoted to Prima Ballerina. Dolin went on to invite Carla to dance *Giselle* as a guest of the London Festival Ballet in 1959, with John Gilpin dancing Albrecht. He asked her again and again to show him her arabesque because it so much reminded him of Olga Spessivtseva's. Kenneth McMillan, John Cranko, and Lynn Seymour were in the audience, applauding wildly. When asked how it felt, Fracci admits that it was difficult to gauge her feelings because she had sprained her ankle in rehearsal and received an injection of pain medication. She does recall that as a young dancer, she was eager to take on the challenge and approach it without nervousness, understanding that it had to be fresh and real to be a success. She was embarrassed by what reviewer Oleg Karensky wrote: that the last Giselle (there were three casts) was the best, that "the baby ballerina" was incredible. It was during this period that she learned that the better part of wisdom came with the understanding that daily barre is the dancer's bread and butter.

Carla was in Level Four when Vera Volkova assumed the director-ship of La Scala for one year. Volkova began to give her private classes. Later in the early 60s, when Volkova went to the Royal Danish Ballet in Copenhagen, she invited Carla to accompany her. Carla decided to accept Volkova's invitation and continued taking class with her there, where she danced the balcony scene from *Romeo and Juliet* as well as *La Sylphide* with Erik Bruhn. In 1961, Lucia Chase invited Bruhn to dance with ABT. He agreed to join the company under one condition: that Carla Fracci be invited also. She went with Erik to the United States to dance *La Sylphide* and *Giselle* with ABT. In 1966, at La Scala, she danced Gelsomina, the iron-spined but waif-like character in the ballet *La Strada*, inspired by Federico Fellini's film of the same name. Her partner was Mario Pistoni. There is a film of a 1968 Giselle performance, which features Fracci, Bruhn, Bruce Marks, Toni Lander, Ted Kivitt, and Eleanor D'Antuono in the leading roles. By 1971, having found her place at ABT, Fracci left La Scala, but not before having had the chance to partner with Paolo Bertoluzzi. She felt that the company did not use her frequently enough, and the work they were doing was not nearly as interesting to her as the roles ABT was giving her, even as that company was suffering financial hardships. When Fracci joined the company, there were facilities for the school, but no company rehearsal studios. The dancers would be given various addresses at which to rehearse. On one occasion, Fracci and Bruhn were given an address for a *Giselle* rehearsal. When they arrived, it turned out that it was a nightclub. Incredulous at first, and then having a good laugh over it, they pushed aside tables, chairs, and barstools, and proceeded to rehearse. While she was at ABT, Carla was able to work with Hugh Laing, and danced Antony Tudor's *Lilac Garden*. Erik and Carla's partnership entered into a friendly competition with Margot Fonteyn's and Rudolf Nureyev's, and Fracci tells of how audiences would catch one couple's performance before the intermission and then move on to another theater to see the other couple dance.[4]

While at ABT, Fracci was privileged to see Sonia Arova dance *Don Quixote* with Bruhn, while she continued to be his *Giselle* partner. She also danced *Raymonda* and John Butler's *After Eden*. In 1974, she danced the role of Civilization in Ugo dell'Ara's reconstruction of Luigi Manzotti's *Excelsior* at the Maggio Musicale Fiorentino (Florence May Music Festival). She danced in a Madrid production of Jose Limon's *The Moor's Pavanne* with Bruce Marks. John Butler created the title role of *Medea* on her for the Spoleto Festival, which she danced with Mikhail Baryshnikov in 1975. Her 1981 performance in Alfred Rodrigues' *Mirandolina* showed her coquettish side. Fracci interrupts the quiet recitation of her repertoire to offer reminiscences about Butler, whom she describes as a "fantastic man," with whom she shared a close relationship. After his death, Fracci was very moved to discover that Butler had left her a painting.

Retracing her steps, Fracci tells of how Cranko was invited to La Scala by Esme Bulnes. When he saw Carla, he said, "I want this girl!" He created Juliet on her with Mario Pistoni as Romeo, and then invited her to dance the ballet in London. Eventually he invited Fracci to follow him to Stuttgart, but at the age of 20, she felt that it would be too difficult to leave her family and La Scala. It had been a big decision and one that she regrets "a little bit," but she nonetheless feels lucky that she was able to dance his *Romeo and Juliet* there, and in Venice at the Lisa La Verdi Open Air Theater. Fracci was a guest in Cranko's home in London, and felt the loss of "a great choreographer" acutely when he died. "He was a genius for me and there are so many other things...he left his ballets to Dieter Graf. We were all such close friends when we were young—all living together in the same house."[5] The "little bit" of regret may in part stem from knowing that it had been Cranko's wish to set *Onegin* on Fracci, which was instead created on the extraordinary Marcia Haydée. Still, Fracci had an opportunity to dance the role of Tatiana in *Onegin* at La Scala, and in New York with Erik Bruhn, who taught it to her, and it remains one of her favorite ballets.

For Fracci, working with Anton Dolin was one of the greatest pleasures of her career. She views herself as a continuator of Dolin's teaching. He taught her how to see the characters and locate their gestures in the spectrum of countervailing feelings that inhabit their inner lives. She insists that is it not sufficient to be satisfied with being a great ballerina, as some dancers are: one has an obligation to transmit the style of Spessivtseva, for example, or Markova. One must thoroughly master the difference between Giselle in the first act, when she is girlishly shy and experiencing her first feelings of love, and who she becomes in the second, when she is both a spirit and an instrument of rectitude, while still able to access her own trove of forgiveness and fortitude.

Dolin showed Fracci how to build a costume, create the makeup, and arrange her hair to support the character in both of its embodiments.

> He took me to the tailor to find the right kind of tulle and shared his idea of the design and shape of the costume based on the kind of line it would show, and

taught me how to comb my hair to best present my profile onstage. I was so spoiled by him that afterwards I went all the way to London to buy silk tulle![6]

She then relates a story about back of house inventiveness: Fracci is scrupulous about checking her costume before a performance to make sure that all is as it should be. One evening, she found that her silk tulle tutu had been sent out by the dresser to be dry cleaned. It had shrunk into a perfectly round ball! A seamstress had been sewing a costume for the dancer Eleanor D'Antuono who was about the same size as Fracci. Within moments, they grabbed D'Antuono's costume and reworked it into a costume for Fracci. As she speaks of D'Antuono, her eyes brighten and she says, "You know that girl was fantastic—so smart! If someone was injured, you could pull her into the dressing room, put her in that injured dancer's costume, push her out onto the stage, and she would dance the role perfectly with no rehearsal!"[7]

While Fracci likes to refer to *Giselle* as her "warhorse," she returns again and again to a single idea: Never think that just because you have danced a ballet many, many times, you can take it for granted. "No!" she says emphatically.

> Always look and learn, especially from your guests. "How does she approach the role? What does she bring to it from her culture?" Never think, "This is it, I'm finished [learning the role]." To believe and think is to learn, to notice and observe that, "Ah, this one is Russian, so very strong technically and beautiful." There are so many approaches to learn from.[8]

It could be said that the commitment to perpetual reassessment became Fracci's fulcrum across the length and breadth of her career. Early on, she made the decision to continually expand and enhance her vocabulary as a dancer and an actress, helped immeasurably by the eye, humor, and creative sensibilities of her husband, Beppe Menegatti. Her capacities to create characters were seen in such roles as Lady of the Mountain in Loris Gai's *The Stone Flower* (1973), and as the Fairy in his *Le Baiser de la Fée* (1975). When she danced Medea with Baryshnikov, Fracci crossed from the ethereal and mythical to the real, cultivating an earthy rootedness in which to grow the gnarled passion and vengeance that ends up defining her character. In 1982, Fracci played Giuseppina Strepponi in an Italian television serial about the life of Giuseppe Verdi, later taking an English-language version to England, the United States, and other English-speaking countries. She played the famous dancer Tamara Karsavina in the 1980 film *Nijinsky*, directed by Herbert Ross, and has played major roles in television productions in Italy and other countries. The documentary "An Hour with Carla Fracci" was shown on Italian television in 1973.[9]

Fracci's facility and range as a dancer and actress made possible her unflinching portrayal of the Accused (Lizzie Borden) in Agnes De Mille's *Fall River Legend*. In Naples, at the Teatro San Carlo and Teatro

Mercandante, she has collaborated on projects with her husband that produced *Nijinsky Memorie di Givinezza, Cocteau-Opium* (1989), and *Eleonora Duse-Isadora Duncan: Adieu et au Revoir* (1991). Because of her tremendous theatrical range, the critic Clive Barnes called Fracci "the Duse of Dance."[10] In part, she credits accolades such as Barnes' to her collaboration with Beppe Menegatti, who generated so many of the ideas that formed the spokes in the wheel of her rounded career. Fracci says,

> In my life, and in my career, I did not only *Giselle*; I did movies, television, modern dance, I did "Can Can" and then the dramatic and passionate roles. I'm not just Giselle, because I have always done a broad range of characters and ballets and so I am never lost without *Giselle*, my warhorse. Gaining other experiences made me grow in certain ways, so that I brought much more to the traditional ballets when I returned to them: Working in film made the story ballets richer experiences when I danced them onstage.[11]

She recounts what it was like to dance and act in "Midsummer Night's Dream," in which she played Titania. Ferruccio Soleri played Oberon, and Gian Carlo Giannini was chosen by Menegatti to play Puck. "We have to use our body *and* our brain, because it is with the brain that you express and find the character," says Fracci.[12]

She makes the point that what a dancer does in the studio is one thing, and it is not the same as what the dancer does on stage.

> When I am onstage, I am not Carla Fracci. I am interpeting the character I am dancing. I do not plan what I do. I must have the freedom to discover as I dance. When I danced Giselle in the movie version, the director came to me, very angry, and said, "Why are you doing that in my movie?" Of course you follow the choreography, but you respond to what it says to you and what your partner makes you feel. In *Giselle*, each of the two acts is very different. In the first act, you are a country girl. In the second, you are a spirit. If you understand it, you don't have to be realistic. In what I had with Erik Bruhn, we did not have to speak.. We had an understanding. We didn't have to say, "You do this; I'll do that." Something happened onstage without us even knowing what. The technique has to be there, but you don't have to show it as you would in the studio. It is more important to show "What is behind that developpé á la seconde?" or "This arabesque is floating because she doesn't really touch the ground." So it is the kind of reading that you arrive at and decide on and that determines the kind of coordination of arms and legs, what is inside the port de bras and what is inside of you. Let your body breathe so you don't get tired. Go with the combination and the steps, but in between you have to let your body go, even if you risk making a fool of yourself, present yourself to the audience in a generous way. I demonstrate these things when we do *Sylphide* or *Giselle* and you can immediately see the way the dancers react when they are learning, but you arrive at a certain point where they have to make it their own. It's not nice to say, "I did it *this* way," because it has to be theirs. Even the counts. Do you say, "Can you do a six, [an entrechat six]?" when what you are concerned about is the quality

not the quantity? It is *a trasmettere*, the transmission, the handing down of the tradition, from [Carlotta] Grisi forward to today. We have to take care care of that because it's precious, like a diamond that gives off a certain light, keeping what we were taught. The freedom of the body changes over the generations. The legs have to both have and lose the technique to achieve the line and the feeling. You must always listen to the music like it's the first time because it gives you inspiration, and you must look in your partner's eyes because you will respond differently than you did the night before. So I had different experiences with Erik, Rudy or with Vasiliev, because each of those men came from a different culture and worked with a different concept, and you must value what they each have, and respond to it.

Anton Dolin taught Fracci the details of the Giselle role according to the Russian dancer's interpretation: the position of the neck, and how she bows to the Myrtha, Queen of the Wilis, the style that has been handed down, and which Fracci strongly insists must be retained. Because being invited to dance as a guest with a company offers the opportunity to absorb the traditions of that company and the special lessons its ballet masters can share, Fracci places a great value on taking full advantage of such invitations by arriving with an open mind. She cites such teachers as William Griffith at ABT and Olga Preobyshenska in Paris to illustrate her point.

I was never very sure of my feet, and so I had to work to develop them, and you start anew in that process with each teacher when you are a guest: Whether in Cuba or Australia, you have an opportunity to grow and develop yourself, meet new audiences, and take on new challenges. It is not so easy when you are young and you hear that you have a beautiful face or costume. No, you have to work to show that you are also strong, and that is where the teacher is so important. You have to develop an eye that sees what you need to fix on and offstage the next day, to correct the spine, the legs, the feet. Never let yourself go because you have achieved a certain position! You will never attain perfection, but taking class is what keeps you from losing ground by working daily and interacting with the people who have a richness that can give you the conceptions of the role: Read the play if you dance *Romeo and Juliet*. It is hard to believe, but there are dancers who never do. How else can you understand what is happening between Romeo, the father and Tybalt? Read it! Read it! Read it! You don't have the words, so your gestures must capture them because you are speaking with your body.[13]

The difficulty of conquering a character on one's own is what has prompted Fracci to surround herself with those who can offer her images, corrections, and the role's historical background.

If one fantasizes that Giselle had been twins and the ballet had instead been called "Les Gemelles Giselles" [The Giselle Twins], the cast that comes to mind would be Fracci and Alicia Alonso, both of them renowned for their interpretations of the peasant girl and the wili she inhabits when she dies. To illustrate the importance of gesture in the portrayal of a character, Fracci relates a story about Alonso, with whom she has shared a longstanding friendship. She begins by saying that Alonso is now blind, and on an occasion when Fracci was dancing *La Sylphide* at a Paris gala, Alonso was seated in the balcony. At a post- performance party, Alonso complimented Fracci on her work, saying, "I of course couldn't see *you*, but I saw your wrist, only your wrist!"[14] The use of the wrist was exquisite, and that made even the blind Alonso able to "see" the character. The point, Fracci explains, is that every element onstage assumes a meaning, and while one may be naturally very beautiful as was Fonteyn, the light in her eyes made her more so; where Markova might not have been naturally beautiful, her lightness endowed her dancing with beauty, making her fascinating to watch. In Fracci's first full-length ballet role as Cinderella, she had to dance with a broom. "I had to be shy with the broom, then more daring. I had to see the broom as a living person in order to make it work. Everything, even a broom, must be invested with life and meaning."[15]

She goes much deeper when she comments on her experience dancing the role of Juliet.

I remember *Romeo and Juliet* by Tudor. It was a masterpiece. I had a small pas de deux that I found very difficult. Then I saw that there were so many characters onstage, all intent on making Juliet marry Paris, someone she didn't love. Then they came with the white dress that I would wear at my wedding, and I discovered right at that moment that to put on that dress would be my death. Marrying a man I did not love! Suddenly I was in tears. Tudor liked that moment. He never allowed anyone at rehearsals, but he and Beppe were very close and Beppe was there, and heard Tudor say, 'That dress!' It was such a strong moment. The dress represented everything that was the tragedy of this girl. If you have the strength inside to feel that, then the music is a part of it. There is no secret. It's just you, the approaches that you take, the decision to keep doing new roles and to discover who you are in them. Without them, you won't find yourself, the suffering that you don't know you are capable of, to gain an understanding of who you are—that part of yourself you don't know, and that every life is not the same. For me to do this, I have to really concentrate before I go onstage. I need my rest; I cannot speak, I have to warm up in a state of calm to conserve my energy, to protect myself. Sometimes it is tiring to speak, and dancing is like an exam in a way. If you are dancing the same role every night, you have to pay attention so that you have the excitement, agitation, and you want to do better each time, to get inside of what you are doing. Maybe because the audience admires you, they follow you [from venue to venue], and I don't want to dance the same way twice. I always want to find something to grab onto, and the strength to carry the performance by involving everyone on the stage, and not be selfish. I always want to bring everyone with me, and you can see whether you have succeeded in this by the reaction of the corps de ballet.[16]

There is a quiet moment when Fracci finishes, and she is seeking me out and asking me questions with her eyes. Do I get what she is saying? Is her English strong enough to convey what is so difficult to say even in one's own tongue? At this moment, this classically beautiful woman has opened up to share and savor with me the flavors and textures of her own experience, as if it were a heavenly picnic basket filled with delicacies. The quiet energy in her voice strains past fatigue to convey what is so historically and artistically important. It plumbs the depth of her special beauty, affirming the hard-earned lessons she has chosen to impart with her words.

She goes on to discuss other roles in which dancers must convey more than a single feeling or emotion. Sometimes they are contradictory, and the audience must be bidden to see the character's inner conflict.

You know, Juliet, she has everything, there is every material that you can think of: classical style, love, passion, drama, death. It is so full of material with which to work and show, all in one ballet! There's that moment when she runs and her cape is flying and really *she* is flying to get help from the apothecary. There are other roles with that kind of scope: Medea, Salome, Dali. For me, when I danced *La Primavera Romana de la Signora Stone* [The Roman Spring of Mrs. Stone], I danced a very complicated woman of 50, who is hoping to turn back the clock by taking on a lover who is young, a new love, but really a gigolo, and she knows this. I utilized the same kind of dramatic flashbacks as in *Romeo and Juliet* to evoke the conflict. Her husband has died, and now she discovers a passion that she has never known with her husband, and in a way it's a pity for her, but in another way, she has a fantastic moment, with so much to project and perceive. "I am old with wrinkles, but I am waiting for him." It's a moment every woman has had or can imagine. There is the strong wish to have that man and be young, but she discovers her own truth and rejects him, and doesn't let him touch her, though she longs for him, but finds the inner strength to say "No." Yes, they give you the choreography, but there's a gesture you have to find that says "I will suffer, I will die, but *No!*" She fights herself and resists; she feels the need of this man that she loves as strongly as the conflict she has, but she pulls herself together. Cranko did the choreography, but I had to find the gesture, as I did with *Medea*.[17]

Now it is I who wants to turn back the clock. My close friend and former High School of Performing Arts classmate Margaret Marchisio Luca is married to Carlo Romairone, who is originally from Genoa. When I asked him what he might like to know about Fracci, he said, "Ask Carla Fracci why she left the United States to return to Italy when her career here was so promising." I posed Romairone's question to Fracci.

She said,

I returned to Italy because I felt that this was my home and I didn't want to lose my relationship with La Scala, and I wasn't permanent there because

Even though ABT had invited me to be permanent, it was the same feeling as when Cranko invited me to join Stuttgart when I was younger. I had my theater, my security, language and family in Italy. The company [ABT] in America was wonderful: I received a lot of affection and esteem, and I can still feel it today. From time to time, my name appears in the paper. I was on the front cover of *Dance Magazine* with the headline "Romantic Ballerina." Clive Barnes called me the "Duse of Dance," and the way the critics followed me, and people waited for me to dance, even when I was just doing something short, like the pas de deux from *Flower Festival in Genzano* with Erik! The house was full all the time, but I knew I had so much to do in Italy, and I'm proud of what I accomplished. I began to guest outside of La Scala, which was the gold standard, but I had to do more to progress, to reach out to people in the smallest provinces, so instead of doing something like "Carla Fracci and Friends," I did the repertoire I knew and I worked like crazy to do it! Yes, I could have been dancing at La Scala instead, but we found beautiful theaters, danced on the piazzas, in churches, and not only to do the work, but to educate, because these audiences didn't go to La Scala, and couldn't afford the tickets.

In any case, I knew I would never leave America altogether because I cherished the experience of working with Erik Bruhn, Royes Fernandez, and Fernando Bujones. Words can't express how much I gave and how much I received—the excitement and richness of it. People came and said, "God bless you that we could see you tonight; your inspiration and the memory of your dancing helps us get through a difficult week." For the housewife who is stuck at home, she would be transported, and the feeling would stay with her and she would dream about it.[18]

Our discussion was interrupted by a knock at the door. Gillian Whittingham, the ballet mistress at Teatro dell'Opera arrived with the bad news that a dancer cast in that evening's performance of *Swan Lake* had been injured. Conferring briefly, Fracci and Wittingham decided that they would choose a student to cover and make their selection during company class. Fracci turned to me and said, "Just like me—when Verdy couldn't dance—an opportunity!" I asked if I might observe company class, and was warmly invited to do so.

Fracci takes barre every day with the company to maintain the continuity of her life as it has always been. She has come to Rome to shape the company into a better instrument and leads by example. In describing her forced departure from La Scala she said, "La Scala can be a box or a prison." After La Scala, Fracci directed small companies in Naples and Verona before assuming the directorship of Rome Opera Ballet. At Rome Opera, apart from almost every dancer being Italian, company class is heterogeneous, with dancers young and old. Of the upper rank dancers, at least two are Eastern European and another is Cuban. Their training gives them a stamina lacking in most of the Italian-trained dancers. By the Grand Allegro, all the dancers except a shank of male dancers and the young woman from Cuba who danced Odette/Odile the previous evening have peeled off and left class. It has been a challenge for Fracci to convince dancers whose contract requires that they take only three classes a week to actually show up for those classes, and with regard to the bigger picture, that their technique is compromised by taking any fewer than five. Fracci goes to a full split on the floor at the end of barre. The dancers are clearly impressed, but many who are half her age do not do a split or remain past Center for Grand Allegro.

In our earlier discussion, Fracci has recounted her experiences as an actress. She explains the difference between acting onstage where everything an actor does is very large, and acting before a camera, where the director is more interested in the detail and the work the actor does with the eyes and the voice. She said that being Milanese, her vowels are not considered round enough, impeding theatrical diction. When she played the role of Giuseppina Strepponi in ''Verdi,'' she worked with just the subtlety of a tiny smile to convey the character. It didn't come easily: She reminded her director Renato Castellani that she hadn't yet signed her contract, and perhaps he could still find an actress better suited to the role. Castellani insisted that she continue, and it went so well that whenever they were shooting one of her scenes, the crew would predict a short day with an early quitting time. Fracci's acting career enabled her to work with such actors as Alan Bates, Ronald Pickup, and George La Pena. The collaborations with such directors as Herbert Ross and Castellani, as well as with Dolin and Cranko, gave her an opportunity to contribute influence that went beyond her dancing to their artistic choices. She describes a moment in *Romeo and Juliet* when Juliet realizes that Romeo has taken his life believing that she has taken hers, and knows that she needs courage to join him in death. She wanted to take Romeo's torpid arm and put it around her, but first she stopped to ask Cranko whether it would be okay, and he said, ''Yes, of course.'' She attributes his willingness to give her such license to the profound mutual understanding that developed side by side with their friendship over the years.

Beppe Menegatti is charming, well-read, imaginative, interested in everything, and exudes a generosity of spirit fueled by his irrepressible creative energy. Over coffee in the Teatro dell'Opera canteen, he reminisces about Alicia Alonso and tells me that he and Carla will be visiting her in Cuba in two weeks' time. The mention of Cuba leads us to a discussion of world politics, and before I know it, Beppe has invited me to join Carla and him for dinner at their Rome apartment built into a ruin overlooking the Coliseum. Over a dinner that night where Gillian Whittingham, the company's ballet mistress, and Barbara Gronchi, Fracci's niece and aide de camp, are present, Fracci talks more about her partnerships, returning to a story about Rudolf Nureyev. ''My God, he was so rough with me!'' ''How so?'' we ask in unison. ''He. . .'' and she hesitates, searching for the right word in English. Failing to find it she finally says, ''He *bruscatami*, dragged me between his legs! One of the other dancers cried

Carla Fracci in *Giselle*. **Photo credit: Judy Cameron.**

because of the way he handled her!" We are all puzzled by her choice of
the verb "bruscare." We all know the noun "bruschetta" in Italian, and
Gillian, Barbara, and I know the adverb "brusque" in English, but are still
confused. Beppe leaves the table and returns toting a massive Italian-
English dictionary. It defines "bruscare" as the rough brushing of a horse.
Beppe's reading of the definition leaves us no choice but to collapse in
laughter at the idea of Rudy handling Carla so brutishly, fully aware that
she cherishes other memories of his generosity and kindliness.

We speak again of Erik Bruhn and the rare love that ballet partners
discover for one another for which there is no equal. We look at photos
of Fracci and Beppe's son, Francesco, who is an architect, and his wife,
Dina and their two year old grandson, Giovanni, who when asked
recently which CD he would like to buy, chose an opera recording. Beppe
raises the names of several dancers from San Francisco and Houston
whom he would like to bring to Rome Opera as guests. He asks my

opinion of his ideas for future ballet season programs. It's an evening that holds the promise of being unforgettable, making you fear that if you overstay, there will be too many delightful details to recapture and treasure when it is over. We discuss commitment to the discipline of revolutionary activism. "Does it require too much sacrifice?" Beppe wonders aloud. Earlier in the day Fracci has raised and dismissed the same question about the life of a ballet dancer. The revolutionary and the artist share a desire to leave the world a better place than they found it. This is a privilege, not a sacrifice. She and I exchange glances, smile and agree that no, it does not, especially if one's commitment and discipline are placed in the service of bringing to the fore the best that humankind can create for itself and future generations.

Notes

Chapter 1

1. "Danseur Noble," *Time*, New York, May 5, 1961, p. 1.
2. John Gruen, *Erik Bruhn, Danseur Noble* (New York: Viking, 1979), p. 34.
3. Ibid., p. 40.
4. Ibid., p. 53.
5. Ibid., p. 62.
6. Ibid., p. 89.
7. Ibid., p. 101.
8. Ibid., p. 75.
9. Ibid., p. 90
10. Ibid., p.105.
11. Ibid., p. 107.
12. Ibid., p.124.
13. Ibid., p. 131.
14. Ibid., p. 123.
15. Ibid., p. 122.
16. Ibid., p 173.
17. Ibid., p.131
18. Ibid., p. 138
19. Ibid., p. 163.
20. Ibid., p. 169.

Chapter 2

1. Beatrice Siegel, *Alicia Alonso: The Story of a Ballerina* (New York: Frederick Warne & Co., Inc., 1979), p. 50.
2. Ibid., p. 41.
3. Ibid., p. 48.
4. Ibid., p. 47.

5. Ibid. p. 48.

6. Ibid., p. 68.

7. Ibid., p. 72.

8. Ibid., p. 125.

9. Ibid., p. 126.

10. Ibid., p. 126.

11. Interview with Laura Alonso by author, Pacifica, California, April, 2004.

12. Interview with Lupe Calzadilla by author, San Francisco, July, 2006.

13. Beatrice Siegel, *Alicia Alonso: The Story of a Ballerina* (New York: Frederick Warne & Co., Inc., 1979), p. 154.

14. Ibid., p. 153.

15. *Alicia*, Created and produced by Frank Boehm, Gordon Weisenborn, Director, Yale Wexler, Executive Producer, Robb Orr, Film Editor. Terpsichore Productions. 1983.

16. Ibid.

Chapter 3

1. Diane Solway, *Nureyev: His Life* (New York, William Morrow and Company, Inc., 1998), p. 543.

2. Ibid., p. 23.

3. Ibid., p. 25.

4. Ibid., p. 34.

5. Ibid., p. 48.

6. Ibid., p. 57.

7. Ibid., p. 67.

8. Ibid., p. 71

9. Ibid., p. 73.

10. Ibid., p. 82

11. Ibid., p. 94.

12. Ibid., p. 134.

13. Ibid., p. 144.

14. Ibid., p. 138.

Chapter 4

1. John Rockwell, "Sadler's Wells Makes U.S. Debut," *New York Times*, October 10, 1949, p. 20.

2. Margot Fonteyn, *Margot Fonteyn: Autobiography* (New York: Knopf, 1976), p. 14.

3. Ibid., p. 15.

4. Ibid., p. 16.

5. Ibid., p. 29.

6. Ibid., p. 34.

7. Ibid., p. 36.

8. Ibid.

9. Ibid., p. 38.

10. Ibid., p. 47.

11. Ibid., p. 51.

12. Ibid., p. 58.

13. Ibid.

14. Ibid., p. 63.

15. Ibid., p. 64.

16. Ibid., p. 70.

17. Ibid., p. 89.

18. Ibid., p. 106.

19. Ibid., p. 111.

20. Meredith Daneman, *Margot Fonteyn: A Life* (New York: Viking, 2004), p. 207.

21. Margot Fonteyn, *Margot Fonteyn: Autobiography* (New York: Knopf, 1976), p. 138.

22. Ibid., p. 205.

23. Ibid., p. 208.

24. Ibid., p. 210.

25. Ibid., p. 216.

26. Meredith Daneman, *Margot Fonteyn: A Life* (New York: Viking, 2004.) p. 522.

27. Ibid., p. 515.

28. Ibid., p. 522.

29. Ibid., p. 523.

30. Ibid., p. 559.

31. Ibid., p. 576.

32. Ibid., p. 578.

33. Ibid., p. 580.

Chapter 5

1. John Rockwell, "Baryshnikov is Overwhelming," *New York Times*, August 4, 1974, p. 85.

2. Barbara Aria, *Misha, The Mikhail Baryshnikov Story* (New York: St. Martin's Press, 1989), p. 9.

3. Ibid., p. 16.

4. Ibid., p. 20.

5. Ibid.

6. Ibid., p. 27.

7. Ibid., p. 32.

8. Ibid., p. 33.

9. Ibid., p. 35.

10. Ibid., p. 88.

11. Ibid., p. 99.

12. Ibid., p. 101.

13. Toba Singer. Interview with Bruce Marks, criticaldance.com, August, 2002.

14. Barbara Aria, *Misha, The Mikhail Baryshnikov Story* (New York: St. Martin's Press, 1989), p. 117.

15. Ibid., p. 120.

16. Ismene Brown, "I hate authority—I like to make my own mistakes," Telegraph.co.uk, February 2, 2004.

17. Joan Acocella, "Loners," *New Yorker*, December 12, 2005, p. 114.

Chapter 6

1. V. Svetloff, *Anna Pavlova* (New York: Dover Publications, Inc., 1974), p. 162.
2. Walford Hyden, *Pavlova* (Boston: Little, Brown, and Company, 1931), p. 20.
3. Ibid., p. 29.
4. Walford Hyden, *Pavlova* (Boston: Little, Brown, and Company, 1931), p. 24.
5. Ibid., p. 29.
6. Ibid., p. 31.
7. V. Svetloff, *Anna Pavlova* (New York: Dover Publications, Inc., 1974), p. 148.
8. Walford Hyden, *Pavlova* (Boston: Little, Brown, and Company, 1931), p. 59.
9. Ibid., p. 106.
10. Ibid., p. 122.
11. Svetloff, *Anna Pavlova* (New York: Dover Publications, Inc., 1974), p. 156.
12. Ibid., p. 158–9.
13. Walford Hyden, *Pavlova* (Boston: Little, Brown, and Company, 1931), p. 153–4.
14. Ibid., p. 245.

Chapter 7

1. Anna Kisselgoff, "Dance: A Surprising Houston Ballet," *New York Times*, April 8, 1981.
2. Li Cunxin, *Mao's Last Dancer: A Memoir* (New York: G.P. Putnam's Sons, 2003), p. 17.
3. Ibid., p. 53.
4. Ibid., p.178.
5. Ibid., p. 211.
6. Ibid., p. 276.
7. Ibid., p. 299.
8. Ibid., p. 321.
9. Interview with Li Cunxin by author, San Francisco, October 13, 2004.

Chapter 8

1. Don McDonagh, *New York Times*, January 31, 1972, p. 23.
2. Gelsey Kirkland, *Dancing on My Grave* (New York: Doubleday, Inc., 1986), p. 65.
3. Ibid., p. 66.
4. Ibid., p. 70.
5. Ibid., p. 71.
6. Ibid., p. 78.
7. Ibid., p. 94.
8. Ibid., p. 97.
9. Ibid., p. 103.
10. Ibid., p. 106.
11. Ibid., p. 112.
12. Ibid., p. 120.
13. Ibid.

14. Ibid., p. 138.

15. Ibid., p. 209.

16. Ibid., p. 222.

17. Ibid., p. 243.

18. Gelsey Kirkland and Greg Lawrence, *The Shape of Love* (New York: Double-day, 1990), p. 69.

19. Ibid., p. 70.

20. Ibid.

21. Ibid.

22. Ibid., p. 106.

Chapter 9

1. Don McDonagh, "Dance: Ailey's Cuban Encore," *New York Times*, May 13, 1967.

2. Toba Singer, "Teacher's Wisdom: Lázaro Carreño," *Dance Magazine*, December, 2004, pp. 81–82.

3. Interview with Lázaro Carreño by author, March 17, 2004, Houston.

4. Octavio Roca, "Ballet Nacional de Cuba-Alicia Alonso Interview," Havana Journal, *Miami Herald*, February 23, 2004.

5. Interview with Lázaro Carreño by author, May 21, 2004.

6. Toba Singer, "Teacher's Wisdom: Lázaro Carreño," *Dance Magazine*, December, 2004, pp. 81–82.

7. Ibid.

Chapter 10

1. Natalia Makarova, *A Dance Autobiography* (New York: Alfred A. Knopf, 1979), p. 174.

2. Ibid., p. 22.

3. Ibid., p. 41.

4. Ibid., p. 49.

5. Ibid., p. 80.

6. Ibid., p. 81.

7. Ibid., p. 97.

8. Ibid., p. 113.

9. Ibid.

10. Ibid., pp. 116–117.

11. Ibid., p. 168.

12. Ibid., p. 169

13. Email interview with Natalia Makarova by author, December, 2006.

14. Ibid.

Chapter 11

1. *International Encyclopedia of Dance*, vol. 5, ed. Selma Jeanne Cohen (New York: Oxford University Press, 1998), p. 204.

2. Maya Plisetskaya, *I, Maya Plisetskaya* (New Haven: Yale University Press, 2001), p. 6.

3. Ibid., p. 7.
4. Ibid., p. 22.
5. Ibid., p. 30.
6. Ibid., p. 74.
7. Ibid., p. 111.
8. Ibid., p. 149.
9. Ibid., p. 219.
10 Ibid., p. 222.
11. Ibid., p. 246.
12. *International Encyclopedia of Dance*, vol. 5, ed. Selma Jeanne Cohen (New York: Oxford University Press, 1998), p. 206.
13. Ibid.

Chapter 12

1. Luke Jennings, "If you see one thing..." *London Observer*, March 5, 2006.
2. Rafael Estefania, "El salta de Carlos Acosta," BBCMundo.com, November 7, 2005, p. 1.
3. Ibid.
4. Margaret Putnam, "Houston Liftoff: Cuban Born Carlos Acosta is Making an International Career at Houston Ballet and Britain's Royal Ballet," *Dance Magazine*, March, 1998, p. 3.
5. Christine Toomey, "Manna from Havana," www.timesonline.co.uk, May 15, 2005, p.1.
6. Ibid., p. 5.
7. Margaret Willis, "The King of Hearts," *Dance Magazine*, May, 2005, p. 36.
8. Mike Dixon, "Carlos Acosta," *Critics Circle*, www.nationaldanceawards.com, 2002, p. 2.
9. Interview with Carlos Acosta by author, London, January 4, 2005.
10. Martha Sánchez, "Sueños y Desafíos," www.islasi.com, June 5, 2005, p. 2.
11. Interview with Carlos Acosta by author, London, January 4, 2005.
12. Ibid.
13. Ibid.
14. Ibid., p. 11.
15. Interview with Lauren Anderson and Andrew Edmonson, Houston, June 17, 2005.
16. Ibid.
17. Ibid.
18. Ibid.
19. Ibid.
20. Ibid.
21. Ibid.
22. Ibid.
23. Telephone interview with Tiekka Prieve by author, June 3, 2006.
24. Ibid.
25. Ibid.
26. Ibid.
27. Ibid.
28. Ibid.

29. Christine Toomey, "Manna from Havana," www.timesonline.co.uk, May 15, 2005, p. 2.
30. Interview with Carlos Acosta by author, London, January 6, 2005.
31. Ibid.
32. Ibid.
33. Ibid.

Chapter 13

1. Rick Nelson, *Miami Star Tribune*, October 25, 2000.
2. Rachel Howard, *San Francisco Chronicle*, December 13, 2001.
3. Marilyn Tucker, *Contra Costa Times*, May 1, 1999.
4. Interview with Muriel Maffre by author, San Francisco, October 17, 2005.
5. Ibid.
6. Ibid.
7. Email interview by author with Monique Maffre, October, 2006.
8. Interview with Muriel Maffre by author, San Francisco, October 17, 2005.
9. Ibid.
10. Ibid.
11. Ibid.
12. Ibid.
13. Ibid.
14. Ibid.
15. Ibid.
16. Ibid.
17. Ibid.
18. Ibid.
19. Ibid.
20. Ibid.
21. Email interview by author with Monique Maffre, October, 2006.
22. Interview by author with Claire Sheridan, San Francisco, July 22, 2006.
23. Ibid.
24. Email interview by author with Monique Maffre, October, 2006.
25. Ibid.
26. Ibid.
27. Ibid.
28. Ibid.
29. Ibid.
30. Ibid.
31. Ibid.
32. Interview with Muriel Maffre by author, San Francisco, November 19, 2005.

Chapter 14

1. Barbara Milberg Fisher, *In Balanchine's Company* (Middletown, CT: Wesleyan Press, 2006), p. 170.
2. Interview with Arthur Mitchell by author, New York, October 9, 2006.
3. Tobi Tobias, *Arthur Mitchell* (New York: Crowell, 1975), p. 8.
4. Interview with Arthur Mitchell by author, New York, October 9, 2006.

5. Toba Singer, "Arthur Mitchell at San Francisco Performing Arts Library with Sheryl Flatow and Brad Rosenstein, January 2004," criticaldance.com, January 28, 2004.

6. Ibid.

7. Interview with Arthur Mitchell by author, New York, October 9, 2006.

8. Tobi Tobias, *Arthur Mitchell* (New York: Crowell, 1975), p. 17.

9. Interview with Arthur Mitchell by author, New York, October 9, 2006.

10. Toba Singer, "Arthur Mitchell at San Francisco Performing Arts Library with Sheryl Flatow and Brad Rosenstein, January 21, 2004," criticaldance.com, January 2004.

11. Barbara Milberg Fisher, *In Balanchine's Company* (Middletown, CT: Wesleyan Press, 2006), p. 149.

12. Ibid.

13. Hilary B. Ostlere, *International Encyclopedia of Dance: A Project of Dance Perspectives Foundation*, vol. 3, Selma Jeanne Cohen, Ed. (New York: Oxford University Press, 1968), p. 436.

14. Interview with Arthur Mitchell by author, New York, October 21, 2006.

15. Valerie Gladstone, "DTH Celebrates the Big 30," *Dance Magazine*, October, 1999, p. 70.

16. Ibid.

17. Hilary B. Ostler, *International Encyclopedia of Dance: a project of Dance Perspectives Foundation*, vol. 4, Selma Jeanne Cohen, ed. (New York: Oxford University Press, 1968), p. 436.

18. Ibid., p. 72.

19. Interview with Arthur Mitchell by author, New York, October 21, 2006.

20. Valerie Gladstone, "DTH Celebrates the Big 30," *Dance Magazine*, October, 1999, p. 72.

21. Interview with Arthur Mitchell by author, New York, October 21, 2006.

22. Valerie Gladstone, "DTH Celebrates the Big 30," *Dance Magazine*, October, 1999, p. 72.

23. Ibid.

24. Ibid.

25. Interview with Arthur Mitchell by author, New York, October 9, 2006.

26. Ibid.

27. Valerie Gladstone and Alexandria Dionne, "DTH Dancers Suffer Defeat: Mitchell Seethes over Strike," *Dance Magazine*, May, 1997, p. 16.

28. Kate Mattingly, "Happy Ending for DTH: New York season imminent," *Dance Magazine*, 1997, p. 23.

29. Interview with Ikolo Griffin, San Francisco, November 28, 2006.

30. Ibid.

31. Ibid.

32. Ibid.

33. Ibid.

34. Ibid.

Chapter 15

1. Lorenzo Arruga, "Perché Carla Fracci?" *Blowup*, 1974, p. 63.

2. Interview with Carla Fracci by author, Rome, October 18, 2006

3. *International Encyclopedia of Dance*, vol. 3, Selma Jeanne Cohen, ed. (New York, Oxford University Press, 1998), p. 57.
4. Ibid.
5. Ibid.
6. Ibid.
7. Ibid.
8. Ibid.
9. *International Encyclopedia of Dance*, vol. 3, Selma Jeanne Cohen, ed. (New York, Oxford University Press, 1998), p. 61.
10. Ibid.
11. Ibid.
12. Ibid.
13. Ibid.
14. Interview with Carla Fracci by author, Rome, October 18, 2006.
15. Ibid.
16. Ibid.
17. Ibid.
18. Ibid.

Bibliography

Abreu, Andres. "Fidel attends Carlos Acosta's choreographic debut." www.
granma.cu, February 17, 2003.

Acocella, Joan. "Loners." *New Yorker,* December 12, 2005.

Amirrezvani, Anita. "Longtime Alonso," *Contra Costa Times*, February 11,
1999.

Aria, Barbara. *Misha, The Mikhail Baryshnikov Story.* New York: St. Martin's Press,
1989.

Arruga, Lorenzo. "Perché Carla Fracci?" *Blowup,* 1974.

Baldini, Lucia. *Carla Fracci: immagini 1996-2005.* Florence: Le Lettere, 2005.

Brown, Ismene, "I hate authority—I like to make my own mistakes."
Telegraph.co.uk, February 2, 2004.

Campoy, Ana and Anar Desai. "Ballet: Cuba's Enduring Revolution." *Cubans
2001*, journnalism.berkeley.edu, April 5, 2002.

Carman, Joseph. "Harlem Troupe Faces Uncertain Future." *Dance Magazine*,
December, 2004.

Chesini, Luciano. *Carla Fracci: Presentazione di Vittoria Ottolenghi.* Rome:
Gregoriana, 1970.

Collins, Kareyn D. "Does Classicism Have a Color?" *Dance Magazine,* June,
2005.

"Dance with Destiny." www.theage.com.au, September 1, 2003.

Daneman, Meredith. *Margot Fonteyn: A Life.* New York: Viking, 2004.

Dixon, Mike. "Carlos Acosta." *Critics Circle*, National Dance Awards, 2002.

Dunning, Jennifer. "Charles Engell France, 59, A Presence in Ballet World, Dies."
New York Times, December 29, 2005.

Estefania, Rafael. "El salta de Carlos Acosta." BBCMundo.com, November 21,
2001.

Fisher, Barbara Milberg. *In Balanchine's Company.* Middletown, CT: Wesleyan
Press, 2006.

Fonteyn, Margot. *Margot Fonteyn: Autobiography.* New York: Knopf, 1976.

Fukushima, Rhoda. "The Facts on Backs—Health and Fitness for Life." *Dance Magazine*, April, 2002.

Gargiulio, Giuliana. *Carla Fracci dall A alla Z: tra pubblico e private*. Naples: grauseditore, October, 2005.

Gladstone, Valerie. "Saluting Arthur Mitchell: DTH Celebrates the Big 30." *Dance Magazine*, October, 1999.

Gladstone, Valerie and Alexandria Dionne. "DTH Dancers Suffer Defeat: Mitchell Seethes Over Strike." *Dance Magazine*, May, 1997.

Glentzer, Molly. "Houston Ballet Star-Turned Broker: Li Cunxin Choreographs Another Career with a Book of Personal and Professional Memoirs." *Houston Chronicle*, March 28, 2004.

Gold, Sylviane. "Misha's World." *Dance Magazine*, February, 2006.

Gruen, John. *Erik Bruhn, Danseur Noble*. New York: Viking Press, 1979.

Gruen, John. "Natalia Makarova: Off Her Toes." *Dance Magazine*, January, 1993.

Hyden, Walford. *Pavlova*. Boston: Little, Brown, and Company, 1931.

International Encyclopedia of Dance. Selma Jeanne Cohen, ed. A project of the Dance Perspectives Foundation, New York: Oxford University Press, 1998.

Jennings, Luke. "If you see one thing…" *Observer*, March 5, 2006.

Kendall, Elizabeth. "Company as Community: DTH at 20." *Dance Magazine*, June, 1989.

Kinetz, Erika. "Born on 37th Street, but Headed for Buffalo." *New York Times*, June 4, 2006.

Kirkland, Gelsey. *Dancing on My Grave*. New York: Doubleday, Inc., 1986.

Kirkland, Gelsey. *Shape of Love*. New York: Doubleday, 1990.

Levin, Jordan. "Revolutionary Moves." *Los Angeles Times*, January 11, 1998.

Li, Cunxin. *Mao's Last Dancer: A Memoir*. New York: G.P. Putnam's Sons, 2003.

Lydon, "Straight from the Heart: Gelsey Kirkland." *Dance Magazine*, September, 2005.

McDonagh, Don. "Ailey's Cuban Encore." *New York Times*, May 13, 1977.

McDonagh, Don. "D'Amboise 'Fantasy' Given with Clifford and Miss Kirkland.'" *New York Times*, January 31, 1972, p. 23.

Machado, Lola Huete. "Maya Plisétskaya: Los encantos del cisne." *El País*, Madrid, December 23, 2005.

Marriott, Bruce. "Carlos Acosta: Principal, The Royal Ballet." www.ballet.co.uk, November, 1998.

Martin, John. "Sadler's Wells Makes U.S. Debut." *New York Times*, October 10, 1949, p. 20.

Martínez, Reny. "Carlos Acosta con el Ballet Nacional de Cuba: Memorable y accidentado Apolo." www.danzahoy.com, November 7, 2005.

Mattingly, Kate. "Happy Ending for DTH: New York Season Imminent." *Dance Magazine*, July, 1997.

Parry, Jann. "Short of a Few Male Ballet Dancers? Try Conscription." *Guardian*, December 21, 2003.

Plisetskaya, Maya. *I, Maya Plisetskaya*. New Haven: Yale University Press, 2001.

Poletti, Silvia. "Fracci Takes Control in Rome." *Dance Magazine*, December, 2000.

Popovich, Irina. "Maya Plisetskaya: A Balletic Lethal Weapon." therussia journal.com, May 31, 1999.

Putnam, Margaret. "Houston Liftoff: Cuban-Born Carlos Acosta is Making an International Career at Houston Ballet and Britain's Royal Ballet." *Dance Magazine*, March 1, 1998.

Roca, Octavio. "Ballet Nacional de Cuba-Alicia Alonso Interview." Havana Journal, *Miami Herald*, February 23, 2004.

Roca, Octavio. "The World's a Stage for Cuban Ballet." *San Francisco Chronicle*, February 1, 1998.

Rockwell, John, "Conservatively, Baryshnikov is Overwhelming!" *New York Times*, August 4, 1976.

Rockwell, John, "Sadler's Wells Makes U.S. Debut." *New York Times*, October 10, 1949, p. 20.

Romano, Irene. "Carla Fracci." danzadance.com, 1999.

Sánchez, Martha. "Sueños y Desafios." www.islaí.com, June 5, 2005.

Seibert, Brian. "Minding Mr. Mitchell's Baby." www.villagevoice.com, October 12, 2004.

Siegel, Beatrice. *Alicia Alonso: The Story of a Ballerina*. New York: Frederick Warne & Co., Inc., 1979.

Sims, Caitlin. "DTH Boasts Balanced Books for 1995." *Dance Magazine*, May, 1996.

Singer, Toba. "Interview with Bruce Marks." criticaldance.com, August, 2002.

Singer, Toba. "Arthur Mitchell at San Francisco Performing Arts Library with Sheryl Flatow and Brad Rosenstein, January 21, 2004." criticaldance.com, January, 2004.

Singer, Toba. "Teacher's Wisdom: Lázaro Carreño." *Dance Magazine*, December, 2004.

Spear, Dean and Francis Timlin. "A First Among Equals." Interview with Muriel Maffre, criticaldance.com, March 11, 2006.

Solway, Diane. *Nureyev: His Life*. New York: William Morrow and Company, Inc., 1998.

Svetloff, V. *Anna Pavlova*. New York: Dover Publications, Inc.

Tablada, Carlos. "The Creativity of Che's Economic Thought," *New International*, No. 8, "Che Guevara , Cuba and the Road to Socialism." New York: 408 Printing and Publishing Corp., 1991.

Tobias, Tobi. *Arthur Mitchell*. New York: Crowell, 1975.

Toomey, Christine. "Manna from Havana." www.timesonline.co.uk, May 15, 2005.

Victor, Thomas. *Mikhail Baryhnikov and Carla Fracci in* Medea: *The Making of a Dance*. New York, Holt, Rinehart and Winston, 1976.

Wallach, Maya. "Maya Plisetskaya's Love Affair with Spain." www.worldani.com , May 1989.

Willan, Philip. "Critics say restoration has ruined La Scala." *Guardian*, December 10, 2002.

Willis, Margaret. "The King of Hearts." *Dance Magazine*, May, 2005.

Unpublished Documents

Application for Admission Part I by Muriel Maffre to LEAP program at St. Mary's College, Moraga, California, provided by Claire Sheridan, program administrator (undated).
Ballet Dancer's Motivation by Muriel Maffre, August 27, 2000.
"Ballet Mori: A Ballet Conducted by the Earth," News Release, January, 2006.
"One Portrait: Homer," by Muriel Maffre (undated).
Carla Fracci, Note Biografiche (undated).

Interviews

Carlos Acosta, by author, London, January 4, 2005.
Carlos Acosta, by author, London, January 6, 2005.
Laura Alonso, by author, San Francisco, April 25, 2004.
Lauren Anderson and Andrew Edmonson, by author, Houston, June 17, 2005.
Lupe Calzadilla, by author, San Francisco, July 15, 2006.
Lázaro Carreño, by author, Houston, March 17, 2004.
Lázaro Carreño, by author, Houston, May 21, 2004.
Carla Fracci, by author, Rome, October 16, 2006.
Carla Fracci, by author, Rome, October 18, 2006.
Ikolo Griffin, by author, San Francisco, November 22, 2006.
Li Cunxin, by author, San Francisco, October 13, 2004.
Bernard and Muriel Maffre, by author, Paris, October 10, 2005.
Isabelle Maffre by author, by email, October, 2006.
Monique Maffre by author, by email, October, 20065.
Muriel Maffre by author, San Francisco, September 17, 2005.
Muriel Maffre by author, San Francisco, November 19, 2005.
Natalia Makarova by author, by email, December, 2006.
Arthur Mitchell by author, New York, October 9, 2006.
Arthur Mitchell by author, New York, October 21, 2006.
Tiekka Prieve, by author, by telephone, June 3, 2006.
Claire Sheridan by author by email, July 16, 2005.

Film

Alicia, produced and directed by Frank Boehm et al., Terpsichore Productions, Chicago, 1986.
Giselle, produced by Unitel Film-und Fernsehproduktionsgesellschaft & Co., directed by Hugo Niebeling, Munich, and TVE, Madrid, 1969.

Index

ABT. *See* American Ballet Theatre
Acocella, Joan, 70
Acosta, Carlos, 119, 120, 153-67, 218
Acosta, Pedro Acosta, 153, 155, 156, 157
Adam, Adolphe, 21
Adams, Diana, 190
Ailey, Alvin, 68, 132
Alenikova, Estella, 35
Alfimova, Marguerite, 36
Allan, Christopher, 12, 13
Allende, Isabel, 54
Alonso, Alberto, 17, 39, 115
Alonso, Alicia, xiv, 7, 8, 15-28, 16, 23, 113, 115-17, 119, 122, 159, 206, 207, 210, 213, 214, 217; Erik Bruhn on, 7
Alonso, Fernando, 17-20, 21, 24, 25, 28, 115-16, 122, 158
Alonso, Laura, 18-21, 26, 27, 214
Alvarez-Camba, Rodrigo, 117
Alvin Ailey American Dance Theater, 117
The American. *See* School of American Ballet
American Ballet Company, 19
American Ballet Theatre, 117, 119; Alicia Alonso and, 22, 24; Carla Fracci at, 202-3; Erik Bruhn and, 5-6, 8-9, 10, 12, 13; Gelsey Kirkland and, 104, 107-9, 111; Mikhail Baryshnikov and, 66-70, 106-8; Natalia Makarova and, 131-36; Rudolf Nureyev and, 39, 42
American Dance Company, 190
Ananiashvili, Nina, 160
Anaya, Dulce Wohner, 24
Anderson, Lauren, 120, 159, 160, 161, 162, 218
Anderson, Nina, 167
Ansermet, Ernest, 51
Appleby, Basil, 56
Araujo, Loipa, 117
Aria, Barbara, 61
Arias, Querube, 56
Arias, Roberto E. (Tito), 48-56
Arova, Sonia, 4-5, 7, 11, 41, 202
Arslanov, Albert, 31-33
artistic directors, 4
Arts Educational School in London, 119
Ashton, Frederick, 47-49, 51, 53, 55, 131, 165, 201
Astafieva, Serafina, 45, 48
Astafieva studio, 45, 46
Atkinson, Brooks, 19
Australian National Ballet, 98, 120

Averty, Karine, 174
Avila, Homer, 182, 183
Babilée, Jean, 138, 151
Bailey, Pearl, 188
Bakhtinyarova, Zaitouna Nureevna,
    33
Balanchine, George, 9-10, 12, 19, 23,
    42, 61, 67, 69, 97, 100-101, 103-6,
    109, 113, 122-23, 132, 133, 134, 136,
    165, 185, 188, 189, 190, 191, 192,
    194, 219
Balanchine, Geva, 102
Ballet Alicia Alonso, 24
Ballet Caravan, 18, 19
Ballet de Camgüey, Lázaro Carreño
    and, 116
Ballet de Rhin, 119
Ballet Nacional de Caracas, 117
Ballet Nacional de Cuba, 25-27, 119;
    Carlos Acosta at, 156; Lázaro
    Carreño and, 113, 116-17, 119
Ballet Russe de Monte Carlo: Alicia
    Alonso and, 8, 25; Maria Tallchief
    and, 9; Muriel Maffre at, 172, 173
Ballet Society. *See* New York City
    Ballet
Ballet Theatre (New York), 5, 8; Alicia
    Alonso and, 16, 20, 22. *See also*
    American Ballet Theatre
ballon, 3
Bandit, 97
Baretta, Caterina, 73
Barnes, Charles, 19
Barnes, Clive, 54, 62, 66-67, 205, 209
Barnes, Patricia, 66
Baron Von Kessenich, 43
Baronova, Irina, 22
Bartok, Bela, 187
Baryshnikov, Aleksandra (Shura), 57,
    60, 69, 70
Baryshnikov, Anna Katerina, 70
Baryshnikov, Mikhail (Misha), xv, 9,
    57-70, 95, 97, 103, 104-9, 111, 113,
    116, 130, 136, 137, 156, 203, 204, 215;
    on Rudolf Nureyev, 35
Baryshnikov, Nikolai, 57
Baryshnikov, Peter, 70

Baryshnikov, Sofia-Luisa, 70
Baryshnikov and Company, 69
The Baryshnikov Center for the Arts,
    70
Bates, Alan, 210
Batista, Fulgencio, 25
Baylis, Lillian, 46
Beck, Hans, 5
Beijing Dance Academy, 85, 89, 90, 96
Béjart, Catherine, 119
Belinskaya, Stanislava, 74
Bello-Portu, Jean Baptiste, 176
Belsky, Igor, 61
Belt, Byron, 101
Ben Stevenson Academy, 117, 120
Bennington College in Modern
    Dance, 187
Bentley, Muriel, 20
Berezov, Nikolai, 146
Bergman, Ingrid, 151
Beriosova, Svetlana, 131
Berlin, Christina, 64, 106
Berlioz, Hector, 130
Berman, Joanna, 175
Bertoluzzi, Paolo, 202
Bessy, Claude, 12, 40, 171
Bintley, David, 182
Bissell, Patrick, 108-9
Black, Maggie, 101-4, 106
"the Black Queen," 55
BNC. *See* Ballet Nacional de Cuba
Boada, Joan, 119
Boatwright, Christopher, 174, 177, 196
Boehm, Frank, xiv, xv, 28
Bogatyrev, Alexander, 147
Bolm, Adolph, 20
Bolshoi Ballet (Moscow), 33, 36, 37,
    65-66; Maya Plisetskaya and, 145,
    152
Borden, Lizzie, 204
Bosch, Aurora, 117
Bosl, Heinz, 50
Boston Ballet, 120
Bosustow, Grace, 45
Bosustow's Academy, Miss, 44
Bournonville, Antoine, 1
Bournonville, August, 1, 5

Bournonville technique, 1, 3
Bowers, Bill, 187
Brae, June, 45
Brandenhoff, Peter, 182
Brik, Lilya, 150
Brito, Amparo, 117-18, 118
Broughton, Brook, 182
Broughton, Shirley, 187
Brown, Ismene, 70
Brown, Karen, 193
Browne, Leslie, 68, 107
Bruce, Christopher, 160
Bruhn, Erik, 1-13, 2, 8, 26, 39, 41, 53,
    129, 132, 189, 200, 202, 203, 205, 206,
    209, 211, 213
Buckle, Richard, 42
Bujones, Fernando, 102, 119, 156, 209
Bukharin, Nikolai, 143
Bulnes, Esme, 201, 203
Bush, Barbara, 96
Bush, George, 98
Bush, George W., 120
Bussell, Darcie, 165
Butler, John, 188, 189, 190, 203
Butler, Martha, 120, 160
Byron, Lord, 42

Cabreza, Cheka, 140
Cage, Betty, 9
Callas, Maria, 135, 201
Calzadilla, Lupe, 27, 157, 214
Candler, Randy, 176
Carreño, Alihaydee, 119
Carreño, Dayana, 117
Carreño, Jose Manuel, 115, 119
Carreño, Lázaro, 113-24, 158, 217
Castellani, Renato, 210
Castro, Fidel, 26, 52, 54, 156, 157
Ce, Zhang, 94, 95
Cecchetti, Enrico, 22, 73, 80, 101
Central Performing and Arts
    University, 5-7, 90
Century Theatre, 76
Chaboukiana, Vakhtang, 38
Chabukiani, Vaxtang, 146
Chairman Mao, 85, 88-91, 93-95, 97
Champion, Gower, 187

Chanel, Coco, 151
Chaplin, Charlie, 150
Chappell, William, 46, 50
Charisse, Nanette, 188
Chase, Lucia, 5, 7, 8, 13, 20, 23, 27, 69,
    108, 136, 202
Chauviré, Yvette, 12, 151, 172, 201
Cherniavsky Trio, 79
Chernov, Michael, 111
Cisneros, Evelyn, 175
Clifford, John, 102, 104, 105
Clinton, William Jefferson, 192
Cocteau, Jean, 67
Cooper, Duncan, 198
Corales, Jesus, 119
Costravitskaya, Vera, 34
Covent Garden, 77
Cragun, Richard, 50
Cranko, John, 11, 137, 202, 203, 208,
    209, 210
Croce, Arlene, 42, 108
Cuban National Ballet. *See* Ballet
    Nacional de Cuba
Cullberg, Birgit, 8
Cunningham, Merce, 68, 187
Cunxin, Bridie, 98
Cunxin, Cuncia, 89
Cunxin, Cunsang, 92
Cunxin, Cunyuan, 91-92, 94
Cunxin, Li, 85-98, 120, 163, 216
Cunxin, Sophie, 98
Cunxin, Thomas, 98
Cuthbertson, Lauren, 165
Czar Alexander, 74
Czarina Maria, 74

Dakun, Gao, 91
Dali, Salvador, 151
D'Amboise, Jacques, 102-3, 196
Dance Theatre of Harlem, 111, 191-98
Daneman, Meredith, 47
Danilian, Leon, 18
Danilova, Alexandra, 102, 106
D'Antuono, Eleanor, 27, 202, 204
Daoud, Muhammad, 146, 150
Davesne, Alain, 172
Davis, Blevins, 5, 7

de Arrendondo, Antonio Martínez, 15
de Avila, Maria, 119
de Falla, Manuel, 50
de Lavallade, Carmen, 188
de Mille, Agnes, 20, 23, 28, 193, 204
de Valois, Ninette, 11, 41, 46, 47, 48-49, 53, 55, 56
del Hoyo y Logo, Ernestina, 15
Delanou, Nelly, 170
DeMille, Agnes, 63
Diaghilev, Sergei, 47, 49, 72, 75, 76, 179
Didlot, C., 72
Dimitriew, Vladimir, 19
Dolgushin, Nikita, 38, 128
Dolin, Anton, 20, 22, 47, 201, 203, 206, 210
Dolinskaya, Yevgenia Ivanovna, 142
Domingo, Placido, 135
Dowell, Anthony, 50, 100, 108, 129, 135, 136
Drigo, Richard, 74, 80
Drury Lane, 77
DTH. See Dance Theatre of Harlem
Duato, Nacho, 119, 165
Dudinskaya, Natalia, 36, 38, 128, 129, 130, 131
Duncan, Isadora, 18, 74, 75
Dunham, Kathryn, 4

Edmonson, Andrew, 159, 160, 161, 162, 218
Eglevksy Ballet School, 106
Eglevsky, Andre, 22
Egorova, Lubov, 49
Eilber, Janet, 54
Eisenstein, Sergei, 146
Ellington, Duke, 132
Elliott, Kristine, 179
Engels, Johan, 93
English National Ballet, 120; Carlos Acosta at, 158
Ergorova, Natalia, 79
La Escuela Vocacional del Arte, 156
Esquivel, Jorge, 27, 28
E.T. Ballet (Barcelona), 119
Etheridge, Jeannette, 42
Etheridge, Marika, 42

Evdokimova, Eva, 158
Evteyeva, Elena, 130
Fadeyechev, Nikolai, 147
Fallis, Barbara, 22
Farmer, Frances, 68
Farrell, Suzanne, 9
Father Gapon, 74
Faubus, Orville, 190
Fedorova, Alexandra, 20, 22, 59
Feijoo, Lorena, 119, 157
Feijoo, Lorna, 119, 157, 165
Fellini, Federico, 202
Fenster, Boris, 37
Fernandez, Royes, 24, 26
Ferran, Jose, 172
Fielding, Marjorie, 18-19
Finney, Truman, 172
Fisher, Barbara Milberg, 190
Flitch, J.E., 73
Fokin, Mikhail, 80, 81
Fokine, Irine, 51, 101
Fokine, Leon, 20
Fokine, Michel, 16, 20, 22, 59, 74
Fonteyn, Margot, 4, 11, 35, 41-42, 43-56, 64, 102, 135-36, 193, 201, 202, 214, 215
Forsythe, William, 165, 174
Fracci, Carla, 12, 58, 199-212, 220; Erik Bruhn and, 7, 12
Fracci, Marisa, 199
France, Charles, 70
Franchetti, Raymond, 172
François, Douce, 42
Frangiopolo, Maria-Marietta, 61, 63
Frangiopolo, Marietta, 130
Franklin, Frederic, 120, 193
Fraser, John, 66
French, Ruth, 47

Gable, Christopher, 50
Gades, Antonio, 28
Gai, Loris, 204
Gandhi, Indira, 146
Gao, George, 94-95
Gapon, Father, 74
García, Marta, 117
Garcia, Pilar, 107, 108

Garland, Robert, 194
Gerdt, Pavel, 73, 74
Geva, Tamara, 102
Giannini, Gian Carlo, 205
Gibson, Richard, 180
Gielgud, Maina, 120
Gil, Jean-Charles, 174
Gilman, Howard, 67, 107
Gilpin, John, 201
Giussani, Paolina, 201
Glazunof, Alexander, 76, 80
Goberman, Max, 24
Godkin, Paul, 19
Göethe, Johann Wolfgang von, 35, 42
Goldberg, Ken, 180
Golden Green Hippodrome, 78
Goleisovsky, Kasyan, 148
Gollner, Nan, 20
Golubin, Slava, 145, 146
Gontar, Victor, 149
Gontcharov, George, 45
Gonzales, Juan Carlos, 157
González, Dania, 117
González, Ofélia, 117
Gosling, Maude, 35
Gotesky, James, xiv, xv, 113-14, 118
Goubé, Jennifer, 117
Goubé, Paul, 117
Govrin, Gloria, 191
Graf, Alicia, 198
Graf, Dieter, 203
Graham, Martha, 18, 54, 68
Gregorieff, Serge, 51
Griffin, Ikolo, 195, 196, 197, 198, 219
Griffith, William, 206
Grisi, Carlotta, 128, 206
Gronchi, Barbara, 210, 211
Gudunov, Alexander, 147
Guevera, Che, 52
Guillem, Sylvie, 42, 165
Gulyayev, Vadim, 130
Guofeng, Hua, 95
Gurri, Delfina Pérez, 17

Haigney, Cathy, 103
Harkness, Rebekah, 120
Harris, Dale, 108

Hatoyama, Itsiro, 150
Haydée, Marcia, 203
Hearns, Willie Mae, 185
Helpmann, Robert, 49, 55
Hermann, Jane, 70
Hernandez, Royes, 209
High School of Performing Arts (New York), 187-88
Hightower, Rosella, 7, 22, 41-42, 53
Hildebrand, Karen, 121-22
Hillaire, Laurent, 42
Hines, Gregory, 69
Hinkson, Mary, 187
Hippodrome, 76
Hitler, Adolf, 56, 58
Ho, Chiu, 90
Hoadley, Nancy, 99
Hookham, Felix, 43
Hookham, Felix John, 43-44
Hookham, Hilda Fontes, 43, 45-47
Hookham, John, 55
Hookham, Margaret (Peggy), 43. *See* Fonteyn, Margot
Hormigon, Laura, 119
Houston Ballet Company, 56, 98, 113-14, 119, 120; Carlos Acosta at, 159, 161
Howard, David, 104-5
Humphrey, Doris, 18
Hurok, Sol, 22, 25, 49, 135, 151
Hyden, Walford, 81-82

Idzikowski, Stanislav, 48
Igualada, Dulce Maria Quesada, 153
Imperial Ballet, 74
Imperial School, 73
Ivanov, Lev, 73
Ivanovsky, Nikolai, 127

Jacquelin, Claudie, 171, 172
Jimenez, Alfredo, 53
Joffrey, Robert, 187
Joffrey Ballet, 102
Johansen, Svend, 73
Johnson, Virginia, 193
Jones, Marilyn, 120

Jude, Charles, 42
Jules, Perrot, 102-3, 105
Kaiser Wilhelm, 76
Kaplan, Mickey Jarson, 109
Kapralis, Yuris, 60
Karensky, Oleg, 202
Karinska, Mme Barbara, 189
Karkar, Edward, 135
Karnilova, Maria, 18, 20, 27
Karsavina, Tamara, 47-48, 51, 204
Kaye, Nora, 7, 19, 20, 55
Kehlet, Niels, 13
Kelly, Desmond, 50
Kelly, Sean, 164
Kennedy, Jacqueline, 35, 42
Kennedy, John F., 115
Kent, Allegra, 9
Kersley, Leo, 28
Kharchevnikova, Manya, 83
Khrushchev, Nikita, 35, 40, 59, 149, 150
Kidd, Michael, 19
King, Alonzo, 174, 175
King Edward, 76
King, Martin Luther, 191
Kirkland, Gelsey, 7, 9, 66-68, 97, 99-111
Kirkland, Jack, 99
Kirkland, Johnna, 99, 100
Kirkland, Marshall, 99
Kirov Ballet, 37, 39, 40, 41, 62-63, 65-66, 68-69, 103
Kirov School, 32, 36
Kirstein, Lincoln, 9, 19, 187, 188, 189, 190, 192
Kisselgoff, Anna, 85
Kivitt, Ted, 202
Kolpakova, Irina, 64, 130, 131
Koltsova, Tatyana, 63, 64-65
Komorova, Helen, 24
Kondratov, Yuri, 145, 147
Konstantinovna, Elena, 32
Kovarskaya, Bella, 60
Kriza, John, 20
Kschesinskaya, Mathilde-Maria Feliksovna, 36, 48, 73-74, 75
Kyast, Lydia, 48
Kylian, Jiri, 159

La Pena, George, 210
La Scala, 6, 209
Labis, Attilio, 50
Lacotte, Pierre, 40, 172, 173
Laing, Hugh, 202
Lambert, Constant, 50
Lanchbery, John, 56
Lander, Harald, 4, 5, 6, 159
Lander, Toni, 6, 12, 202
Lange, Jessica, 68-70
Langley, Suzanne, 97
LaRouche, Helga Zepp, 109
LaRouche, Lyndon, 109-10
Larsen, Niels Bjørn, 6
Latvia State Opera and Ballet Theater, 59
Latvian Opera and Ballet Theater Company, 60
Lavrovsky, Mikhail, 128
Lawrence, Greg, 109, 110
Le Clercq, Tanaquil, 189
LEAP (Liberal Education for Arts Professionals), 179-80
LeClercq, Tanaquil, 9
Legnani, Pierina, 73-74, 80
Lenin, Vladimir, 49, 93
Leningrad Ballet, 40
Leningrad Choreographic Institute (St. Petersburg). See Vaganova Choreographic Institute
Leontyeva, Maria Mikhailovna, 145
Lester, Keith, 45
Levitin, Grisha, 149
Lifar, Serge, 5, 151, 172
Limon, Jose, 54, 203
Lixie, Ma, 93
Llorente, Ana, 113
Llorente, Marielena, 117
Lloyd, Paula, 24
London Festival Ballet, 201
Lopokova, Lydia, 47
Loring, Eugene, 20, 22
Luca, Margaret Marchisio, 208
Lueng, Chen, 91
Lujun, Wang, 92
Lurgenson, Ksenia Losifovna, 62

Lydon, Kate, 111
Lyons, Leonard, 36

Machado, Gerardo, 18
Mackey, Elizabeth, 97-98
MacLeary, Donald, 129, 135
MacMillan, Kenneth, 54, 153
Madame Mao, 85, 89, 97
Madsen, Egon, 50
Maffre, Bernard, 169, 171
Maffre, Chan, 170
Maffre, Isabelle, 170, 182, 183
Maffre, Monique Berteaux, 169, 170,
    171, 172, 175, 182, 218
Maffre, Muriel, 169-83, 218, 219
Magallanes, Nicholas, 25
Makarova, André-Michel, 137
Makarova, Dina, 66, 106
Makarova, Natalia, 7, 8, 13, 36, 67, 97,
    102, 104-6, 114, 125-38, 217; on Erik
    Bruhn, 13
Mandela, Nelson, 194
Manzotti, Luigi, 203
Marcos, Ferdinand, 54-55
Marcos, Imelda, 54-55
Markova, Alicia, 7, 8, 22, 26, 45, 47,
    201
Marks, Bruce, 12, 67, 202, 203, 215
Marshall, George, 146
Martin, John, 9, 15
Martínez, Cuca, 16, 25
Martínez, Enrique, 24
Martínez, Menia, 35, 38
Martinioni, Edda, 201
Martins, Peter, 42, 66, 69, 105-6, 111
Marx, Karl, 93
Maryinsky Theatre, 32, 62-63, 65, 71,
    73, 75
Mason, Monica, 110, 111
Massine, Léonide, 5, 22, 49
Mathis, Clover, 179
Maule, Michael, 24
Maximova, Ekaterina, 36, 141
Mayakovsky, Vladimir, 129
Maynard, Olga, 20
Maynor, Dorothy, 191
Mazzuchelli, Estorina, 201

McBride, Patricia, 9, 69
McDonagh, Don, 99, 113
McKayle, Donald, 187
McKendry, Mary, 98
McKenzie, Kevin, 70
McLeary, Donald, 50
McMillan, Kenneth, 165, 202
Medina, Buenaventura, 55, 56
Mendes, Josefina, 117
Menegatti, Beppe, 201, 204, 205, 207,
    210, 211, 212
Mercé, Antonia, 17
Merrild, Karl, 3
Messel, Oliver, 49
Messerer, Asaf Mikhailovich, 139,
    141, 144, 145
Messerer, Mikhail Borisovich, 139
Messerer, Rakhil, 139, 143, 144, 145
Metropolitan Ballet (London), 4
Metropolitan Opera House, 76
Meyer, Yvonne, 172
Meyerhold, Vsevolod, 127, 142
Michel, Carl, 193
Mikhailov, Mikhail, 127
Mikhailovich, 127
Miñana, Christina, 172
Minkus, Leon, 74
Minz, Sasha, 38, 66
Mitchell, Arthur, 185-98, 219
Mitchell, Arthur Sr., 185
Mitchell, Willie Mae, 187
Mordkin, Mikhail, 18, 20, 76
Mordkin Ballet Company, 18
Moreau, Jacqueline, 171
Moreton, Ursula, 46
Moscow Choreographic School, 142
Motte, Claire, 40, 171
Moylan, Mary Ellen, 7
Muhan, Lin, 96
Musil, Karl, 50

Nagata, Mikifumo, 50
Nagy, Ivan, 13, 50, 104, 132, 136, 158
Nagy, Marilyn, 104
Nasser, Gamal, 146
National Ballet (Washington, D.C.),
    120

National Ballet of Brazil, 190
National Ballet of Canada, 119
National Ballet of Mexico, 119
National Ballet School (Cuba). *See* Ballet Nacional de Cuba
National Conservatory for Advanced Studies, 171-72
Nazretdinova, Zaitouna, 32
Neary, Patricia, 9
Nedviguene, Gennadi, 179
Nehru, Jawaharlal, 146, 148
NEPmen, 130
Neumeier, John, 132
New York City Ballet, 9, 19, 66, 69, 100, 101, 102, 103, 105, 106, 108, 109
Newman, LaTanya, 187
Nicholson, Jack, 68
Nijinksa, Bronislava, 9, 20
Nijinsky, Vaslav, 36, 62
Niles, Mary Ann, 189
Nín, Joaquin, 21
Noriega, Gen. Manuel, 56
Norman, Jessye, 42
Novikoff, Laurent, 76
Nuñez, Guillermo, 116
Nuñez, Marienela, 165
Nureyev, Rudolf, 10-11, 12, 29-42, 50, 53-56, 62, 64, 66, 102, 104, 107, 113, 131, 165, 202, 206, 210, 211, 214
Nureyeva, Farida, 29-34
Nureyeva, Hamet, 29-34
Nureyeva, Lilya, 31, 39
Nureyeva, Rosa, 32, 38-39, 42
NYCB. *See* New York City Ballet

Oblakov, Alexander, 73
Old Vic and Sadler's Wells (Vic-Wells) school, 45-46
Oliphant, Betty, 12
Opera House, 31
Osato, Sono, 22

Packer, Randall, 180
Pahlavi, Shah, 146
Panov, Valery, 34, 63, 64
Paris Opera Ballet, 119; Muriel Maffre at, 169, 171

Parker, Janie, 98, 120, 160, 163
Parkinson, Georgina, 52, 108
Parkinson, Tobias, 108
pas de deux, 7
Pavlakos, Lenore, 195
Pavlova, Alla, 38
Pavlova, Anna (Nura), 44, 47, 62, 71-83, 216
Pavlovna, Elizaveta, 142
Peter the Great, 60, 72
Petipa, Gerdt, 73
Petipa, Marius, 47, 73, 74, 80, 81
Petit, Roland, 51, 67
Phifer, Cassandra, 195
Pianowsky, Michael, 83
Pickup, Ronald, 210
Pierce, Benjamin, 169, 177, 178, 180, 181
Pioneer Palace, 33
Pissarev, Vadim, 173
Pistoni, Mario, 202, 203
Pleasant, Richard, 5, 20
plié, 3
Plisetskaya, Alexander, 141, 145
Plisetskaya, Maya, 36, 63, 139-52, 217
Plisetski, Azari, 27
Plucis, Harijs, 49
Polish Opera Ballet (Lodz), 119
Pontois, Noëlla, 107
Possokhov, Yuri, 173, 180, 181
Preobrajenska, Olga, 48, 73, 75, 79, 206
Prieve, Tiekka, 120, 162, 163, 164, 218
Prince Charles, 55
Prince Ranier, 68
Pro Arte Musical, 16-17, 24
Psycho Ballet, 27
Pushkin, Alexander, 35-39, 60-62, 64, 116
Pushkin, Zenia (Xsana), 38
Pyari, Viktor, 33

Qing, Jiang, 85, 90-91, 94-95, 97
Queen Elizabeth, 42
Quesada, Berta Acosta, 153, 154
Quesada, Marilin Acosta, 153

Rachinsky, Petr, 64

Radziwill, Lee, 35
Ratmansky, Alex, 173
Rayet, Jacqueline, 172
Rayneri, Laura, 17
Raynolds, Rothay, 73
Reagan, Ronald, 98
Reed, Janet, 22
Rencher, Derek, 110
Rich, Virginia, 190
Riga Choreographic Institute, 59, 60
Riga School of Opera and Ballet
    Theater, 59
Rilke, Mainer Maria, xv
Rimbaud, Laun, 42
Rinehart, Lisa, 70
Rivera, Chita, 191
Robbins, Jerome, 19, 20, 68-69, 97, 102,
    104-5, 136, 190
Rockwell, John, 43, 57
Rodrigues, Alfred, 201, 203
Rodzianko, Irina, 131
Rojo, Tamara, 153, 165
Romairone, Carlo, 208
Rosenthal, Jean, 189
Ross, Herbert, 204, 210
Royal Ballet (London), 56, 67, 110, 119;
    Carlos Acosta at, 157, 165; Natalia
    Makarova and, 131, 135
Royal Copenhagen Ballet School, 2-3,
    5
Royal Danish Ballet, 4, 6, 9, 120; Carla
    Fracci at, 202
Royal Swedish Ballet Company, 12
Royal Winnipeg Ballet, 119

SAB. See School of American Ballet
Saddler, Donald, 22
Sadler's Wells Ballet, 4, 6, 49, 120
Saint, Clara, 35, 40
San Francisco Ballet, 193; Maffre at,
    174-78
Sandre, Didier, 171
Sarofim, Louisa, 96
Sassoon, Janet, 137
Saunders, Kellye, 198
Savva, Marina Petrovna, 35
Scannell, Dawn, 120

Schanne, Margrethe, 201
Schaufuss, Peter, 108, 156
Schiller, Ana Sofia, 109
School of American Ballet (SAB), 19,
    100, 104; Arthur Mitchell at, 188
Segura, Felipe, 25
Selassie, Haile, 146
Semenov, Victor Alexandrovich, 142
Semenyaka, Ludmila, 158
Semyonova, Marina, 147
Sergava, Katherine, 20
Sergeyev, Konstantin, 39, 64, 116, 129,
    130, 131
Serrano, Luis, 119
Serrano, Lupe, 7, 25
Sevillano, Trinidad, 110
Seymour, Lynn, 202
Shafer, Richard, 107-8
Sharafoutdinova, Alfia, 39
Shchedrin, Rodion, 148, 150
Shearer, Moira, 4
Shelepin, Alexander Nikolayevich,
    150, 151
Shelkov, Valentin, 34-35, 38, 125
Shellman, Eddie J., 194
Shepard, Sam, 70
Sheridan, Claire, 178, 179, 180, 219
Shiripina, Elena Vasilievna, 127
Shook, Karel, 187, 190, 191
Shorer, Suki, 9
Shu, Zhang, 94, 96
Shurr, Gertrude, 187
Siegel, Marcia B., 107
Simón, Pedro, 28, 117
Sinatra, Frank, 187
Sinclair, Janet, 28
Sisova, Alla, 36
Smakov, Gennady, 62, 137
Smith, Damian, 179
Smith, Oliver, 70
Smolny Institute, 127
Smuin, Michael, 193, 196
Sohm, Jim, 178
Sokolova, Eugenia, 73
Soleri, Ferruccio, 205
Solodovnikov, Alexander, 147, 148
Soloviev, Yuri, 36, 40, 69

Sombart, Alexander, 137
Somes, Michael, 47, 51, 51-52
Somoza, Anastasio, 54
Spessivtzeva, Olga, 47, 102, 202
St. Petersburg's Leningrad
    Choreographic Institute. *See*
    Vaganova Choreographic Institute
Staff, Frank, 5
Stalin, Joseph, 33-35, 58-59, 63, 127,
    130, 138, 142, 143, 144, 147, 148, 149
Stanislavsky, Konstantin, 127
Stanislavsky theater, 36
Steinberg, Ben, 24
Stevenson, Ben, 96, 97, 119-20, 158,
    159, 160, 161, 164
Stravinsky, Igor, 190
Strepponi, Giuseppina, 210
Stroganova, Nine, 20
Stuart, Muriel, 19
Stuttgart Ballet, 11
Suárez, Rosaria, 117
Svetloff, V., 71

Taglioni, Maria, 128, 148
Tallchief, Maria, 7, 9-11, 12, 39, 41, 189
Tan, Yuan Yuan, 179
Taras, John, 5, 42, 102
Tchaikovsky, Pyotr Ilyich, 42, 46-47,
    71, 80, 106, 138, 145
Tcherneicheva, Lubov, 51
Tchernichov, Igor, 63, 129, 130
Tchernishova, Elena, 137
Teacher Song, 85
Teatro Municipal (Rio), 119
Teatro Real (Madrid), 119
Terrero, Alberto, 156
Terry, Walter, 10, 11, 151
Tetley, Glen, 136, 160, 189
Tewsley, Robert, 160
Texas Ballet Theatre, 119
Tharp, Twyla, 68
Thesmar, Ghislaine, 172
Thomas, Rasta, 198
Tikhomirnova, Irina, 26
Tito, Marshal, 146
Tomasson, Helgi, 63, 104, 174, 176,
    177, 180, 193, 196

Toropov, George, 45
Torrado, Oscar, 119
Toumanova, Tamara, 19
Trefilova, Vera, 79
Trotsky, Leon, 93, 142
Tudor, Antony, 20, 68, 101, 107, 132,
    165, 202, 207

Udeltsova, Anna, 32
Ufa Ballet, 32, 33, 37
Ufa Opera House, 33
Ulanova, Galina, 26, 36, 52-53, 63, 129,
    130, 141, 145, 146, 147, 148, 151
Ullate, Victor, 119
Universidad Compultense de
    Madrid, 119
Urrutia, Manuel, 52

Vaganova, Agrippina, 6, 34, 68, 91,
    101, 111, 143, 145, 146
Vaganova Academy, Lázaro Carreño
    and, 113
Vaganova Choreographic Institute,
    34, 60-62, 103, 116, 121-22, 123, 124,
    125; Lázaro Carreño and, 113
Vallarino, Anabella, 56
van Dantzig, Rudi, 42
van Schayk, Toer, 42
Van Vooren, Monique, 55
Vasiliev, Vladimir, 36, 141, 148, 206
Vaussard, Christiane, 169, 171
Vecheslova, Tatiana Mikhailovna,
    128
Verdi, Giuseppe, 204
Verdy, Violette, 9, 201, 209
Verne, Jules, 31
Vestris, Auguste, 63
Vic-Wells Ballet, 46, 47
Victor Dandré, 79
Vines, Delia, 115
Virsaladze, Simon, 40
Visconti, Luchino, 201
Vladimiroff, Pierre, 19
Voitovich, Elena, 33
Volkenstein, Mikhail, 35
Volkova, Vera, 6-7, 10, 45, 49, 53, 201,
    202

Wall, David, 50, 55
Wang, Jean, 91
Warbug, Edward M.M., 19
Watts, Heather, 105
Wayne, John, 50
Weidmann, Charles, 18
Weiqiang, Zhang, 96
Welch, Garth, 50, 120
Welch, Stanton, 120, 169
Whittingham, Gillian, 209, 210, 211
Wilde, Patricia, 9
Williams, Donald, 196, 197
Williams, Stanley, 104

Xiao, Chen, 92-98
Xiaoping, Deng, 94-95

Xiongjun, Chong, 94

Yakobson, Leonid Veniaminovich, 63,
    129, 130, 142, 145, 149, 151
Yanowsky, Zenaida, 165
Yarborough, Sarah, 191
Yavorsky, Nikolai, 15-17, 115
Yimou, Zhang, 97
Youskevitch, Igor, 8, 23, 24, 26
Yu, Sien, 87
Yuen, Chen, 91, 93

Zanfretta, Enrico, 18
Zedong, Mao, 146, 148, 216
Zongshu, Zhang, 97
Zukov, Yuri, 177

About the Author

TOBA SINGER is the Dance Selector and Senior Program Director of the Art and Music Center of the San Francisco Public Library. She graduated from New York City's High School of Performing Arts, and has lived and written in Boston, Baltimore, Washington, D.C., Richmond, Virginia, and Charleston, West Virginia. She has been a steelworker, chemical refinery operator, presser and sewing machine operator and airlines worker. Her articles have been published in the *Charleston Gazette*, *San Francisco Chronicle*, *Dance Magazine*, *Dance Europe*, voiceofdance.com, and criticaldance.com. Singer produced "Dance to Live, Live to Dance," and served on the board of Robert Moses' Kin dance company. She studied dance with Svetlana Afanasieva, Nina Anderson, Perry Brunson, Cora Cahan, Jane Dudley, Richard Gibson, Zory Kara, Donald McKayle, Françoise Martinet, Augusta Moore, Gertrude Shurr, and Kahz Smuda. Her son James Gotesky dances with the Houston Ballet.